Advance praise for

Laboring in the Shadows

"This fascinating, moving, and revelatory text is an urgent intervention into the canon of critical race studies. Baldridge draws on a wealth of research to explore the history and present-day realities of Black youth workers, revealing the tokenism, microaggressions, and anti-Black racism that provide a backdrop to the deep commitments and rich contribution that they make, not only to the youth, but to society at large."

—David Gillborn, author of *White Lies: Racism, Education and Critical Race Theory*

"Bianca J. Baldridge shines an important light on the often-overlooked contributions of Black youth workers, their resilience as they adopt innovative teaching methods and 'freedom dreaming' to empower the youth they serve. This book challenges us to recognize the strength and significance of Black youth workers, offering hope and insight into the transformative power of community care. A must-read."

—Roberto G. Gonzales, University of Pennsylvania

"Bianca Baldridge reminds us of the centrality of youth workers as educational professionals, illuminating the power and generative nature of what they contribute to our economy and society . . . a stellar contribution."

—Gloria Ladson-Billings, University of Wisconsin-Madison

Laboring in the Shadows

Laboring in the Shadows

PRECARITY AND PROMISE IN BLACK YOUTH WORK

Bianca J. Baldridge

STANFORD UNIVERSITY PRESS
Stanford, California

Stanford University Press
Stanford, California

Portions of chapter 2 were originally published in Bianca J. Baldridge, "Negotiating Anti-Black Racism in 'Liberal' Contexts: The Experiences of Black Youth Workers in Community-Based Educational Spaces," *Race Ethnicity and Education* 23, no. 6 (2000), and are reprinted by permission of the publisher, Taylor & Francis Ltd, http://www .tandfonline.com.

Library of Congress Cataloging-in-Publication Data
Names: Baldridge, Bianca J. (Bianca Jontae), 1983– author.
Title: Laboring in the shadows : precarity and promise in Black youth work / Bianca J. Baldridge.
Description: Stanford, California : Standard University Press, 2026. | Includes bibliographical references and index.
Identifiers: LCCN 2025038791 (print) | LCCN 2025038792 (ebook) | ISBN 9781503640351 (cloth) | ISBN 9781503644892 (paperback) | ISBN 9781503644908 (ebook)
Subjects: LCSH: African American youth workers. | Social work with African American youth. | Precarious employment—United States.
Classification: LCC HV3181 .B35 2026 (print) | LCC HV3181 (ebook)
LC record available at https://lccn.loc.gov/2025038791
LC ebook record available at https://lccn.loc.gov/2025038792

Cover design: Lindy Kasler
Cover art: Charly Palmer, *Demand with Love* (2025), acrylic on canvas; Charly Palmer Collection, Atlanta, Georgia

The authorized representative in the EU for product safety and compliance is: Mare Nostrum Group B.V. | Mauritskade 21D | 1091 GC Amsterdam | The Netherlands | Email address: gpsr@mare-nostrum.co.uk | KVK chamber of commerce number: 96249943

Contents

Preface: Journeying to Youth Work

Sitting cross-legged on the opaque linoleum floor of the school assembly room, I listened to a group of high school and college students from an organization focused on youth leadership development. As a seventh grader, I was impressed that young people not much older than me had the confidence to stand in front of disinterested middle schoolers, presenting information to us like my teachers did, but in a more engaging and fun way. Near the end of their workshop, they enthusiastically shared that if we enjoyed their activities that day, we would also like their weeklong summer program on a college campus. A few seconds after they mentioned the summer program, I felt a tap on my shoulder. I turned to find Mrs. P. crouched beside me. "I think it would be great if you could go," she whispered. I was intrigued and felt special that a teacher had singled me out for what seemed like an exciting opportunity, but I also wanted to appear disinterested in case my peers did not find it as interesting as I did. She viewed me as a "leader," and that felt good. That summer, I, along with roughly twenty other middle and high school students from Westside, my small K–12 magnet school in Los Angeles, spent a week in a summer program on a California college campus. A few hundred students representing high schools from around the state attended this week-long program. My classmates and I quickly realized that our school brought racial diversity. We were placed in small groups of six to eight students for the week and were the only Black and Latine students in our groups. But we always managed to find each other during mealtimes for familiarity and comfort.

Our school was one of the magnets in the Los Angeles Unified School District and strived to create racial diversity by maintaining an equal percentage of students across different races. However, racial diversity was more apparent in the elementary grades, while the population shifted to predominantly Black and Latine in the middle and high school grades. Most Black and Latine students came from predominantly Black and Latine neighborhoods in South Central and East Los Angeles. We woke up at dawn and spent an hour on the school bus traveling to a small, quirky magnet school by the beach.

By the time I attended that summer program, I had been a student at the magnet school for nearly two years. Before that, I went to Horace Mann Middle School, my local school just a few blocks from my house in South Central Los Angeles. One afternoon in sixth grade, however, my brother and I came home from school to find our parents waiting for us with excitement. This was unusual because we always arrived home before they did. They informed us that we would be going to a new school and wanted to take us for a drive to show us. Learning that my brother and I would be moving to a new school was unexpected and unwelcome news. Our parents had not mentioned considering a move away from our neighborhood school. The first emotion I felt was shock, quickly followed by disappointment. I was finding my stride and beginning to thrive at Horace Mann; I was fond of most of my teachers and planning to try out for the basketball team the following week. I had made friends and was asked to be someone's girlfriend (although I can't recall his name), but I never saw him again, thanks to my parents.

The new school my parents took us to that day was located by the beach. It had around four hundred to five hundred students in total, from kindergarten through twelfth grade. Although I was reluctant to change schools, I became intrigued by what I discovered once I started. Many aspects were different. We addressed teachers by their first names, and the magnet focus was environmental science, which allowed us to spend a lot of time exploring the nearby beaches and canals. This school turned out to be a unique place, feeling distinct from the traditional, large, comprehensive middle school I had previously attended. The differences initially felt exciting during my first years. Once I entered my eighth-grade year, the school shifted our magnet focus from environmental studies to leadership in order to empower students to lead and engage in social change. The emergence of the leadership focus exposed deeper weaknesses within the school. One of its most significant failures was its inability to prepare the predominantly Black and Latine high school student body for higher education or viable career pathways.

My school did not provide everything I needed to be prepared for college, but the leadership component through the youth nonprofit offered a powerful pathway to youth work. The school struggled to meet the requirements of the University of California system and did not offer honors or advanced placement courses. However, some teachers sought me out for academic opportunities and encouraged me to take classes at a nearby high school to help fulfill these requirements. At the same time, according to my older brother, no one at the school discussed his options post-graduation until the second semester of his senior year. My classmates were intelligent and creative but were not strongly encouraged to consider their futures after high school. This reality has always been a source of pain for me—to recognize now that teachers and school staff targeted me for opportunities while being unaware of or dismissing other students' interests. I took courses at a nearby large comprehensive high school to qualify for the UC system. I earned approximately fifteen credits between Santa Monica College and Southwest Community College, taking courses in Black studies, sociology, criminal justice, and biology.

Throughout high school, I became involved with the nonprofit organization that helped transform our school into a leadership magnet. I began traveling throughout the state, leading workshops at high schools and community-based organizations with teenagers like me and sometimes with classroom teachers, school administrators, or leaders from other youth-serving organizations. I was engaging in what I would now call youth work. The program focused on guiding groups through nonviolent communication, strategic planning for student government, and supporting students' efforts to improve their schools and neighborhoods. The group also attempted to discuss issues of racial and gender justice, although these efforts were not well executed. Through my work in this organization, I gained a vast toolkit of teaching and facilitation skills that I still use today. As a young leader, I became more confident and comfortable in my own skin. Many of my experiences and exposure within this program were invaluable and inspiring, leading me to think big and create a vision for myself without limitations. However, there were also serious problems that I couldn't fully see at the time. While working for this program, I was recognized as an exemplary student, someone who had "overcome" the difficulties in my family and "dangerous" neighborhood. Other students and adult program staff members spoke about me in ways that today I would identify as deeply problematic: Racial microaggressions were common, and judgments about my home life were made. At the time, I did not have the language of anti-Black racism or paternalism to express my discomfort with the comments I heard. However, this program's problematic framing of my life as a teen followed me into adulthood as a youth development professional. Later, when I was applying to various jobs and graduate schools in my early twenties, a program director wrote a letter of recommendation for me. But the words in this letter made my stomach turn. "Every young person from the inner city should be like Bianca," it said. "Bianca lived in a single-parent home and traveled over two hours to get to school," the letter continued, along with other descriptions of my "bad" neighborhood. I'll never forget these sentences.

The problem is that the stories about me were exaggerations, and many were not true. For one thing, it did not take me two hours to get to school. It was also false that my neighborhood was a "bad" neighborhood. Although news reports about South Central Los Angeles often portrayed it with almost exclusively violent imagery, this represented a singular narrative that overlooked the richness of my community. My brother and I could walk three blocks to spend time with my mother's parents, and we were less than two miles from my father's parents, who lived in Inglewood. We lived in a solidly working-class Black neighborhood. My neighbors were small business owners or held various jobs in education, health care, and city and state services. My block was filled with children my age; we played football in the streets, ran from lawn to lawn with super-soakers, and freely rode our bikes around the neighborhood. We hosted an annual summer block party where my dad would barbeque for the entire block; the neighbors would bring side dishes that reflected the diversity of the Black diaspora and our community. Approaching our block parties, one could smell my dad's smoky barbeque, my next-door neighbor's Nigerian jollof, and beef patties prepared by my neighbor across the street, a Jamaican food supplier to local restaurants in the city.

There was gang activity, and there were certain blocks my parents wanted us to avoid. When we first arrived, the neighbors directly across the street had a son named Darnell, who sometimes sold drugs outside their home. I later learned that my dad and two other fathers on the block had a few words with Darnell to ensure the safety of the children in the area. Of course, I found out about this when I became an adult. Not long after that "conversation," Darnell and his family moved away. Still, there was much joy and freedom to roam our block and simply be kids. After school and during the summer, we would go from house to house, playing basketball in backyards, enjoying video games, or exchanging cassette tapes and, later, CDs. Although there was a time when my mother was solely responsible for parenting after my parents divorced, I spent most of my childhood with both parents, and I maintain a close relationship with my father today. Watching the program director attempt to gain favor in that letter, despite these inaccuracies, broke my heart. At that time, recommendation letters were not submitted online; recommenders would mail hard copies in a sealed envelope to be included with the paper application or sent separately. I shouldn't have read the letter, but I had an extra copy and was encouraged to review letters written on my behalf by this program director when I was a high school student. So, I didn't think it would be a big deal, but I now understand that it constituted a breach of trust. Even so, I'm grateful that I did. Although painful, it validated many feelings and the discomfort I encountered while working in this organization.

The letter was filled with stereotypes and made me out to be "exceptional," somehow better than other Black youth in my community.[1] What hurt most is that I cared deeply for this program director, whom I had met when I was thirteen; they cared for me, too. But, instead of seeing me for who I was—a young person raised by a loving Black family and community who believed in the power of education and service to others—the letter evoked white supremacist tropes about Blackness that are typical in youth work organizations. The worst parts of the letter positioned the program I spent so much time working for, a program I valued as my savior, as my rescuer. But I didn't need rescuing.

Sociology, Black studies, and education provided me with the language to understand my experiences and journey into youth work, particularly the narrative of Black exceptionalism imparted by organizations that fostered critical skills yet overlooked my humanity. Reconciling the various, sometimes conflicting emotions I encountered while trying to grasp how I could feel empowered by my experiences while also feeling harmed or belittled represents a paradox in youth work that I have grappled with throughout my career. My early journey into youth work revealed the promise of the field—the educational support, empowerment, increased self-efficacy, and significant relationships developed with non-parental adults. This journey also illuminated the paradoxes and contradictions within youth work that are linked to the deficit constructions of Black youth who are viewed as needing containment or "fixing" through after-school education. Nevertheless, it was my journey to youth work and experiences as a youth worker and researcher that exposed the precarity faced by those who sustain and uphold the field—youth workers.

————

For many, youth work is a vocation of love. However, it is also a job—and a profoundly precarious one at that: underpaid and undervalued by policymakers and the public. Youth work is one of the most essential educational and social professions in the United States today because many of our most vital social institutions, including the economy, education, and the family, depend on it. Despite its importance, many people, if asked, cannot even define what a youth worker is. I can, however, guarantee that you know or have met a youth worker. You may not have recognized them by that title, but you likely know someone who works with young people outside of school hours. Youth workers are adult professionals who support young people's academic, social, and personal development, often in informal settings, such as after-school programs, youth organizations, and community-based education spaces.[2] If the label of youth worker doesn't resonate with you, you might be more familiar with the programs that parents and young people depend on for care, safety, activities, nutrition, and academic support after school or during the summer months. These programs come with various names, including after-school, out-of-school time, youth development programs, community-based educational spaces, and youth organizations. The individuals who work in these programs are youth workers—and they are among the most crucial professionals in the United States.[3] Youth workers are trusted, non-parental adults who guide young people as they develop essential aspects of their identities. They play a vital role in the lives of children and adolescents.

Youth workers are essential to the education and youth development workforce. Yet, their work often remains invisible to those outside the communities and programs where they serve. This invisibility is not accidental—it is imposed upon them. It reflects a society that fails to value their contributions, even as it renders them indispensable. This invisibility also affects other professions—teachers, health-care workers, family caregivers, and gig workers. For youth workers, particularly Black youth workers, this invisibility arises from the precarious nature of nonstandard employment and is steeped in the paradoxes of US history—of living, working, and surviving in a world where anti-Black racism is a social reality.[4] *Laboring in the Shadows* focuses on Black youth workers as a microcosm of vulnerable youth workers engaging in the field to understand how they navigate anti-Black racism in the field. Anti-Black racism is a system of structural oppression rooted in anti-Blackness, as theorized by Black studies scholars and taken up by scholars of education and sociology, defined as the disregard and disdain for Black people, Black culture, and ways of being—and ultimately, the positioning of Black people outside of humanity.[5]

Estimates suggest that there are 2.53 million youth workers in the United States, which is only 650,000 fewer than the number of full-time equivalent (FTE) classroom teachers.[6] However, this number may not fully reflect the size of this workforce, as many volunteer and part-time positions exist in various locales where young people are confined or need support. Many youth workers face inadequate and failing social and economic networks that put them at risk and leave them unprotected from many forms of harm. Youth workers in organizations and education agencies that receive public funding, such as school districts, hospitals, or city or state programs, have a more straightforward pathway to organize and unionize alongside other vulnerable essential workers. However, a significant percentage of youth workers are employed by organizations that primarily rely on private philanthropy—and these youth workers encounter precarious circumstances. Nevertheless, these youth workers are not dispensable—they are essential workers, like those in health care, early childcare, nannies, or school paraprofessionals—they are crucial to how society functions.[7] Yet they remain largely unprotected against the pathologizing forces of unregulated capitalism. They are rendered vulnerable and often exploited.[8] Policymakers generally understand youth workers as care and education workers (even though their legitimacy as educators is frequently overlooked)[9] and typically view their work—like schoolteachers and those in care-based nonprofits—as "noble" or a "labor of love,"[10] which ultimately furthers their exploitation. For youth workers, this kind of work is indeed a "labor of love." But too often, this commitment is used to justify their exploitation.

Youth workers find the work rewarding. It allows them to engage with incredible young people and have the chance to shape their lives in formative ways. However, this type of work can be unstable, forcing youth workers to labor in precarity, with their plight primarily hidden in the shadows. The same social realities that undermine the well-being of Black youth and Black youth workers also create the urgency of youth work. It is a cycle of precarity and paradox that Black youth workers have struggled against and within for generations.[11] This book reveals the precarity, paradoxes, and promise of youth work in community-based organizations by exploring the professional and personal lives of dedicated youth workers.

Youth workers operate within the broader education and care work landscape, yet labor in the shadows. As you read this book, I hope you recognize the value of youth work in our society through the dedication and determination of youth workers. Throughout the pages of this book, you will encounter Black youth workers from every region of the country who have committed their lives to supporting the educational futures of Black and other marginalized youth. Despite their deep commitment to this work, they face challenges–some that are common in the profession, such as instability, low wages, and burnout—alongside those that are unique to them as Black youth workers navigating anti-Black racism in the field, including leadership ceilings, retaliation, and the need to protect Black students from deficit and paternalistic framing and treatment within organizations. Yet, despite these challenges, which are not unique to Black educational life and movement work, the Black youth workers you'll meet in this book remain steadfast in their commitment to Black youth, continuing the legacy of the work done by Black educators and activists before them.

Acknowledgments

Writing *Laboring in the Shadows* has been a long journey. I wasn't sure this book would be completed. Between the initial idea and the writing of these chapters lies loss, grief, and the struggle to be well. There were days when looking at a computer screen made me nauseous and profoundly fatigued. Fighting to be well and to heal was necessary. I had to carve out space to heal, even if that meant disappointing others. Considering this, I want to thank the people and places that honored and safeguarded my desire to be well and who have been with me on this journey. Thank you to my partner in life, John Diamond, and my sister-scholars: Keisha Allen, Sosanya Jones, Terrenda C. White, and Blanca E. Vega. To my walk-and-talkers, meme sharers, fellow joy-seekers, wise council, "no" committee members, and those who help me keep my vibe right: Fenaba Addo, Angela Rose Black, Erika C. Bullock, Brittney Bolden, Alyson Edwards, Lisa Ellis, Ja'Dell Davis, Kim Diamond, Aaliyah El Amin, Tikia Hamilton, Tarsha Herelle, Erica Hewitt, Marc Lamont Hill, R. L'Huereux Lewis McCoy, Gabi Oliveira, Afia Opantiri, Linn Posey Maddox, kihana ross, Suz Switzer, Erica Turner, Chizoba Udeorji, Cidna Valentin, Melissa Valle, Shirin Vossoughi, Derron Wallace, Tanya Wiggins, Ron Williams, Maisha T. Winn, and the Literary Collective PVD (you know who you are ☺).

I am sincerely grateful to Prudence Carter, John Diamond, Shawn Ginwright, Jarvis Givens, and Stacey Lee for spending many hours with me to strengthen this book. Thank you for pushing me, thinking with me, and, most importantly, believing I could pull this off! Your feedback has been tremendously invaluable. To Chris Lura: Thank you for believing in this project and supporting me once again!

To my community at the Center for Advanced Study in the Behavioral Sciences (CASBS)—this book would not have come to life without the time and space to read, reflect, write, and talk through the tensions of writing this book. I am immensely grateful to the incredible, special, and hard-working staff members who provided everything I could need or want. CASBS was a dream and one of the most significant honors of my career. Thanks to my wonderful cohort mates for their thoughtful questions. I want to give an extra shout-out to my fellow fellows who dedicated extra time to helping me think about this book and encouraging me along the way: Mary Lopez, Young Mie Kim, Santi Furnami, Stephán Vincent Lacrin, Faranak Miraftab, Gabe Winant, Ceren Budak, Emily Penner, Andrew Penner, Erica Robles Anderson, Micah Musculino, Jen Morton, and Peter Ferreto. To Louise Aronson and Sarah Cody, our discussions about the parallel tensions and precarity in education and health care were insightful, albeit depressing (lol). I also must thank Woody Powell and Sarah Soule for their guidance, feedback, and suggestions, which were tremendously valuable in crafting this book. During my time at CASBS and Stanford, my connections with colleagues and students—even briefly—helped me view this project in new ways. I'm grateful to Alfredo Artiles, Brian Cabral, Judy Chu, Matt Clair, Michael Hines, Jacquelyn Hwang, Ruth Milkman, Alexandros Orphanides, Eujin Park, and Maria Velazquez.

Throughout my journey, many generous colleagues from my former Department of Educational Policy Studies at UW Madison, current colleagues at Harvard University, and mentors and thought partners from various institutions have been exceptionally giving with their time. They listened to me vent, provided feedback and references, and sent notes of affirmation and encouragement—thank you. I especially want to thank Ebony Bridwell-Mitchell, Gretchen Brion-Meisels, Derrick Brooms, Karida Brown, Kevin Clay, Tania de St. Croix, Sarah Dryden Peterson, John Eason, Rich Furman, Nancy Hill, Andrew Ho, Tony Jack, Roberto Gonzales, David Johns,

Amanda E. Lewis, Meira Levinson, Irene Leifshitz, Karen Mapp, Jal Mehta, David Pedulla, Noliwe Rooks, Sandra Susan Smith, Bridget Terry Long, Amy Stuart Wells, Naomi Mae. Joseph Nelson, Sakeena Everett, Ashley Smith-Purviance, Daphne Watkins, Abby Orrick, Zenzile Riddick, Christian Walkes, and Maricruz Vargas Ramirez, Adriana Umaña Taylor, and Christina Villareal. To Karen Pittman and Dana Fusco, thanks for creating a pathway to talk about youth workers' contributions to society. To Ashley Morrow and Brooke King-Harris, I can hardly do anything without you; I truly appreciate your support! Thank you to the HGSE colleagues who offered me excellent advice during Wine and Wisdom—those early pieces of feedback significantly expanded my project! To HGSE leadership, Jimmy Kim and Mary West, I truly appreciate your support. I am incredibly grateful for Dean Nonie Lesaux's encouragement and the generous backing of the Dean's Faculty Fund.

Having the opportunity to discuss this book while writing was a valuable exercise that profoundly shaped my thinking. I am grateful to Torry and Maisha Winn and the Transformative Justice in Education Center; Roberto Gonzales and Alex Posecznick and the Penn Ethnography Forum; Brian Brown and the Race, Inequality, and Language in Education (RILE) Speaker's Series; Kathryn Moeller and Amilcar Pereira and the Transnational Anti-Racism in Education Research & Exchange Programme.

My name is on this book's cover, but a large community of colleagues and students made the research for this book possible. First, I'd like to thank my colleagues and collaborators on the Equity and Out-of-School Time project: Daniela DiGiacomo, Ben Kirshner, Sam Mejias, and Deepa Vasudevan. You are all brilliant scholars and wonderful people. I am honored to work alongside you. Second, I am thankful to Bronwyn Bevan for believing in our work. Last but certainly not least, I am grateful for every student who dedicated time and energy to data collection and organization in the early stages of the project: Virginia Downing, Carl "CJ" Greer, Pablo Aquiles Sanchez, Edom Tesfa, Tina Brote, Teo Garipey, and Ayomi Wolf. I want to thank Marlo Reeves, Wallace Grace, Jaylah Bateman, Darion Allen, Tyriek Mack, Ella Sklaw, Amina Iro, Shilpa Maddikunti, Jessica Huemann, and Tashiana Lipscomb for their contributions to the projects that shaped this book. In the final phase of this study, I am most grateful for my extraordinary team at the Critical Youth Work Collective (CYC). I am indebted to your commitment to valuing humanizing research, critical youth work pedagogies, and honoring youth workers and community-based youth work. To Angela R. Black, thanks for keeping me grounded. To my student team: Michelle Amponsah, Moisés G. Contreras, Angel Cox, Woohee Kim, Shantá Harrington, and Georgina Rivers, thank you all for your hard work. I am incredibly grateful to Zora Haque and Nora Ngo Mitchell for your careful attention to this work in its final stages. I would have been lost without your diligence. Thank you! To those I might have forgotten to mention, please blame my head and not my heart.

I am grateful for the support from the National Academy of Education/ Spencer Foundation Postdoctoral Fellows Program, the Spencer Foundation's Scholar in Residence Program, and the Wallace Foundation. I appreciate Stanford University Press and my incredible editor, Marcela Maxfield. Thank you, thank you, thank you. I'm so thankful for your support. I also want to thank Justine Nicole Sargent for your kindness, Cathy Mallon, Derek Gottlieb, and all the SUP staff for making this book possible. To Charly Palmer, whose incredible and moving art, *Demand with Love*, graces the cover of *Laboring in the Shadows*: I am grateful for you and your contributions to artistic expressions of Black intellectual life, survival, thriving, and movement building.

I'd like to conclude as I began—by thanking my loved ones, family, and friends. I'm grateful for my biological and chosen family, who keep me grounded and always remind me of who I am. Thank you to my loving parents and the wonderful young people in my life: Zahra, Zion, Mecca, Lincoln Allen, Obasi, and Zafir. I must especially thank my brother, Brandon (a phenomenal educator and youth worker)—I love you dearly. To Baylor, I feel blessed to be your bonus mom; you make me proud. Again, to my partner, John, thank you for your love, support, and unwavering belief in me.

To all the youth workers who have spoken with me and my team over the years, I am in awe of you. I honor you and am deeply grateful for your presence on this earth. The young people, families, and communities you serve are fortunate to have you. Thank you for your vision and your freedom dreams.

Precarity, Paradox, and Promise

Joy's energy and her, well, joy are contagious.[1] She smiles widely as she discusses dedicating her life to working with young people. "Working with youth is my passion," she tells me while sharing the story that led her to a twenty-five-year career working with youth. As a tenth grader growing up in the Northeast, she began tutoring elementary students after school in a youth program, followed by a summer reading program, and then she began working with younger children in the dance ministry at her church. She left the Northeast for the Midwest to attend college. "I had good parents, but not rich parents," she shares through laughter. This reality encouraged her to pursue a lucrative career in marketing after college. She moved back to her home city, pursued internships with IBM, and landed a job at Xerox, but she was unhappy. "I was like, this is so boring! I do not like this. It wasn't challenging." Despite her unhappiness, Joy's supervisor had plans to promote her, but she had other plans. She decided to pursue graduate study in education since she had always loved working with youth.

Since that graduate program, Joy has held almost every job one can have in education. She has been an elementary school teacher, a math and literacy coach, a curriculum and instruction coach, directed a Head Start program, and worked for large school districts and charter school systems. When we met, she oversaw middle-school programming for a mixed media program as part of a national youth development organization in the Midwest. With an expansive career in schools and youth organizations, Joy preferred youth work in community-based organizations. She "needed autonomy" and did not want to be bogged down by the "standardization" schools are expected to uphold. As someone who exudes joy in talking about young people, Joy still craved breaks and time off because youth work can be all-consuming. "It becomes so engulfing and overwhelming that sometimes I have to take a break . . . I literally have to. My daughter wouldn't be raised if I didn't do that, right? My husband will be so mad at me, you know, because it becomes my life in a way." Despite the intensity that youth work can bring, guiding children and youth through academic, social, and personal development during non-school hours, Joy sees youth work as a way to reinvent herself. "You get to reinvent yourself, and every day is different." Reflecting on how youth work and youth workers are regarded within the broader societal and educational landscape, Joy says, "How we think about education, like it doesn't necessarily happen from that 8 to 3 time in school. That's not necessarily the only place where education takes place. A lot of it honestly takes place in the after-school space, because the kids are more open to taking risks and trying new things. And you know, being wrong and starting the process over." What Joy communicates here has been long established through decades of rich research about the positive academic and social outcomes of participating in after-school and community-based programs.[2]

Joy continues and connects society's dismissal of the after-school space to its disregard of those who hold up the field: youth workers. "I think a lot of that mindset shift has to happen before we can get to a *real* place of talking about what should a youth worker make." Joy's point is well taken here. How society regards youth workers, those who care for our children and youth when they are not in school, reflects our narrow view of learning as only being within school spaces. But what is the youth work landscape, and who are the people who work within this field? How does youth work within community-based settings support our economy, family, and school systems? How can we as a society claim to care for children and youth but do very little to support those who care for them? How do social forces like race and class shape youth workers' experiences? What are the features of this labor that require Joy to take time off? As Joy eloquently states, our view of education and learning must expand. Doing so allows our vision of who can be an educator to expand, and then, perhaps, we might be able to see all those who contribute to the learning and development of young people in this country and beyond. By truly seeing them, we can understand the ways they nurture, support, and expand the minds of youth—and we can also begin to see, understand, name, and disrupt the precarity and harm they face. Youth workers—the volunteer, part-time, or full-time staff in these programs—are essential to American social, political, economic, and educational life. However, they labor in the shadows within a rewarding yet unstable field, with layers of precarity shaping their personal and professional lives. This precarity is exacerbated for Black youth workers who seek to help Black youth navigate anti-Black racism in society. *Laboring in the Shadows* provides an interior view of the lives of Black youth workers and encourages a deeper look into the precarity and promise that shape their lives and the field.

Seeing Youth Work(ers)

Young people spend more time outside of school than inside school.[3] Roughly 10 million children and youth in the United States participate in community-based educational spaces (CBES),[4] that is, after-school programs, out-of-school time programs, youth organizations, and so on. For nearly a century, community-based after-school programs have supported the education system in providing supplementary services to youth and allowing families to continue working past school hours.[5] The field is far-reaching and supports many vital sectors important for the care and well-being of young people, families, neighborhoods, and the economy. Youth work occurs within a variety of settings, including national programs with regional locations like the Boys and Girls Clubs of America; independent grassroots organizations like Brotherhood Sister Sol in Harlem, New York; cultural institutions like museums, libraries, and theater spaces; early childhood centers; city and county agencies like youth detention centers and parks and recreation centers; faith-based spaces; group homes; federally funded college preparatory programs like Upward Bound; or programs that cater to young people who are unhoused where youth workers canvass city blocks providing basic needs like food and clothing. Each sector has its own funding structure, different approaches to youth engagement, and criteria for hiring and training youth workers.

We only have estimates of how many youth workers exist in the US. The Association of Child and Youth Care Practice estimates about two and a half million youth workers,[6] other estimates are lower.[7] There are considerable gaps in our understanding of the field, and youth workers exist across many sectors, making it difficult to calculate their number accurately. Information about the racial backgrounds, gender, and class status of youth workers is lacking, thus contributing to their invisibility and vulnerability in the workforce. As this book reveals, this precarity can be extreme for Black youth workers. The precarity in this form of labor induces paradoxes structured into youth work today, further exacerbating this instability.[8] *Laboring in the Shadows* shines a light on this precarity and invisibility while also demonstrating the power and promise of youth work as a sustaining and necessary force in Black educational and social life.

PRECARITY AND INVISIBILITY IN SHADOW WORK

When looking at community-based nonprofit youth organizations and the labor of youth work professionals, the metaphor of the shadow is particularly apt. Most youth-serving programs operate as nonprofit organizations. Nonprofit youth work organizations are not government-run organizations, but they serve a critical civic function. As a result, they exist as part of what scholar Jennifer Wolch has described as the *shadow state*—the institutions or programs outside the state that support citizens and their sociopolitical lives. The shadow state emerged in the United States alongside the rise in volunteer sectors involved in direct social services previously provided by the state through New Deal and Great Society programs.[9] The shadow state comprises organizations and programs that essentially take care of people as a complement or supplement to the state. In most cases, the shadow state makes up for what the state lacks or refuses to provide.[10]

Like those employed at many other nonprofits in this shadow state, youth workers' labor consistently goes unacknowledged and often remains invisible to those outside nonprofit youth work. A similar precarity exists for those serving as school paraprofessionals[11] or medical assistants;[12] however, the field in which they work—school systems and health-care systems—are recognizable systems of American life. Although not without inequity, hierarchies, and harm, these systems are known and part of everyday discourse. Youth work, however, does not enjoy this same recognition. The structure of youth work varies from organization to organization, contributing to a lack of general awareness of how the organizations function. And yet, millions of Americans rely on these programs to care for children, support adolescents, complement school systems, and make up for what schools cannot provide. In the US, youth work organizations serve as a social safety net for youth, and youth workers are vital to youths' development, care, and safety. However, community-based, youth-serving organizations do not function without youth workers' labor.

In a critical analysis of the shadow state, scholar and activist Ruth Gilmore makes the case that organizations and programs committed to disrupting structural and systemic oppression, or those that support the most marginalized, operate in the shadow of the shadow state.[13] In other words, social and education programs that step in to take care of society's most vulnerable and that support their disruption of systems that harm them—People of Color, children, immigrants, women and nonbinary folks, queer people, those who experience immense poverty, for example—operate within the shadow of the shadow state. Networks of formal and informal organizations operating in the shadows, caring for the most vulnerable, means that those individuals working within these spaces are also vulnerable. This vulnerability places workers in these spaces in precarious situations; they are more likely to experience burnout, overworking, low wages, lack of health benefits, and high stress levels.[14] Within this vulnerability is an invisibility from working in the shadows within programs and organizations that are not readily recognized by most of society. While there may be cursory knowledge about the existence and benefits of youth centers or extracurricular programs students may have access to after school, youth work occurs across many contexts.

In a national study I led for the Wallace Foundation, my colleagues and I attempted to bring some order to the complexity of the field of youth work. Some parts of youth work are much more visible than others. Based on our research and speaking with youth work professionals and stakeholders, some who are featured in this book, we have mapped fifteen contexts where youth work can occur (see table 0.1). We see these contexts not as fixed but malleable. They include pre-K–12 schools; national organizations and associations; independent local organizations; higher education settings; federal and state, city and county, faith-based, and cultural institutions; street-based and outreach; home, leisure, and neighborhoods; health and wellness organizations; elite college preparatory and private pay-to-participate programs; digital spaces; and intermediary and capacity-building organizations that support many youth-serving organizations at the city and state levels.

TABLE 0.1   Youth Work Landscape: Sectors, Contexts, and Examples.

Sectors and Contexts	Examples
School districts	School district providers, extracurricular activities, community schools, after-school programs
National programs	Boys and Girls Club, YMCA/YWCA, Camp Fire, etc.
Independent programs	Grassroots programs, neighborhood youth programs independent from national programs, etc.
Cultural institutions	Museums, libraries, theaters, zoos
Higher education	Upward Bound, GEAR Up, university and community partnerships, etc.
Faith-based	religious and spiritual institutions, camps, etc.
Associations and affinity groups	Rotary clubs, fraternity- and sorority-sponsored youth programs, etc.
City and county providers	Juvenile detention centers, parks/recreation, summer youth employment programs, shelters, etc.*
Federal and state	Group homes, partisan youth programs, state-wide leadership development programs, etc.*
Home and neighborhoods	Barbershops and salons, homeschool collectives, skate parks, laundromats, malls, etc.
Elite high school/college prep programs	A Better Chance, Oliver Scholars, Prep for Prep, Beacon Academy, etc.
Street-based outreach	Programs targeting unhoused youth, canvass neighborhoods to support youths' basic needs,
Health and wellness	Mental health programs, sexual health groups, support groups*
Digital	Chat rooms, digital programs, online affinity spaces
Private pay-to-participate	Private tutoring programs, elite sports groups, for-profit learning centers, private music centers
Intermediary	Capacity building, city and state after-school networks, professional development/advocacy

*Juvenile detention centers, group homes, shelters, and mental health programs (inpatient and outpatient) may be led and funded by counties, states, philanthropic groups, and independent programs.

Source: Author.

In each of these contexts, there are many spaces and formal or informal programs operating during after-school hours, weekends, summer programming, or supporting youth who may be disconnected from formal schooling or need immediate resources and care. The ecology of the youth work landscape is vast, heterogeneous, and diverse philosophically, financially, and pedagogically. Some programs are tethered to federal and city government, while others are connected to cultural institutions like libraries, zoos, museums, or faith-based spaces where it is a common practice to offer youth programming for academic support and recreation alongside cultural and spiritual development. The diversity of the field provides youth and families with options to meet their needs and interests. At the same time, this diversity in the landscape presents challenges for categorization, professionalization, and structural support for this work and for youth workers who hold up the field.[15]

Youth work programs are an essential part of civil society but are not formal state institutions or part of the family structure.[16] An important interplay exists between youth work organizations, schools, and families. Sometimes, you will hear people say that youth-serving organizations meet a need for young people that families and schools do not fulfill. This may be true in some circumstances, but a more asset-rich framing would be that these spaces can enhance what young people are provided at home and school. But because youth work organizations exist in this intersection between what schools and families provide youth, they are in the complex position of helping youth navigate all the pressures and problems associated with school and family life—including financial and domestic struggles and the structural inequalities they can face in the formal educational system. To illustrate this, let's walk through a typical day of a young person on their way to a program after school to meet a youth worker. Young people start their day at whatever home they have. For some, this will mean beginning their day surrounded by family members/guardians. For others, such as those facing poverty, abandonment by parents, or other difficulties, it might mean starting their day at a friend's house or a shelter. No matter where they start, however, they will carry any struggles with them wherever they go during the day. After leaving home or wherever they might have slept that night, they enter a form of schooling. While at school, they will have many experiences with their peers, teachers, and administrators—these experiences might reduce or augment any struggles they are facing.

As many scholars have documented, for Black youth and other marginalized young people, a school can be a site of terror and suffering, and the efforts to process and navigate any violence or suffering they face will become part of their state of mind during the day.[17] At the same time, outside of school—either on the way to school from home in the morning or while making their way from school to a youth program after school—they will witness, experience, and encounter many things that may further weigh on any struggles they may be facing. When youth finally reach the program after school, they will carry all the emotions they have witnessed and experienced through all those junctures—home, family, and neighborhood. Youth workers—who may not be state employees, may not have pensions, frequently do not have health insurance, and are almost invariably underpaid—are then tasked with creating a space for students to process or decompress from all they have experienced that day. Doing this work without a living wage is challenging for many youth workers you will meet in this book. According to the Economic Policy Institute, a living wage should provide people with enough income to support themselves without falling below the federal poverty line.[18] This entails that a full-time worker should earn an adequate income that will allow them to cover the cost of their family's basic needs according to their geographic location.[19] Structural and organizational support of youth should entail that they earn a living wage to support themselves and their families. But many youth workers are part-time and are tasked with helping students make concrete steps for their future, including academic support, and mentoring them through their worries, insecurities, and complicated and ever-evolving identities as they come of age. As they do so, youth workers will engage students in activities and dialogue, offering strategies and tools to support them. Through this work, these youth programs and the staff working there will make up for what schools fail to provide—including repairing the harms from the structure of schooling.

Despite this critical work, society remains disengaged from the work that youth workers actually do. The public, politicians, and even school educators do not always recognize or have clarity about youth workers' identities, their skills, or an understanding of their pathway to this work.[20] Within the field, and for school systems that partner with youth-serving organizations, there is immense praise for youth workers' knowledge about youth, their skills, and the connections they make with youth.[21] However, some of these things remain elusive.[22] It is a paradox that fuels precarity in the field of youth work. America depends on after-school programs, even as it neglects and underinvests in their work. The structural forces that cause hardships for families and the impact of systemic inequality within schools often fall on community-based organizations and their staff.[23] Youth work as a field and its workforce are responsible for solving structural problems, with little recognition or support, leading to great precarity that I detail throughout the book.

MAKING SENSE OF NONPROFIT SECTOR YOUTH WORK

Youth work occurs within and across diverse organizations and agencies. However, the majority of youth work programs take place within nonprofit organizations. The heterogeneity of these organizations provides youth and families with various programs to participate in, but this diversity creates some unique challenges for the field and those who work in these spaces. Although there are similarities across organizations and how youth workers engage with young people in these settings, funding structures, leadership, philosophy, and approaches to engaging youth vary.

As nonprofits, community-based educational organizations share tax-exempt status, sometimes leading people to believe these organizations share the same purpose.[24] The reality is more complicated. Although nonprofit organizations indeed have explicit missions to serve the public or have a clear "social purpose,"[25] the nature of these organizations' work and their impact vary dramatically between organizations. Because of the vast number of nonprofits in the United States—especially those that support education[26]—and their role in providing essential services not provided by the state, some researchers have described nonprofits as the "organizing infrastructure of civil society."[27] They are created, led, and used by many people across the political spectrum.[28] Sociologist Woody Powell has written about how the legal and social framing of nonprofits implies firm boundaries in the nature of their public function; however, nonprofits range from public service, education, volunteer organizations, and charities to professional and social associations.[29] Powell notes how the concept of a "sector" can imply that all organizations in that ' sector" have a fundamental similarity in their social role. However, this impression is flawed, as it fails to account for the work they actually do or provide for organizational members and the public. Some nonprofits produce millions of dollars, for example, while many struggle to keep their lights on and the doors open.[30]

The general public may not always remember that public and private colleges and universities, faith-based institutions, foundations, and philanthropic agencies all benefit from the same nonprofit designation that provides them with tax-exempt status. However, this same tax and legal status, for example, is also given to shelters that provide services to those who are unhoused, neighborhood arts-based programs for the elderly or young people, and bare-bones drop-in tutoring programs for teens. But the work these organizations do is often profoundly different and often with competing political or cultural objectives.

In the public imagination, nonprofit workers are framed as "do-gooders" who engage in this work for the common good or because they love it. They are then framed as "noble," which often justifies their low wages, inhumane working conditions, and long, grueling hours because they "love what they do."[31] People pursuing careers in education, school systems, or community-based educational spaces are the quintessential workers defined by this framing. Those who work with children are pegged as doing valuable and necessary work. And yet, teachers have organized for higher salaries and rightly complained about the time and personal money they put into their teaching, often at the cost of their well-being.[32] Educational scholars have written about teachers' multiple roles in schools, especially those underfunded and neglected by the state.[33] We ask teachers to teach students, be social workers, nurses, and security guards, and now carry weapons instead of passing sensible gun laws. Although powerful, teachers' unions are sometimes framed as greedy and unworthy of the demands they request because they "should want to teach" even under the most stressful, untenable conditions.[34] The same thing happens to youth workers outside of school contexts who seek better working conditions, as if expecting better wages or more secure jobs contrasts with the "nobility" of their work. People's instinct to criticize this kind of demand as inappropriate, however, is directly tied to the do-gooder and noble characterizations so frequently associated with education and nonprofit work. As the journalist Sarah Jaffe highlights in her 2021 book, *Work Won't Love You Back*, this framing of "suffering for the cause" speaks to the notion that those who do good in the world for young people or other vulnerable populations should want to do these jobs for free or little pay because they can be incredibly rewarding, meaningful, and fulfilling.[35] And, as Joy reminds us, it can also be overwhelming.

This view of nonprofit workers encourages a cycle of precarity for workers and leads the economic and social value of certain kinds of work to be ignored or dismissed. Nonprofit organizations centered on care work or education, and those that organize for civil rights and social justice are essential to society. Jaffe describes this as a "labor of love ideology" in which people's devotion to their jobs, particularly those in human services, care, and education work, continues to be exploited in these professions due to neoliberal ideology that positions them as worthy only of the wages and protection an unregulated market offers them. Jaffe and numerous labor and political economy scholars have discussed how the integration of neoliberal logic in public policy—including notions of individualism, choice, and privatization—fuels precarity for nonprofit workers by encouraging society to adopt minimally regulated market-based approaches for the provision of social services.[36] For those who work in nonprofit jobs (as well as working-class jobs, menial labor, etc.), the impact of this is severe, and they can face a deep precarity that the general public and policymakers position as an individual choice rather than an indictment of a system predicated on adherence to capitalism that reproduces harm, exploitation, and poverty.[37]

Today, because of the broad integration of these ideologies in the American legal and cultural imagination, nonprofits dedicated to serving fundamental social needs—including human services, education, care work, social justice, and political education—are nested within a cycle of financial dependency, paternalism, infiltration, and sabotage. Scholars refer to this cycle as the nonprofit industrial complex (NPIC).[38] The negative impacts of this cycle are most prevalent for programs and workers who are part of grassroots, politically inclined, and social justice–oriented organizations. In a popular edited volume organized by the group INCITE! Women Against Violence, entitled *The Revolution Will Not Be Funded*, scholar and activist Dylan Rodriguez refers to this nonprofit industrial complex as "the industrialized incorporation of pro-state liberal and progressive campaigns and movements into a spectrum of government-proctored non-profit organizations."[39] However, the industrial incorporation of nonprofits has underwritten and encouraged a crisis for youth workers—a cycle of precarity built into the DNA of the nonprofit system itself.

For most, education and learning are often synonymous with schooling. Teachers are positioned as the sole bearers of knowledge and the only adults who can teach young people. As such, anyone outside of the traditional schoolteacher role or outside of school systems is not often considered an educator or pedagogue in the same way.[40] However, as other scholars and I have documented, this is incorrect. Youth work professionals don't just "work with kids"; they are key actors in a system of education and care work that is meaningful and necessary for young people's education and social development.[41] However, youth workers exist within a fluid and multifaceted profession that is not entirely stable, which creates a challenge for policymakers and the public to categorize their labor. This can lead to precarious labor marked by low wages, instability, discrimination, inadequate to no benefits, or immense debt.

The institutional arrangement of youth-serving programs and organizations creates a particular instability in the youth work profession. Youth-serving programs can exist within and be facilitated by various institutions, systems, and organizations. Youth workers are situated within these spaces, from school districts to independent organizations, faith-based institutions, local government, city programs, and cultural institutions like libraries and museums. This means youth workers are subject to a complex variety of employer approaches for hiring, wages, and leadership development. For youth workers, however, these diverging approaches among organizations lead to serious challenges and paradoxes they must face in their professional and personal lives. However, these are not challenges that youth workers themselves can solve—they result from broader sociopolitical systems, including racial capitalism, and how youth development in the US is arranged and facilitated mainly by nonprofits and grassroots community-based youth organizations.

Paradox and Promise in Youth Work

My older brother is a special education teacher in Los Angeles. He has three children—two are in middle school, and one is in elementary school. For those familiar with the Los Angeles landscape, you know that getting through rush hour traffic is a nightmare. My brother depends on after-school programs because he cannot leave work to pick up my nieces and nephew. Like many other parents in the US, my brother relies on school-based and community-based after-school programs to engage children after school, support them with homework, feed them, and allow them opportunities to play, learn a new skill, or hone existing talents. My brother's experience is common for most American families. Families rely on these spaces to continue working past school hours and have peace of mind that their children are safe, engaging in activities they enjoy, and connecting with their peers and positive adults.[42] Despite this reliance and dependence on youth work, there is an invisibility and perhaps a taken-for-granted unconscious disregard for the field and youth workers. The societal reliance on youth work and underinvestment is a paradox that needs unpacking.

I see multiple paradoxes integrated into youth work. First, a paradox exists in which youth workers remain largely invisible and unrecognized despite massive public reliance on them from families, schools, and the economy. After-school and community-based youth organizations are recognized as a complement to formal schooling. However, they are rarely included in educational decision-making and struggle for funding, and those who uphold the field tend to be an afterthought.[43]

Secondly, a paradox exists within the occupational identities[44] of youth workers trapped in a cycle of "noble" and necessary work that leads to financial and professional precarity imposed on them even as they serve an essential civic function. They are essentially exploited for their commitment to working with youth. The profession of youth work is often considered a "calling." As this book explains, Black youth workers frequently follow a certain pattern when they enter the profession. Many youth workers feel called or even obligated to support their communities and young people in the same way they were supported when they were younger—to "pay it forward." A commitment to Black education, liberation, and free futures for Black youth consistently inspires them. This commitment guides their work and sustains them as they navigate the kind of complex precarity that this book outlines. *Youth worker* is a term that is legible in most spaces in the US and abroad in places like the United Kingdom, Ireland, and Sweden. Scholars like Deepa Vasudevan have noted that *youth workers* can function as an umbrella term for a wide range of positions in the lives of youth, including coaches, community-based educators, mentors, counselors, teaching artists, cultural workers, and tutors.[45] While the occupational identities of youth workers vary[46] and have shifted over time and are mainly dependent on the sector they work within, what holds is that the commitment these workers make to the profession is not always rewarded in money, appreciation, or respect. The commitment to nonprofit work, like youth development, furthers the exploitation of its workers because of neoliberal logic that indicts workers for what they cannot manage instead of the capitalist system that keeps workers suffering.[47]

This contradiction between personal dedication and the scope of recognition and compensation workers receive is built into the system of youth work today. As the journalist Sarah Jaffe argues, many Americans, including nonprofit organization workers, hold jobs they mostly enjoy because they want to give back to their communities or support worthy causes. However, they maintain this sense of meaning even while receiving low wages, struggling to make a sustainable living, and being vulnerable to mistreatment. Jaffe outlines how workers in jobs and careers considered noble or a "labor of love" are typically the most exploited.[48] Education and care professions, like health care, are always regarded as noble, righteous, and essential. We praise individuals for their work, particularly their sacrifices, and ability to do their jobs without little recognition or support. However, as this book explains, for youth workers, like others who work in these "noble" professions, this lack of support has concrete and dangerous consequences, including low wages, housing instability, lack of benefits, food insecurity, looming debt, or the inability to unionize.

These challenges manifest in different ways depending on the nature of youth work. While some youth workers hold part-time and full-time positions where they engage with students during after-school hours during the week, those involved in youth detention centers, group homes, or shelters may find themselves working every day of the week or make themselves available for students twenty-four hours a day. Long hours, low wages, minimal protections, and a high risk of harm and exploitation consistently leave workers in this field in precarious positions.[49] Still, youth workers find themselves in these positions out of a sense of commitment to community, obligation, or simply because they love engaging with young people. They are often torn between their responsibilities to young people and community and the precarious situations that threaten their livelihoods. Black youth workers, who work in predominantly white-led organizations, face specific forms of exploitation, including anti-Black racism, which they must navigate as they attempt to push back against the deficit framing of Black youth as needing to be saved or fixed by programs.[50] For Black youth workers, it is a paradox with agonizing implications for their professional identity: to pursue a calling to support and engage Black youth means working in a field that often exploits them.

Finally, a paradox exists in the nonprofit organizational model where youth workers must navigate deficit-framing of the racially minoritized and multiply marginalized prompted by the political, social, and historical context undergirding the nonprofit sector, constructions and moral panics about youth, and racial and class logics that engender contradictory routines and youth engagement in the context of organizations.[51] Youth work organizations are among the most important sites for learning and personal growth for young people in the United States. Their pervasive place in the lives of American youth means that what happens in these programs has significant implications for the broader development of America's children.

Literature on youth work within multiple disciplines, including education, public health, sociology, and social work, sometimes risks positioning youth work outside formal schools in opposition to schools, thus creating a false dichotomy of *good* and *bad* or *affirming* and *stifling*. I have suggested in previous work, and still hold, that Black community-based youth work generally provides a safer physical, emotional, and psychic space for Black youth—an opportunity to receive second and third chances to make youthful mistakes and gain direction on navigating difficult academic and social experiences.[52] However, like all social institutions existing within an unjust world, paradoxes and contradictions exist, and community-based youth programming is not exempt.[53]

Community-based youth work organizations exist within a broader sociopolitical context that can shape how programs are constructed, how programming is developed, and how youth workers and young people experience programs.[54] As such, community organizations can both disrupt and reproduce anti-Black racism, paternalism, colonial mindsets, and kid-fixing discourses.[55] Like all organizations, these spaces do not continuously operate within a dichotomy. Sometimes, youth programs often frame Black youth as inherently deficient and in need of saving. On the other hand, sometimes they frame Black youth through a more asset-based approach, treating them as brilliant and capable young people who may be navigating challenging circumstances in their lives. However, it is more frequently the case that programs include a mix of these frames; they can hold multiple logics and approaches to youth work at once. This paradoxical framing of Black youth is widely integrated into youth work organizations today. This reveals the contradictions that define what it means to provide educational and care work within a system of structural oppression. Because of the significance of youth work organizations in the United States today—both in terms of the number of organizations and the opportunities and risks they present—it is vital to identify, unpack, and examine how these paradoxes stem from precarity and how they also induce precarity.

There are numerous challenges that scholars and policymakers still need to address, even for codifying the broader field. Because we only have estimates of how many youth workers exist in the US, and these workers exist across many different organizational types, the number is difficult to fully calculate with precision.[56] It also indicates that information about the racial backgrounds, gender, and class status of youth workers is lacking, thus contributing to Black youth workers' vulnerability. Developing a more statistically comprehensive understanding of youth work will be essential as we address the precarity and paradoxes in the field. Providing more specificity for understanding the plight and needs of youth workers is necessary—Black, Latine, Indigenous, Asian American, Pacific Islander; youth workers from refugee and immigrant backgrounds, from low-income or queer communities. It is imperative that we understand the specificity of their experiences to build organizational and structural support within the field.[57]

The contemporary precarity facing youth workers in the field has connections to the history and formation of formalized youth work in the United States. The precarity and resilience of Black youth workers today can be traced back to Black educational history, which uncovers the power and promise of Black education and Black youth development.

How We Got Here

In the early 1900s, as new definitions of *child* and *youth* were rendered, child labor was banned, and compulsory education became the law, the need for after-school care became apparent.[58] Idle children, especially youth living in poverty, were positioned as a problem by educators, social welfare advocates, and politicians.[59] Early after-school spaces like settlement houses in New York City, the Hull House in Chicago, scouting, and summer camps engaged children in workforce development, citizenship education for European immigrants, play, and gender-segregated social activities.[60] These early spaces—scouting, summer camps, children's clubs, and settlement houses—developed during the Progressive Era. As historical research has shown, these early spaces of after-school care sought to build character, citizenship, and language development for immigrant youth; reinforce gendered tasks and performances; and expose city kids to rural contexts and opportunities for recreation and play.[61] These spaces within policy contexts were organized and facilitated by white middle-class city residents who held assumptions about race, place, class, and gender that informed their engagement with youth.[62] As policy initiatives were established during the New Deal Era, after the Great Depression, programs like the National Youth Administration provided young people the opportunity for employment and learning trades. Still, as educational historian Rachel Klepper suggests, the responsibility of who or what would house after-school programs became a point of contention. With loose policy support, after-school education became the nonprofit sector's work. Offloading this work to the nonprofit sector has created a dynamic of dependency on wealthy philanthropists and a reliance on advocacy for political support, placing these efforts solely on those who work in these settings to advocate for their work.

The model of youth work organizations that most people think of today when they think of "after-school programs" are the ones that have roots in the late 1970s and 1980s. During this time, there was a boom in the creation of after-school programs, fueled by the rise in 501(c)3 nonprofits funded by private philanthropy.[63] These programs were sometimes associated with schools but often run by community-based organizations outside schools. However, the motivation to create and fund these kinds of programs was often driven by fear of low-income and nonwhite youth.[64] Federal reports highlighted the crisis facing youth in the '80s and '90s and declared that the most dangerous time is between 3:00 pm and 6:00 pm.[65] As a result, the programs that were created during this time were often aimed directly at Black, Latine, and youth living in poverty.[66] Although presented as providing academic support for these kids, the reality is far harsher, and these after-school programs consistently acted as sites of control and surveillance.

This targeting of Black and Latine youth became severe during the War on Drugs campaign, a political, cultural, and media campaign by the US government that stigmatized and attacked nonwhite communities with excessive punishments for drug use or possession, leading to the imprisonment of huge numbers of Black and Latine boys and men that would fuel the mass incarceration crisis we experience today.[67] At the same time as this mass imprisonment program was underway, there was a notable rise in organizations in cities targeting Black and Latine youth.[68] During these initial decades of the War on Drugs campaign, there was extensive use of anti-Black framing of youth as "super predators" that were "wilding," a scare campaign that helped white politicians gain votes but that led to state violence against Black Americans.[69] This included public calls for violence, such as, in the '80s and '90s, the anti-Black calls for the death penalty for the now Exonerated Five— the five Black and Latino men who ranged from ages thirteen to sixteen at the time of their false arrests for the 1989 violent sexual assault in Central Park.[70] At the same time, school officials, nonprofits, and politicians advocating youth work programs did so by framing youth programs as spaces of containment for Black and Latine youth, as sites to control "male criminality and female sexuality," as scholar Soo Ah Kwon put it.[71] Today, this vision of youth programs endures. In philanthropy and the public imagination, these programs can still perpetuate the notion that they exist to ensure that "Black girls don't get pregnant and that Black boys don't join gangs or engage in crime."[72]

This view of youth work programs and Black youth during the '70s, '80s, and '90s gained wide traction among the people organizing youth work programs. It led after-school programs to integrate anti-Black and paternalist framing of Black youth as "at risk" and "needing to be fixed" or "saved"—a framing that depicts Black youth as deficient, which shaped how these programs are designed and how the programs engage with youth.[73] This deficit framing has saturated our political and popular discourse, especially within media and film. There is no shortage of white savior films, like *The Principal, Dangerous Minds,* or *Freedom Writers,* positioning Black (and Brown) youth from a position of "lack."[74] There is also a healthy dose of Black male superhero films like *Coach Carter* or *Lean on Me,* where the message is that Black youth, boys in particular, need a "tough love" that leaves them broken and then put back together again by a Black male superhero who coincidently is from the same neighborhood they are, and has returned to rescue all the Black children.[75] Chicano/a/x studies and education scholar Michael Singh theorizes this phenomenon for Latino male educators mentoring Latino boys in schools and community-based organizations.[76] These framings reinforce deeply held anti-Black and gendered stereotypes that ultimately inform funding decisions, marketing approaches, and programming.[77] These social policies and the political and cultural histories driving them shape youth work practice in the United States in ways that are not just racist or paternalistic; they are deeply anti-Black as they render Black children and youth as objects, not humans, to be saved, surveilled, and contained. Youth workers must then navigate these long-standing tensions and paradoxes in the field.

Today, after-school programs and youth work organizations operate all over the country. For several decades, scholarship on youth work and after-school education has highlighted the academic benefits and educational outcomes associated with youth participation in after-school programs like tutoring and mentorship. According to the Afterschool Alliance, an advocacy organization, 69% of youth participating in after-school programs show academic improvement, greater attachment to schools, and improvement in behavior.[78] Beyond academic gains and where most of my work has been situated, these programs support young people's identity development, greater self-efficacy, a stronger sense of self, and the ability to create change in their schools and neighborhoods.

Recovering Youth Work in Black History

The class-based prevention narrative of "keeping kids off the street so they cannot commit crimes" would follow after-school programming into subsequent decades and quickly became racialized. During the Great Migration in the early twentieth century, large numbers of Black families from the South moved to the North and West in search of economic opportunity and to escape the Southern violence during the post-Reconstruction and the Jim Crow era. This migration northward led to a considerable growth in the number of Black children attending schools who needed after-school care. But many after-school programs at this time, like those in the settlement houses that targeted children of European immigrant families, excluded Black youth.[79] Youth work in Black communities emerged out of necessity in the face of this kind of segregation, along with the pervasive white violence in schools and exclusion that Black youth faced in spaces of public leisure and play.[80] Adults from the Black community were the ones who stepped in to fill this void, forming community-based organizations to provide education and support Black children—a form of engagement that, because of the social circumstances, aimed to educate for social change and political awareness.[81] To place Black youth workers in their proper historical context, it is important to locate how educators beyond formal school settings sought to educate, nurture, and prepare Black youth for the world. Though there are many, I would like to point to three historical examples in which Black youth work is evident.

FUGITIVITY

The act of pursuing education was a fugitive act once deemed criminal and outlawed for Black people.[82] From the formation of Black Literary Societies[83] to Independent Black Institutions,[84] Black communities have always carved out space for learning, storytelling, and a reclamation of humanity in fugitivity. Historian Jarvis Givens grapples with fugitivity as an act of escape and uses it as an analytic to interrogate Black education as a historical and political act, as well as the critical role of Black educators' determination and belief in education and freedom being inseparably linked together within Black communities.[85] I see community-based educational spaces as fugitive spaces or Black education fugitive spaces, as defined by scholar kihana miraya ross;[86] they are an escape for Black youth from the exclusion, discrimination, and physical, psychic, and curricular violence they may face in school.[87] Before *Brown v. Board of Education*, though with little resources, Black students, teachers, and administrators had nurturing school spaces where Black youth thrived.[88] Black communities have always found ways to educate, nurture, and prepare Black youth for the world as it is.

Historically, outside-of-school spaces were used as sites of learning and sociopolitical awareness for youth to navigate a hostile world. Black churches often served as out-of-school spaces; advocacy organizations and independent Black publications provided educational and sociopolitical literature and activities with Black youth in mind.[89] As Givens explains in *Fugitive Pedagogy: Carter G. Woodson and the Art of Black Teaching*, out-of-school spaces were critical sites of Black pedagogy, which cultivated learning and political identity development. He writes: "Out-of-school spaces were always important sites of Black pedagogy . . . Woodson's Sunday school classroom, sites like the

Wheatley home, black newspapers, and even his Association. Woodson's conviction to support the educational development of black people, particularly as it pertained to their radical and political identities, pushed him to operate in this way."[90] Developing Black children's political identities was essential to understanding and navigating an anti-Black world because a lack of knowledge of the impending threat of white supremacist violence and terror could be detrimental. The pedagogy in community-based programs has always been diverse, but those that specifically help Black youth deconstruct how structural racism and anti-Blackness operate in their schooling experiences and within broader society have been vital.

MARY McLEOD BETHUNE AND THE NATIONAL YOUTH ADMINISTRATION

Following the Great Depression, under the leadership of Franklin D. Roosevelt, the National Youth Administration (NYA) emerged as part of New Deal programs to help bring people out of poverty. From 1935 to 1943, the NYA provided young people, ages sixteen to twenty-five, opportunities for skill development, employment, and education. Mary McLeod Bethune, the formidable education leader, activist, teacher, philanthropist, investor, businesswoman, and founder of the National Council for Negro Women, insisted that the NYA have a division catering specifically to the needs of Black youth, known as the Negro Division.[91] As the first and only Black division head in the cabinet, Bethune worked to provide funds to support Black students in school and created training and employment programs to support young people's interests. She sought to provide education and workforce development opportunities to teens, older teens, and young adults who desired employment and mobility. According to Africana studies scholar Noliwe Rooks, the first programs she created were camps for Black girls and single young women in Chicago, New Jersey, Florida, and North and South Carolina.[92] As a lifelong educator, Bethune understood the importance of cultivating Black agency and allowing young people the opportunity to reach their fullest potential. I like to think of Bethune as a youth worker—a Black educator and leader committed to Black youths' development. Her programs included vocational classes where students were offered stipends for attending, student government associations, civic education, writing development, and instruction in Black history to ensure that students understood their legacies and where they came from. The theme of Black history and political education would recur throughout the struggle for Black liberation and freedom through Black youth work.

Civil rights history also marks a critical time for Black youth development as the struggle for Black freedom continued. The contemporary engagement of Black youth inside community-based educational spaces is rooted in the historical legacy of Black education and spaces of learning Black people created for affirmation and survival. From the Black Panther Party's mission of political education, their Free Breakfast Programs, and Liberation Schools to the Freedom Schools of the Student Nonviolent Coordinating Committee (SNCC) to Black faith-based spaces and Black civil society organizations—preparing Black youth for the realities of an anti-Black world has always been an important practice in Black communities, and it is a practice that has consistently extended beyond formal school spaces.[93]

FREEDOM SCHOOLS, LIBERATION SCHOOLS, AND POLITICAL EDUCATION

Although SNCC's Freedom Schools, the Black Panther Party's Liberation Schools, and other community programs cannot be romanticized—as differences in philosophy and pedagogical approaches to teaching Black children led to discord within the movement—these earlier educational projects played a crucial role in setting the stage for future programs aimed at supporting Black youth.[94] The philosophical and pedagogical approaches to the education of Black youth shifted as politics shifted.[95] SNCC's initial approach relied on white Northerners coming to the South as volunteers to teach, and classes were rooted in the belief that guiding youth through critical questioning of their own realities would develop their social awareness and help them make sense of the world and themselves. As educational historian Daniel Perlstein writes, "The commitment to giving students the opportunity to construct meaning from their experiences drew on the belief that African American students could collectively reshape their world."[96] Pedagogy was open-ended and inquiry-based. On the other hand, the Black Panthers' pedagogy was intentional, explicit, and rooted in radical analysis of society. The focus on transmitting knowledge independent of white American culture characterized their network in Liberation Schools.[97] Despite diverging approaches to educating Black youth, the seeds planted by Black scholars, educators, and activists, along with the pedagogy for educational freedom and self-determination from groups like SNCC and the Black Panther Party, are present today and can be seen within independent Black institutions, including community-based educational spaces committed to preparing Black youth for a world that refuses to see their humanity.[98] Through the legacy of Carter G. Woodson's Saturday Schools, the creation of Black Literary Societies formed due to the exclusion of Black people from formal education, the Negro Division of the NYA, SNCC's Freedom Schools, and the Black Panther Party's Liberation Schools, Black communities have always created spaces of education, deep study of the world, and space to affirm Black humanity.[99]

Black educators and organizing strategists are paramount to movements for Black liberation, and Black youth workers are part of that tradition. *Laboring in the Shadows* speaks to this sometimes hidden historical tradition while celebrating and elevating the parallel experiences of Black youth workers today. Their contributions to Black education and victories in a precarious field need greater political attention and deeper study.

Confronting Black Precarity

Youth work as a field operates within the shadow state, and those committed to social-justice organizing specifically operate within the shadow of the shadow state, deepening the precarity of youth workers and the paradoxes in a field that society relies on, but one that is hidden within the shadows. Placing Black youth work within a historical context can spotlight the specific forms of precarity facing Black youth workers. As Judith Butler explains, precarity is a "politically induced condition in which certain populations suffer from failing social and economic networks of support and become differentially exposed to injury, violence, and death."[100] This condition leads to an increased risk of "disease, poverty, starvation, displacement, and exposure to violence without protection."[101] With the United States' heavy reliance on capitalism, those living in poverty and the working class are regularly working jobs that sustain society and benefit the elite. But these jobs are precarious—and they can be physically dangerous, lack adequate benefits and health-care support, and are prone to disrespect and unsafe working conditions, alongside other harsh conditions that make their labor arduous.[102]

Youth work, as a field, is diverse, has a heterogeneous infrastructure, and is susceptible to significant precarity. Programs engaging young people vary in their scope of work, access, approach to youth development, funding sources, professionalization, and professional learning opportunities. But because of these organizations' social framing, structure, and funding, people working in them confront great uncertainty, high turnover, low wages, and housing instability, among other challenges. Many youth workers struggle to make a living wage. For Black youth workers, the instability of the profession, coupled with how anti-Black racism can be embedded in organizations, remain key drivers of these precarious circumstances.[103] Due to legacies of structural anti-Blackness embedded into law and social institutions, Black workers have always been in precarious employment situations while simultaneously fighting against injustice.[104]

In some ways, the precarious experience of Black youth workers in the profession is not different from that which Black workers face in other occupations. The threat of discrimination and anti-Blackness create tension and racial stress that Black workers have always dealt with.[105] Precarity surfaces in many areas of Black life beyond education, including social services, health care, and housing.[106] Black youth workers, like other Black professionals, must find ways to navigate this—not only to survive personally and professionally but also to support the youth they work with.

Just like Black life is not defined solely by anti-Blackness, precarity and suffering also do not define Black life. The pursuit of justice, freedom, joy, and liberation have always been features of Black life that have grounded Black educational experiences.[107] Black youth workers committed to creating culturally sustaining[108] and emancipatory spaces of learning and development for Black youth know this. Black youth workers intimately understand that their work occurs out of necessity, and even with the inevitability of anti-Blackness, they foster dream spaces, imagination, and healing for Black youth despite the harms they are likely to face in an anti-Black world.

The Projects That Led to This Book

In the summer of 2020—a summer marked by the uprisings against police violence after the killings of George Floyd, Breonna Taylor, and far too many others, as well as the fear of the COVID-19 pandemic—I was approached by the Wallace Foundation to conduct a study about equity in the out-of-school time field. Together, alongside four colleagues and a team of students, we set out to talk with those we identified as "experts" in the field. We held fifty-eight interviews with people connected to youth work: program leaders, frontline youth workers, scholars, and policy influencers who advocated for out-of-school spaces. We also conducted focus groups with a total of thirty-five people. Of these ninety-three people, twenty-seven were Black. As part of our project, we also created a team of youth researchers—high school and college-aged students—to engage their peers about the matters most import-ant to them regarding out-of-school time. As I began coding these data, I realized a pattern emerging from the interviews with Black youth workers, program leaders, and scholars. There were similarities in their motivations for entering the profession, parallel experiences of financial precarity, lead-ership ceilings, and workplace dynamics rooted in tokenism, racial micro-aggressions, and anti-Black racism. They raised similar concerns about the field as my previous ethnographic work in Pleasant Ridge,[109] a predominantly white college midwestern city with immense racial disparities facing Black residents, and especially Black youth.

I conducted ethnographic fieldwork and interviews over four years be-tween 2015 and 2020. I interviewed Black youth workers to understand how they made sense of anti-Black racism and how they supported Black students in their unpacking of racial disparities. In addition to fieldwork, observing twenty-two events in the city addressing racial disparities, I conducted six-teen interviews with youth workers in Pleasant Ridge—fourteen identified as Black. Based on the recurring themes in interviews from 2016 and 2020, I engaged in another round of interviews with Black youth workers and pro-gram leaders across the country to understand how they understood race and anti-Black racism in their work and how the uprisings in 2020 shaped and reshaped their work with Black youth. From these additional fifteen in-terviews, conducted between 2022 and 2023, with Black youth workers from every region of the United States, I bring to the forefront a collection of ex-periences, stories of survival, resistance, and joy within Black youth work. Through the narratives of fifty-five Black youth workers across the country and ethnographic fieldwork in Pleasant Ridge, I explore their interiority as they work with a drive and unshakable commitment to Black educational justice.[110] In the appendix, I offer more details about my research methods.

Black youth workers serve as confidants, educators, and guides to Black students during some of the most challenging times in their lives. *Laboring in the Shadows* captures their maneuvers to work within and through the paradoxes amid the precarity that emerges within the field, their organizations, and their professional identities.

What's to Come

This book takes the reader into the lives of dedicated Black youth workers from every region of the United States to understand their interior lives and how they navigate precarity and contradiction in the field of youth work as they try to support Black youth at the same time. It captures their experiences navigating complicated organizational dynamics that reinforce anti-Black racism; it highlights their personal and professional commitment to Black liberation through education and youth development; and it shows what it means to work to protect Black youth while also trying to protect themselves and their livelihoods.

In the first chapter, I introduce Chris, an extraordinary poet and youth worker from the Midwest, and other Black youth workers from around the country.[111] I weave together the similarities in their motivations for entering youth work, why they choose to work with Black youth, and their expectations of the field. Each strongly desired to "pay it forward," support their communities, and follow their passions for working with youth. They quickly found that youth worker labor can be overwhelming and susceptible to low wages, inadequate benefits, instability, and a lack of respect and recognition for their work. Through their stories, I capture the structural precarity shaping the field and the lives of youth workers. In chapter 2, I turn to Pleasant Ridge, where we meet Brandon, a dedicated youth worker who held two youth work jobs, struggled with housing security, and desperately sought leadership positions to no avail. Pleasant Ridge is a predominantly white midwestern city that boasts it is one of the best places to live and raise a family but has some of the most abysmal statistics showing racial disparities where Black people, and youth in particular, are deeply impacted. Black youth workers in Pleasant Ridge specifically share the challenges of housing insecurity and progressing into positions of power and leadership in white-led organizations. I detail how Black youth workers navigate anti-Black racism in a self-proclaimed liberal city that lauds progressive stances but where Black people find themselves at the very bottom of the social and economic ladder. Through the powerful narratives of Black youth workers organizing alongside Black youth for racial justice, this chapter illuminates their survival working within oppressive spaces and their struggle for power in their respective organizations.

In chapter 3, I again zoom out to the national landscape during what scholar-activist Robin D. G. Kelley calls Black Spring, in which millions of people around the globe protested to demand justice for George Floyd and other victims of police violence in 2020.[112] I make the case that Black Spring was not exceptional and that violence against Black people is ordinary—and in this ordinariness, youth workers are tasked with making space for Black youth to make sense of their witnessing and mourning of Black death. I detail how Black youth workers create the conditions for Black youth to push back—how they fight to resist, fight for self-determination, and fight to dream and imagine the world anew.

Chapter 4 draws on the experiences of Black youth workers who are striving to provide a soft landing for Black youth while enduring anti-Black racism and harm at the same time. Through the experiences of youth workers like Hippolyta and Olivia, I show how they create opportunities for political education, joy, and respite in the context of community-based education as a form of protection against the structural, physical, and psychic harms they face in society. In making space for political education, or to "know and understand the world," and joy, this chapter highlights the strategies employed by Black youth workers to protect Black youth from the harms of anti-Black violence in schools and within the larger society while also trying to seek joy and heal themselves from the enduring trauma of anti-Blackness they face in their workplaces and within their respective cities.

While *Laboring in the Shadows* uncovers the structural conditions that shape youth work organizations and the precarious nature of being a youth worker, and how this precarity is exacerbated for Black youth workers due to anti-Black racism, it is also a book about the essence of Black education and its purpose—political consciousness, self-improvement, and social change.[113] Focusing on change and Black futurity, chapter 5 addresses this directly, capturing Black youth workers' knowledge, depth of experience, and pedagogical expertise as educators and important figures in the educational lives of Black youth despite the precarity and contradictions in the field. In this chapter, I connect youth workers' past, present, and future experiences by allowing them to imagine themselves and their work in the future. Despite the inevitability of anti-Blackness in society, I make the case that *Black youth work is the process of futuring.* To do this work, the youth workers I spoke with deeply believe in the brilliance and agency of Black youth while knowing and understanding what awaits them in a world that constantly disregards their humanity.

Community-based youth workers are vital educators who benefit our society, yet their work is often invisible and delegitimized. They operate in the shadows—they are intercessors, cultural workers, advocates, nurturers, and mentors, among many other roles. However, their work is often unseen, unrecognized, or dismissed altogether. How do we make visible the lived experiences of youth workers made most vulnerable by white supremacy, capitalism, patriarchy, and other systems of power that make work precarious? In the conclusion, I present a call to action for the public, educators, scholars, policymakers, and funders of youth work programs. Youth workers are positioned to be responsible for solving deeply structural problems with little support, recognition, and compensation for their labor. I also highlight the current federal support of youth work, the advocacy of states and local out-of-school time systems, and new research that presents some exciting possibilities for the future of youth work.

An Invitation

In this book's preface, I began with a personal story about my journey to youth work as a teenager, a youth worker, and an engaged scholar. This was not easy for me. I am an ambivert, and sharing my narrative feels not only vulnerable but I also question why anyone would care. Youth work, especially outside of traditional school contexts, has always represented freedom, discovery, joy, and personal power that is sometimes difficult to explain. Growing up in a Black family that celebrated education and as a student of sociology and Black studies, the connections between contemporary youth work and Black educational fugitivity,[114] both historically and contemporarily, are clear. Still, these spaces and the lives of youth workers, especially the most vulnerable, cannot be romanticized. Contradictions exist within the conflicting purposes of education. Paradoxes are a standard part of social life, particularly in a social world where structural inequality is deeply embedded. Black people have always endured the contradictions of America and have had a complicated relationship with freedom, self-determination, and education.[115] There is always precarity in Black life.[116] Through the voices and wisdom of the youth workers I have come to know through writing this book, I hope to provide language and spaces for us all to reflect on the ways the most vulnerable endure precarity while providing a labor and service society depends on.

While reading *Laboring in the Shadows*, I invite you to rethink education beyond school walls and take action to support and invest in youth workers and understand their diverse needs based on their social positioning. My work begs us to consider whose labor matters. I see the work within community-based educational spaces within a long tradition of educational fugitivity for Black people. The Black youth workers in my book teach to transgress[117]—they push beyond the boundaries of systems and paradoxes within the field—as they envision radical possibilities in their work with Black youth. This sense of radical possibility is reflected in the youth workers and program leaders who spoke with me and my team; it's in the power of young people and the strength of emancipatory spaces of learning and care when Black youth workers work alongside Black youth to help them understand the conditions that shape their lives, generate tools to help them push back on systems that harm them, and dream and envision a world anew. I see radical possibilities within the youth workers who shared their stories with me and a love in action[118] that allows them to get up every day and work on behalf of young people for little recognition, little pay, and long hours because they believe in the work they do—and more specifically, because they believe in the brilliance, creativity, and futures of Black youth.

ONE

Working in the Shadows

> We are expected to be martyrs; we are expected to serve nobly and to never question. And if ever we asked for our needs to be met, we're demonized and told that, "Oh, you must not really care about the kids."
>
> —OLIVIA, youth worker

> On college applications, you always hear about the coach, mentor, or person who affected the trajectory in a way that changed this kid's life. But how often do we ask how much was that coach paid?
>
> —CHRIS, youth worker

Chris's love for writing and spoken word led him to Mr. Rashad. While trying to impress a girl, he signed up to participate in a spoken word competition. He didn't get the girl, but he did win the competition. He had always loved writing, specifically poetry, but sharing his work publicly was new. After doing the competition, his passion for performance was unlocked. He began sharing his poetry publicly and met Mr. Rashad, a youth worker and respected community leader who created community-based spaces for young people to practice their creativity and engage in the arts, media, and music making. Mr. Rashad poured his support into Chris, helping him through a time of complicated family dynamics, encouraging him to focus on his academic success, and helping him find a space where he could work on his craft. Chris describes Mr. Rashad as a kind soul and "gentle man" deeply committed to Black youth. Later, Mr. Rashad even hired Chris as a part-time youth worker at a media program housed at a popular national youth organization, where Chris could support other young people interested in media and the arts.

Shortly after Chris was hired, Mr. Rashad unexpectedly passed away. Chris was devastated. Hundreds of young people, including popular artists who cultivated their craft in the community spaces Mr. Rashad created, expressed their grief over his passing on social media. Since Mr. Rashad's passing, however, his memory and spirit continue to live on in Chris's work with youth in the city. Chris was eventually promoted to director of education at the organization Mr. Rashad had introduced him to—a position that Mr. Rashad once held—and Chris continues to be inspired by Mr. Rashad's gentle leadership and advocacy for young people. Chris's journey to youth work began with him being inspired and nurtured by a youth worker—a youth worker he wanted to emulate. Ten years later, Chris proudly carries Mr. Rashad's legacy while building a new, powerful legacy of his own.

Chris identifies as Black and Native American. He is in his late twenties and has long, thick, sandy-brown curly hair. As his image is reflected back to me from the Zoom video, I can see his hair pulled back into a ponytail, highlighting his honey-brown complexion and warm and inviting smile. Chris's energy is lighthearted; he oozes charisma and laughs easily. Yet his seriousness about working with young people is evident when he talks. When I contacted Chris about participating in an interview, his only question to me was about the "purpose" and the "impact" of my research. To Chris, these things mattered, and he wanted to ensure that his values aligned with my work. Chris's "why" for engaging with youth is aligned with others featured in this book. For youth workers like Chris, the primary reason for this engagement was a commitment to Black education, youth, and liberation and upholding a legacy of mentorship by Black youth workers. "Like, I consider myself a part of a legacy," he said. "I'm not giving up that legacy for anything . . . I'm a Black man who was mentored by a Black man who was mentored by a Black man. I'm not going to break that line, you know."

In high school, Chris missed many days because of his passion for spoken word performance. "Once I discovered poetry, I was trying to be the next Saul Williams," he says through laughter. "For a minute, I was touring the country and doing poems in places that made me feel good. But that also led to me not going to school." In the second semester of his junior year, Chris missed seventy days of school. "They kicked me out," Chris says. "In my second semester of junior year in high school, I missed seventy days of school of the available, I think, like ninety-two." Being expelled from school made Chris "disillusioned" with formal education. Like many youth workers across the country, Chris does not have a college degree but plans to attend a few months after our conversation. While there is excitement about attending college, Chris feels like he is "giving up a protest" because going to college to "get saddled with debt" is not a choice he wanted to make after getting kicked out of high school. Despite his resistance in his earlier years, he wants to honor Mr. Rashad, who encouraged him to attend college. He has come to believe that a degree in social sciences and education would help him better serve young people and his organization. Ten years later, he finally plans to attend and hopes to pursue a doctorate eventually.

Chris's desire to continue his education is rooted in his commitment to ensuring livable wages and clear pathways for other youth workers to engage in this work. "Part of the reason I want to go to school is because . . . I'm going to school to get my doctorate . . . I want to ensure that there is a pathway to success for youth workers. A living wage is important, right? A wage—that advancement is important." Ensuring living wages for youth workers is an ongoing effort in some states and cities that have committed to supporting their youth development workforce.[1] Chris understands this and believes that his compensation and development as an educator and professional should be supported because the field is so relied upon by society, and it does not receive as much recognition as it deserves.

> I feel like I should be paid in respect too. I feel like there are so many lives I've touched at this point over my ten years doing the work. There's so many times kids have come up to me and expressed, 'I want to do what you do, I want to walk in the same pathway that you do.' And I think that is so true for youth workers . . . kids whose lives you touch want to touch lives in the same way that you had . . . I want to build a pathway that exists for people like me to go to school, to learn how to do this, to learn how to be better at this.

Chris's perspective on respect, wages, and professional support belies the underbelly of this profession and the symbolic and material precarity facing youth workers.

Like many others featured in this book, Chris's perspectives reflect the other side of the youth work coin. On one side, touching the lives of youth and making an impact is rewarding. On the other side, there is precarity. The lack of respect or recognition Chris speaks of reflects a disregard for this group of professionals.[2] Youth workers face significant challenges in the field, including low wages, inadequate benefits, lack of health care and housing, food insecurity, and looming debt for those with higher education degrees that impact youth workers' personal and professional lives. When Chris started working at the program, he was part-time, "broke," and traveling two hours on public transportation to work. "It was untenable in a lot of ways," Chris told me. Chris was living with his mother and several siblings, and, at the time, he was the only person working in the house. Trying to support his household and confront his grief of losing Mr. Rashad while also trying to "do right by the kids" was overwhelming. "I was juggling a lot," he said. Even though Chris was part-time and loved working with youth, he was not making enough money to support himself and his family. Through some laughter, Chris shared that he was illegally managing a nightclub to make ends meet. "I should not have been doing that. I was far too young to be around so many adults getting drunk." Many youth workers juggle multiple part-time youth work jobs or, like Chris, find other part-time jobs outside of education and youth development to make ends meet, like ride share or the service industry.[3]

Chris's experience is quite common. Chris would arrive at his program around noon, leave around 6:30, and work at the club from 8:30 pm to 2:00 am. "I was busting my behind. I think part of the reason that, well, the only reason I can imagine that youth workers don't stick around is because they're not paid in a way that allows them to live. I was lucky enough to have another gig. You know, I was lucky enough to, in some cases, lean on my art to support me doing the occasional show." Chris continued, "And I also think part of the assumption is that when organizations offer youth worker jobs, they aren't built to support you . . . you put so much emotional labor and put so much physical labor, give your everything to the kids that you see from two to six. But [you] also have another job. So, you can . . . eat and sleep comfortably . . . And you know, it's just imbalanced, right?"

Chris speaks of this imbalance and low wages as critical issues that influence the high turnover rate of youth workers. According to Chris, the part-time status of many youth workers highlights the lack of respect for the work.

"It is not hard, in my opinion, to keep frontline staff. It is not hard to make a youth worker full-time if you care about their development. Right? Have them come in at 10. Maybe have professional development for them? If not, cool, have them develop curriculum for the day, for the week, for the month. Like, I think the assumption is that we have no work for you because there are no kids here. And that's stupid. Preparation is at least half the battle." Chris raises an important point here: Youth development professionals serve as educators, mentors, counselors, and facilitators, among many other roles. They deserve time to prepare and professional learning opportunities to hone their craft, improve weaknesses, and engage in dialogue with coworkers to support their growth and development. However, these opportunities vary according to where a program is situated within the landscape (see table 0.1 in the introduction).

Chris's entry into the field is marked by love and respect for Mr. Rashad, his desire to shape the lives of youth the way Mr. Rashad shaped his, and his belief in the power of working with young people. The instability within the field is evident in Chris's story, and this instability and the precarity it causes can go unnoticed. Youth workers labor in the shadows, and the precarity is not the only thing that remains hidden. The power and benefits of their work with youth, families, and school systems can also be hidden and unacknowledged. This chapter captures the motivations and inspirations for Black youth workers entering the field and the material and symbolic forms of precarity they face as they engage in paradoxical work, including unfair expectations to "fix" societal problems with limited resources, lack of respect, and too few financial resources. Still, youth workers traverse this precarity and the challenges the profession brings, even with its rewards.

Pathways to the Profession

The youth workers and program leaders my team and I spoke with had similar reasons for wanting to engage with youth in community-based educational spaces. Some stumbled into the field or were encouraged by a youth worker like Chris, while others participated in after-school programs and youth centers, received impactful mentorship from youth workers, and wanted to follow in their footsteps. Overwhelmingly, Black youth workers saw their work as a commitment to their communities, wanting to give back, and a way to support Black youths' education and development.

Sheryl has worked with or on behalf of vulnerable youth for thirty years. Born and raised in the Midwest, Sheryl has a kind soul and exudes joy despite all she manages in her home and work life. I came to know Sheryl in a few capacities during my research and engaged work with youth-serving organizations across the Midwest. I learned that Sheryl ran away from home at fourteen years old and lived in a shelter for a period during her teen years. This was her first encounter with youth development work, which led her to want to pursue a career in social work. "I lived in a youth emergency shelter and got very good support from folks that were really youth workers. And from there, [I] decided to go into social work and to pursue things that had to do with children, youth, and families. And so, I have been involved in that work in my entire long, long, long career." Sheryl smiles widely and begins to speak about her love of youth work. "It's the time of promise for me." A time of promise has characterized the field—and it has also been characterized as a time of significant risk.[4] The characterization of risk is most often rooted in the moral panics society has about young people being unsupervised.[5] Much like Sheryl, I see a time of promise and opportunity that captures the possibilities in the field for young people. It is a subtle yet powerful narrative departure from the hyperfocus on the perceived dangers of unsupervised youth and makes a crucial shift to the power of young people's choices and agency.[6] Sheryl perfectly captures this: "So, it's the point where I don't have to focus or even allow the young person to focus on all that has brought them to where they are that they can't control, but that they have enough agency to begin to control their future. And so, for me, that is just an extremely exciting point in life." Sheryl's commitment to youth and their families has been steadfast— from a social worker to director of programs at a youth center to running a state-wide intermediary organization that supports youth development opportunities throughout a midwestern state.

Like many people we spoke with, Sheryl had initial connections with youth work by participating in programs as a teen. These early interactions in youth programs charted the path for her and many youth workers and program leaders featured in this book. For Morris, it was not only the connections he made with youth workers in national programs like the Boys and Girls Clubs and the YMCA but also the programming, exposure, and opportunities that allowed him to see the world differently that made him fall in love with the field. Morris grew up in public housing in the Midwest, and he recalls his first introduction to the field was through the Boys and Girls Clubs at nine years old. "My uncle actually was the director of a local Boys and Girls Clubs site. So, when I [would] leave school, I [would] go there after school. And I remember playing in the game room and that just being a positive experience. [That] was sort of my first entree to, you know, formal after-school, out-of-school time." Youth work became transformational for Morris as a teen when, at sixteen years old, he joined the YMCA. "That definitely changed my life." Morris's reflection on his life as a teenager participating in entrepreneurship workshops and youth-led Black achievement programs made an impression on him because a lot of the programming was "completely youth-led . . . and the message wasn't coming from an adult, it was coming from a peer." The YMCA was three blocks from Morris's house, and prior to joining officially, he had only attended to play basketball with friends or swim occasionally. "So going there and becoming a part of that club, which still exists to this day, was definitely a life-altering decision and, you know, while at that age, me and my friends were either deciding to sell drugs, work legally or do something else. And this was one of the 'something else' that I chose to do that led me, you know, it kept me away from those other decisions, which shouldn't have even been options, right?" Because of his connection to the YMCA, he went on Black college tours and was able "to see a world" outside of the day-to-day of his neighborhood. This exposure for Morris led him to see and understand the "power of out-of-school time programs," he explains. "The connection to a consistent positive, caring adult. That was sort of what I got from that experience, and understanding it saving my own life." Morris, like me and other youth workers, began the role of youth worker as a teen,

> I ended up working at the Y teaching arts and crafts to five-year-olds as a sixteen-year-old. And it was sort of the first time having my talent affirmed, and like, wow, I can actually, be one that my community values . . . a skill that I have and can make money off of it in terms of employment and it's not illegal and so, and, most importantly, the kids I was teaching valued it . . . but it was the first job that I had as a youth worker. And then,

from there, I became a camp counselor, a teen center attendant, and so I sort of was like, wow, actually, you know, perhaps this is a gift or a purpose in terms of working with youth.

Morris minored in education in college and remained connected to youth development. After college, he became involved in a citywide youth initiative focused on increasing civic engagement among youth. Working at the intersection of independent youth development organizations and citywide policy-level work to support young people, Morris has founded and led two independent youth organizations in the city where he grew up—both focused on Black youth activism and civic engagement, empowering youth to transform their schools and communities. In the last several years, he has worked in city government, engaging in violence prevention work and advocating for young people in local policy spaces.

Morris's and Sheryl's entry into the field began with them making a choice to attend programs as teenagers and seek support—Morris for an alternative path as a teen, and Sheryl to escape her home life. Gabi, however, was led to youth programs by her mother. Gabi is a proud Afro-Indigenous queer woman who was born and raised in a major East Coast city. She lovingly reflects that her mother always found a program for her and her siblings to attend. "I've been in youth programs since I was young. So my mother always found programs to put us in, and I'm grateful for that experience because a lot of my after-school experiences contributed to formulating who I am . . . I know how to do well in school, but I didn't have that connection with my teachers where I trusted to talk to them. But with my after-school teachers, I loved them, you know, and they made space for me to show up as myself and be received." In her role as a program coordinator at a citywide independent youth organization catering to Black and Latino boys, Gabi's own journey in her racial and gender identity development shaped how and why she chooses to engage with young people from her city. With immense pride in where she comes from and her identity, Gabi finds comfort and purpose in connecting with youth. "Sharing [with] them my own journey of confidence, of self-awareness of healing, you know, generational traumas, and working through toxic relationship patterns with family and parents to get to a place where I'm fully happy and comfortable with who I am and where my life is." As a youth worker, Gabi can have "honest conversations with youth," and loves community work because of the trust she is able to establish with young people—the same trust she experienced with youth workers when she was a teen. Youth workers often reflect on how they can gain the young people's trust, but Gabi expresses how she became able to trust young people enough to share her life with them. "Because when you work in a center or in a program with young people who trust you, you begin to trust them back and share your life with them . . . and then you start to see patterns . . . and then they want to do things that you've done. They want to experience things you've experienced for the sake of getting closer to strengthening that connection but also validating themselves that I can do this, you know." The "this" Gabi refers to is the life that young people desire for themselves, their educational goals, being comfortable and confident in their skin and their abilities. Chris and Gabi share the desire to continue the legacies and the pathway set by the youth workers who nurtured them. Like Gabi, Chris wants to return the trust, acceptance, and support he received from Mr. Rashad and engage with young people within community-based settings.

Youth workers enter the profession for several reasons, including the opportunity to build meaningful relationships, guide young people, and expose them to opportunities they otherwise may not have. Chris also sees himself as part of a long line of Black male mentorship, and this is a legacy he does not want to break. Another prominent reason Black youth workers give for entering the profession is their awareness of the impact they can have in the lives of Black youth. Olivia, a Black and Samoan educator from the West Coast, has long been invested in school-based and community-based education. As a former classroom teacher, after-school educator, nonprofit youth program creator, and leader, Olivia knows about the power of effective and loving Black classroom teachers and the significance of flexible community-based after-school spaces for Black youth: The subversion, freedom, and ability to enact creativity and joy in these spaces is paramount for her. "What did it for me . . . I had really close relationships. I had a lot of amazing teachers in my life and had really close relationships with many educators. I think for every really terrible educator in my life, I had at least three amazing ones, and so also felt like, I guess, an obligation to repay folks and pay it forward."

The desire to "pay it forward" or obligation and commitment to community or Black education were primary reasons Black youth workers chose youth work as a profession. However, youth work as a profession is complicated, as the field is arranged in such a way that many people do not have the option for full-time employment, livable wages, or the respect they deserve as educators and care workers in the lives of young people. Educators in all places often refer to their entry into the field as a "calling." Committing to youth development is not always rewarded with money, appreciation, or respect. However, there is an expectation for youth workers (and the nonprofit sector) to fix structural problems.

An Expectation to Fix Societal Problems

As I discussed in the previous chapter, nonprofit youth development organizations operate in civil society or the shadow state, engaging in work the state does not provide or making up for what the state has failed to provide.[7] Because of this, funding for youth development organizations is contingent on philanthropic groups and individuals, some private, city, and state grants, and very little federal or public funding. These programs are often overlooked for how they intervene for youth and how their work complements and supplements what occurs at school or in the home.[8] As youth workers labor in the shadows, it also means that the expectations upon them and other social safety programs to alleviate structural problems and subsequent precarity in the profession are also in the shadows—hidden from public view. Historically, after-school programs were seen primarily as sites of safety and care. However, this perspective does not consider the work that youth workers undertake—work that is often stressful. Hillary, a scholar and longtime advocate of after-school programs at the systems level, shares that youth programs "are under a huge amount of pressure." However, the depth and importance of this work takes a toll on youth workers, leading to, as Hillary explains, "enormous pressure and responsibility that we're layering on after-school programs." Many, like Hillary and several program leaders featured in this book, share that youth work "fills in gaps" and the missing pieces that schools and society fail to, cannot, or refuse to provide. Robeson, a Black man in his mid-thirties from the Northeast, has always worked with young people—in national organizations, independent programs, and faith-based programs. Aligned with Hillary's perspective about programs being under a lot of pressure, Robeson speaks to what this pressure feels like as a youth worker. "Youth work is expected to fix societal problems with a wrench. So, like, the issue is actually the economic structure at large, and the offshoots above that structure, intentional and otherwise, and we're supposed to somehow fix that with tape and bubble gum." Robeson's comment captures a fundamental structural problem facing youth work. Youth work is expected to support youth academically, socially, emotionally, politically, and culturally and provide material resources to youth when families and schools are unable. Yet, the lives of the youth workers who hold up these programs with the wrench, the tape, and the bubblegum, as Robeson puts it, are largely unknown.

Organizations within civil society, like nonprofits, are tasked with solving symptoms of more significant structural problems. But this responsibility of "fixing" societal problems through civil society organizations is a trap.[9] Civil society operates as the shadow state, and organizations committed to liberation, social justice, and disruption with revolutionary ideas are in the "shadow of the shadow state," as scholar and activist Ruth Gilmore has put it. These programs are then blamed for failure when they are trapped in a predatory relationship with funders and philanthropists and up against structures that continue to make their work difficult.[10]

To understand youth work today, it is critical to examine the structural issues like poverty that result from capitalism and that shape education and the lives of young people.[11] In addition to working with youth, many youth workers are also directly invested in this urgent interrogation of social structures. Farrah, a longtime youth worker and scholar of youth work practice, began her career focusing on "practice and looking at the components of quality practice," including how youth workers engaged young people. She then spent years studying systemic issues that impact the profession. One area she has explored is the issue of family income—how families of means can afford to pay for after-school enrichment programs for their children. Pay-to-participate opportunities for youth are also part of the landscape but are rarely discussed in the same way as families and youth that rely on free programming as part of youth organizations. Farrah says, "If you have money, then you buy your kids the types of enriching experiences that money buys. So, you know, if you don't have those safe spaces and then the families and the communities don't have the resources to buy the types of enriching . . . experiences that resourced communities have, then what happens to those kids? Well, we already know the answer to that, right?" Having spent many years as a youth worker and, later, a researcher, Farrah believes that when young people don't have the support they need, they detach from schools and are more susceptible to the criminal legal system and other harms.

Farrah's comments encourage us to consider who is responsible for youth in this country. Compared to other countries, the United States has no real national policy for youth, according to Farrah. "Why do we accept that as a society?" she asks. "It's brutal . . . it's just brutal. It's brutal that we accept that. You know that [we] still very much are entrenched in the idea that there's [a] meritocracy in this country . . . and yes, there are lots of stories, and you could write books and novels and produce very touching movies that shows the exceptions and the, you know, pull oneself up from [their] bootstrap[s] . . . and those are very touching." However, as Farrah knows well, these stories conceal a harsh reality in America, and her explanation here echoes Morris's and captures the lack of structural support for young people. Although there are stories of triumph to point to, focusing on these can be misleading, obscuring the realities of structural barriers. It is common for young people to have transformative life-changing experiences within community-based educational spaces due to their time with youth workers, but encouraging and positioning people to be "the exception" is not a solution to serious structural problems. The stories of triumph are common, but, as Farrah puts it, it is "systemically not enough." The existence of these exceptional experiences, Farrah explains, "should not be enough for us as a modern, very well-resourced country." Youth workers are tasked with trying to fill in more than gaps; they are tasked with making up for structural failures shaping young people's schooling experiences and their lives outside school.

Hippolyta, an extraordinary, charismatic, longtime youth worker and military veteran who leads a violence prevention program in the Southeast, regularly goes above and beyond, often neglecting her own needs to be there for youth in her community, providing crucial support for them in the face of the state's failures. Her violence prevention work has been recognized by local government on several occasions. She is seen by the youth she works with as what Black Feminist thinkers and writers describe as an "other mother."[12] During Hippolyta's interview, she received a call from a student who needed transportation to school because the student's school is over six miles away. There is no public or school bus for students to access. After getting off the call, she says, "So I'm their only transportation . . . They shouldn't have to worry about transportation, going to and from school, or wherever. So, that's another sad part. So, you know, I Uber these kids every day." Phone calls from students were a common occurrence during interviews with youth workers who were doing direct service with youth in organizations. Depending on the type of organization, like detention centers, shelters, or residential facilities, youth workers may have to make themselves available at all hours for young people who require support, while others, like Hippolyta, forge the kind of relationships with young people who require a specific kind of support due to unique family circumstances or structural problems requiring intervention.[13]

Morris believes that the state of education and youth development in the United States has everything to do with the lack of structural support and value of young people, which becomes even further complicated by the compounding forces of race, class, gender, and other social categories. He sees that the lack of support for classroom teachers, chronic underfunding and dismantling of public schools, and underinvestment in youth work reflect how society values young people:

> I think it starts at a societal level with our lack of value for young people. Everybody on this planet has been a child at some point and has endured adolescence and youthhood at some point in their life, regardless of race, sexual identity, orientation, or religion. Everybody has been a young person at some point. And for some people, don't ever want to remember that stage of their life, especially if it was traumatic. And other people just grow [up] and forget about it. And unless, and until, people either have a natural sort of inclination and love for young people or they have children of their own, they literally don't give a damn about what happens with children in their society. So, literally, I think our value of young people as a society is one of the greatest challenges and threats to the safety and well-being of children in our community, in our country, and in our world.

If Morris is right, then those who dedicate their lives to supporting young people—classroom teachers, youth workers, and other care workers who support the educational, social lives, and well-being of children and youth—are also not regarded or fully supported beyond lip service that celebrates their nobility and service to youth.

Youth workers' labor that is sometimes unseen, disregarded, or undervalued shapes the precarity they face in the field and speaks to a paradox at the core of the field: As a society, we claim to protect and care for young people, yet we fail to protect those who care for them. This paradox in the field itself leads to greater precarity for many youth workers who experience low wages, lack benefits and health care, and struggle to care for themselves and their loved ones in a profession they love so dearly.

Hidden Precarity in Youth Work

Scholars across the social sciences have examined precarity as a category, condition, and experience.[14] I see precarity as a "politically induced condition,"[15] and as a labor condition or status.[16] Whether as a condition of being, a labor condition, or class identity, precarity is unavoidable under capitalism, and vulnerable populations are made to suffer.[17] In other words, populations that are already made vulnerable experience exacerbated forms of precarity. The United States' heavy reliance on capitalism, those living in poverty, and the working class are regularly working jobs that sustain society and that benefit the elite. But these jobs are precarious—and they can be physically dangerous, lack adequate benefits and health-care support, and are prone to disrespect and unsafe working conditions, alongside other harsh conditions that make their labor arduous.[18] Although it may be argued that precarity is part of the human condition, there is variability based on social positioning and structural oppression.[19]

Youth work, as a field, is diverse, has a heterogeneous infrastructure, and is susceptible to significant precarity. Programs engaging young people vary in their scope of work, access, approach to youth development, funding sources, professionalization, and professional learning opportunities.[20] But because of these organizations' social framing, structure, and funding, people working in them confront great uncertainty and lack of opportunities for advancement, leading to dissatisfaction, burnout, and exits from the field.[21] As shared earlier in this chapter, Chris struggled to make ends meet for his family with a part-time youth work position. He traveled a long distance to work and held a second job to ensure he could support himself and his family. Although his initial role at the organization was part-time, Chris believed that organizations could provide opportunities to invest in youth workers when they are not working with youth so that they could have full-time positions. Chris was one of many youth workers we spoke with who initially struggled finan-cially in the field. Hilario, a thirty-five-year-old Black man with Caribbean ancestry from the Southeast, first came to youth work because of his love for sports. He mentored and coached various youth soccer clubs on the West and East coasts. Hilario holds a bachelor's and master's degree in urban planning and candidly spoke about his "six-figure debt . . . that [he's] still feeling from grad school." He knows that working a nonprofit job will not help him pay off school loans. Despite his knowledge of the Public Service Loan Forgiveness Program operating at the time of his interview,[22] he is convinced that he will "never . . . pay off student loan debt." Federal loan forgiveness programs are helpful for youth workers with student loan debt, but the debt feels crushing and is nearly impossible to pay off on such low wages.[23]

Once Hilario completed school and no longer received student health care, food, and housing, he had to receive public benefits alongside his youth worker job in an expensive major metropolitan city:

> So, I went on public benefits . . . getting SNAP, food stamps for that year, because it's getting paid like [a] little over $500 a month, or $500 per pay-check. So, it's like $1,200 a month, or something like that, to live in [the city], which is very difficult. I did have health insurance, luckily. Yeah, that was a little difficult, just the process to just get food stamps was so illuminating for me, because it was very difficult. And I was like, I have a master's degree, and this is difficult for me. I can't imagine how it is for people who have no choice but to like skip school and start working, who have to work every day, because if they don't, they'll get fired. How are they supposed to do all these steps and do all this stuff to get food stamps, something that they really need? So, I, at least like . . . was able to map out all things I need to do and how to get time off work to like, go to the food stamps office to take care of all the papers and stuff like that. But yeah, I can't imagine for people, other youth workers, having to go through that.

Hilario's sobering reflection clearly shows the reality for youth workers who struggle to make ends meet. At the time, Hilario worked at an independent youth organization, lived with three roommates, and needed public support to eat. This job was paid through the AmeriCorps program—an indepen-dent federal agency committed to public service and volunteerism—where workers in the program receive a stipend or volunteer.[24] "Yeah, so the food stamp stuff, 'cause you know, AmeriCorps, you're paid at like poverty level, so we can't really spend much money. Luckily, the housing that I got was discounted because of how much I was getting paid, but I had to live with it. It could be worse, but I was with three other people, so that could be very difficult at times." Living wages—earning an income that allows someone to support themselves and their loved ones according to the cost of living in their location—is a challenge the field must contend with.[25]

Youth workers come into the profession following their passions. Some are surprised by the low wages, and others expect them. Braylen, a composer and theater artist, began working as a teaching artist. Teaching artists are part of the youth work landscape; as cultural workers and youth development practitioners, they support youth in honing a particular craft or artistic expression.[26] Braylen has worked with many organizations supporting youth during non-school hours in the Southeast and East Coast. "I realized quickly that I could not make my living solely as a teaching artist. I needed something else, and this position opened up to coordinate middle school and high school programs during the weekday," he says. Now, Braylen directs a summer program for over two hundred young people every summer. In his experiences as a youth worker and now program director, Braylen understands that youth work in the nonprofit sector is marked by financial insecurity. "People are stretched really thin—nonprofits are doing a lot for a little. Employees are not always super well taken care of. You know, we don't have the same salaries that people in for-profit work do."

For Bria, a youth worker in the Midwest who works with young people seeking mental health services, low wages weigh on her, often making it difficult to do her job. Bria participated in youth work as a teenager through sports and dance. As an early youth worker, she taught hip-hop dance in independent community-based organizations. With an interest in clinical psychology and social work, Bria is a care coordinator for a community-based organization operating at the county level. In her role, Bria connects youth to the services and people they need to reach their goals, such as mentors or mental health professionals. Bria's connections with youth and families are rewarding and fulfilling for her, but it is hard to make a living. This paradox in youth work is a reality that Bria constantly reckons with:

I do have those connections with youth. I think it's also really a rewarding part of the job and why I do continue to do this work. Because right now, I will be honest, I am not being paid a livable wage. Which, which really, really sucks. But again, it's like, this is the work that I really, really enjoyed doing. I can definitely go into a different profession or go a different route. And, you know, get my phlebotomy license and go into the medical field. I can do that . . . But that's not necessarily the work that I enjoyed doing. I really enjoy working with these kiddos. I think there needs to be a just higher wage for youth workers in general.

The low wages can lead to housing and food insecurity, but more precarity for youth workers can also mean they may not have access to health insurance or benefits. As Robeson reflects on his early days of youth work, he recalls being food insecure while he was in between jobs, but health care has been more of a challenge for him in his career in youth work.

Health insurance, however, that's a lot more of a thing, especially around dental plans. I've had some experiences where I found out that my dental plan, like, you call the number, and the number . . . isn't actually a number for a dental plan. It's trying to sell you stuff while you're on the phone, and then you finally get around to the actual plan itself, and it's basically not a plan. And I think we just don't have a lot in the way of strong health insurance options. Usually, it's a choice between two relatively similar plans . . . We just don't have great insurance in my experience.

Kim, a lifelong youth worker, former elementary school teacher, and now organization founder and director, speaks directly about her desire to keep her organization afloat, pay youth workers a living wage, and her struggles with health care and housing insecurity. When we spoke with Kim, she had recently finished a doctoral program for educational leaders. "I didn't have insurance when I first graduated for like six months." Kim's innovative organization engages young people through music and community service. She partners with school districts for her work, but it can take a while to get paid. "As a new business, districts can take anywhere from thirty to ninety days to pay you [even] with you harassing them . . . So, my bank account looks like a yo-yo—one minute up . . . and then I'm not up. And so that is difficult to create levels of security on all levels, from food, to housing, to all of the things." When Kim spoke with us, she revealed that she technically did not have a home. Kim felt like she could always return to the West Coast to her family but assured us that she had "places to stay." "I'm okay," she told us, but "it's still dysregulating as a new leader . . . I've got probably 30k-plus outstanding from districts right now. I think for our workers, too, I'm mindful. I try to pay them a decent wage. No one with me in after school makes less than $25 an hour. [In] summers, we do stipends. Right now, I think the biggest tension for me is that I'm not giving people benefits, which, if I could, I would." Kim was disappointed that she could not provide her youth workers with benefits, even though she wanted to ensure they were paid well above the minimum wage.

Youth workers like Gabi and Hilario, who happened to work at the same organization, felt supported financially because they coordinated specific programs in their organizations. However, they both reflected on when the work was more challenging. It had been a while since Gabi had suffered from low wages in youth work. "I've not suffered from any of that in a long time, because of my status and where I'm at, in terms of like, what I'm making. I'm a single woman with no kids. So, it was really just me taking care of me. But for youth workers who are [front]line staff, it's a part-time position." To offset this, Gabi shared that her organization looks for people who want to supplement their current work. "So oftentimes we look for people or teachers who want to supplement their work and make extra income. So, we look for teachers, we look for college students who are juggling school or just need some extra money. Unless you are going into leadership regarding youth work, the pay can seem a little inadequate. But oftentimes, when I hire people and when I interview people, they tell me it's not for the money. You know, it's really about the experience and really giving back to the youth."

Giving back to community and pursuing a passion for working with young people does not mean that those who choose to do so must live in poverty. Everyone relies on education and other helping professions, yet those who do the caretaking and the educating are an afterthought. Olivia, who has been a classroom teacher, youth worker, and program leader, speaks to this tension directly. "We are expected to be martyrs; we are expected to serve nobly and to never question. And if ever we asked for our needs to be met, we're demonized and told that, 'Oh, you must not really care about the kids.'" This is true for teachers' unions, vulnerable health-care workers, paraprofessionals, and vulnerable workers in nonprofit settings who seek higher pay, adequate benefits, and protections to do their jobs.[27]

––––––

As a field, youth work is diverse, has a heterogeneous infrastructure, and its workers are susceptible to significant precarity. The field and its workers support the economy by allowing parents to work late with the peace of mind that their children are cared for and engaged in productive activities; it offers opportunities for safety, discovery, imagination, play, and identity development in ways that create lifelong skills for youth to carry with them into adulthood. However, for the adults who do this work, their struggles for recognition, living wages, and stability go unnoticed. Youth workers introduced in this chapter came to the field to continue the legacy of Black mentorship, "pay it forward," to give back to community, and to support youth in their educational journeys and futures. As Morris reflected, as a society that claims to value youth, we do a poor job of caring for those who care for youth. Tracing the pathways of youth workers in this chapter, many began their work in the field, facing low wages, working multiple jobs to make ends meet, relying on food stamps, and facing difficult moments with inadequate health insurance and nonexistent benefits. Those who are now in roles where they have more responsibility in coordinating programming for youth in their organizations or have stepped into leadership roles carry the weight of not reproducing the precarity in the field by striving to pay living wages for their staff.

In the next chapter, I consider how the forms of instability and precarity in the profession named in this chapter impact a group of Black youth workers in the midwestern city of Pleasant Ridge. With ethnographic observations and interviews in a city marked by persistent racial disparities, I detail how Black youth workers navigate anti-Black racism and the struggle for power in their organizations while navigating the challenges brought to light in this chapter, like low wages and housing insecurity. The experiences of Black youth workers and community leaders in Pleasant Ridge capture what it means to maneuver through the organizational paradoxes deeply embedded within their work that further induce precarity in their professional lives.

TWO

Struggle for Power

The US Black workers' future, then, operates in this context of global crisis and can only be solved through organization, strategy, and the fight for power.

—BILL FLETCHER, "Whither the Black Worker?"

Pleasant Ridge is comfortable with the superficial way that it addresses issues of race and will only move when provoked.

—ALEXIS, youth worker

Brandon was born in Chicago, and after his mother passed away in his early teens, he moved in with his older sister. Soon after, Brandon moved to "Pleasant Ridge," a nearby midwestern city, to complete high school. His high school was in a more affluent and predominantly white town adjacent to Pleasant Ridge. He struggled to keep up in school because of the culture shock of a new city and the grief from his mother's passing. Brandon eventually transferred to an alternative school to complete his GED. He earned his GED, moved in with his two sisters and their young children, and desperately sought employment to help support his family. Shortly after completing his GED, Brandon and his family were evicted for having six people live in a one-bedroom apartment. They needed more space, and Brandon desired better employment opportunities.

Brandon found a job answering phones at a credit card company, but soon after, called friends to inquire about other jobs. Brandon reflected on that time: "I've been homeless; I'm not asking anybody for anything. All I want, all I'm looking for is a job," he told me. Eventually, someone in his network connected him with Joy Land, a long-standing daycare and independent after-school program for young children.[1] With a minimal work history, Brandon was thrilled to find a job that he enjoyed and was good at. Brandon radiates charisma and connects easily with others, making youth work the perfect field for him. His experience was transformative, and he remained at Joy Land for several years off and on. Soon after, he began working part-time at a local chapter of a national youth organization.

Like many youth workers in the United States, Brandon stumbled into community-based youth work. While some stumble into the profession, some feel "called." Most youth workers I've spoken to throughout my career describe their commitment to their jobs as a calling to support young people and their communities. Unfortunately, the youth work profession has not always rewarded this commitment. The undervaluing of their work, however, is a common feature of many nonprofits in the United States, including Pleasant Ridge, and it is directly tied to broader political and economic neoliberal logics that inform American educational and economic policy and has long helped prop up racial inequities in the United States. For Brandon, the problems he faced left him overwhelmed, anxious, and struggling financially. He worked part-time at the national youth program, Joy Land, the independent program engaging young children, and in the summer, he took college courses whenever he could fit them in. He and his sisters were renting motel rooms to remain housed. At one point during one of the most financially precarious moments in Brandon's life, he and his family were over the motel room capacity, so he was always frightened of being evicted again. Constantly on edge, Brandon and his sisters eventually found a landlord who would allow all six family members to share a two-bedroom apartment.

When Brandon and I met, he had worked at the national program for roughly eight years. Although his financial situation was more stable, he still encountered periods of financial precarity. Despite being at the organization for several years, Brandon still did not have a full-time position even after being repeatedly told he was "the perfect fit" for various positions. Brandon believed his lack of an advanced degree and racial "tokenism" were barriers to full-time employment at the program. In other words, like other Black youth workers featured in this book, Brandon languished in part-time roles—often front-facing roles engaging with youth directly—but was never employed full-time or advanced to leadership positions. Brandon describes feeling exploited—being underpaid and not being promoted while being expected to share his knowledge and expertise about engaging youth, specifically Black youth, whenever asked. Brandon felt forced to remain in a front-facing part-time position because his supervisors "were probably looking for [an] African American to do [the] job." Brandon's experience differed from Chris's, who was mentored and brought into his organization by Mr. Rashad, a Black man who led the program that Chris now leads. Despite the executive director being Black, the explanations Brandon was given by white people in the program's power structure for not being offered stable positions or promotions range from not having a higher education degree to not being "ready" to take on leadership positions. Black youth workers feel used for their connections to the communities being served, their relationships with youth, and their pedagogical skills. However, positions of power or opportunities to make more money remain elusive.

Brandon's financial precarity and the barriers to finding full-time employment illustrate the challenges that many youth workers face. However, all youth workers may face some precarity, and Black youth workers—much like all Black workers—are subjected to even greater precarity due to the reality of anti-Black racism, systemic racial discrimination from employment structures, and labor exploitation.[2] The broader sociopolitical context of a city like Pleasant Ridge creates a particular layer of precarity, contradictions, and paradoxes experienced by Brandon and other Black youth work professionals featured in this book.

This book shines a light on the lives of Black youth workers living and working in many cities across the United States. However, this chapter draws on ethnographic data and conversations with Black youth workers in Pleasant Ridge. This is a city where racial disparities abound in a context where overt liberal progressiveness is expressed, while deep pockets of structural oppression exist. I spent years engaging with Black youth workers in Pleasant Ridge, observing public events that addressed racism at the local and state levels. Rooted in the experiences of Black youth workers, their stories reveal an ongoing disregard for Black suffering through the structured ignorance of white liberals, a deliberate shutdown of race dialogue with youth by white organizational leaders, and exploitation of Black youth workers' labor. This chapter captures Black youth workers' struggle for power amid financial precarity in a predominantly white college town with immense racial disparities.

Inside Pleasant Ridge

Pleasant Ridge, a quintessential majority-white college town, is known throughout the country for its major university, grand lakes, and for consistently voting for Democratic candidates in a deeply purple state. Leaders in the city hold on tight to a progressive ethos and claims made by long-time residents. Yet, large pockets of racial inequality persist throughout the city, impacting communities of color, especially Black residents. Because of the abysmal statistics suggesting Black youth fall behind in nearly every category of educational and social success, there's no shortage of events: talks, forums, or initiatives focused on discussing the state of racial dynamics and Black people in the city.[3] Racial and economic disparities impact Black and racially minoritized youth and families in the city. With a total population of approximately 5.9 million residents in the state, over 80% are white, with a little over 6% identifying as Black.[4] In the county in which Pleasant Ridge is located, the median annual income for white households is $80,063, while the median annual income for Black residents is $37,815. Economic hardship in the city afflicts many residents of all racial and ethnic backgrounds; however, in recent years, the economic and racial disparities disproportionately impacting Black residents have received local and national attention.

For three consecutive years, I, or a member of my research team, attended Pleasant Ridge's flagship university's "equity conference," where scholars, educators, and city officials or individuals considered experts on issues of "diversity, equity, and inclusion" come to discuss matters of race in the city, state, or nationally. One afternoon, I attended a panel that included a Black male professor from the local university who had been deeply engaged with the local school district, a Black male principal from a neighboring and more affluent school district, and an Indigenous man who was an administrator at a community college outside of the city, but in the state. A Black woman with ties to community engagement in the Pleasant Ridge school district moderated the panel.

When I arrived, I was shocked to find that this session was taking place in the largest room at the venue. Even though I had been attending these events for a few years, I was always surprised by the number of white residents who attended these events, eager to understand racism and who expressed a desire to disrupt it. However, data consistently show that opportunity hoarding among white residents and parents continues to reinforce racial inequity within the city and schools.[5] Residents attending these public forums and similar events multiple times a year signaled a hunger to "know more." However, conversations about race and racism in the city were often held in performative ways and frequently, but without any real systemic change.

Every round table was packed, and as people came in, they lined up against the back wall. I found a space in the back of the room on the floor and began to listen and take notes. Near the end of the session, the moderator shared her feelings about the challenge of remaining hopeful and excited by the work occurring while trying to manage the frequent disappointment she experiences. She then pivoted to a question about priorities and the work that must be done toward racial justice. The local university professor began his response by evoking Derrick Bell, the late critical race theorist and legal scholar. He stunned the room when he said, "I have no deep belief in racial progress." A comment like this is not the norm for a place like Pleasant Ridge, where narratives of progressive change are worn like a badge of honor. I could hear a few audible gasps expressing surprise at his comment. He continued to say that he fights because it makes him "human" and allows him to "live with himself to make spaces more livable for [his] family and his people." He made it clear that disruption is necessary and should occur but firmly stated, as Bell did, that racism is permanent and ordinary in our society and that systems of oppression function exactly the way they're supposed to.[6] This perspective not only "takes the air out of rooms," as he explained, but it goes against the sensibilities of uber-liberal spaces where the measure of goodness is based on perceived acts of antiracist beliefs and practices without deep investment in redistributing power or resources.

In a context like Pleasant Ridge, community-based youth work presents opportunities and challenges for Black youth and educators in all settings, including Black youth workers. For Black youth work professionals who are laboring amid precarity, wages, health care, benefits, opportunities for advancement, and respect for the work can be tenuous and context-specific based on where employment is situated. As stated earlier in the previous chapter, labor precarity for Black and other historically oppressed groups has deep roots in the United States.[7] In addition to access to and opportunity for adequate employment, racial and gender discrimination in pay and promotion and racist harm result in significant costs to physical, mental, and emotional health, and speaking out against racism can lead to intimidation, demotion, retaliation, or job loss.[8]

The city of Pleasant Ridge and the entire state received national attention for its racial disparities and the plight of Black communities. Pleasant Ridge has just over 280,000 residents, of which roughly 75% are white, 8.7% Asian, 7% Latinx, 6.4% Black, 2.9% American Indian/Alaskan Native, and 3.5% of more than two races. Disparities between Black and white residents were the most acute and alarming for many in the city. A 2023 report on the county reports that Black households live on roughly $28,000 a year or less, making them more likely to live below the poverty line. Data also reveal that Black residents in the county of any age were three times more likely not to have health insurance than white residents. Major issues like infant mortality, low on-time high school graduation rates, greater interaction with law enforcement, and more frequent out-of-school suspensions continue to shape the experiences of Black children and youth. Black students make up 10% of students in public schools in the county, but only 4% of school employees are Black, presenting challenges for Black youth to see a reflection of themselves in their classrooms.

Many longtime white residents expressed deep shock about the statistics. However, Black residents were not surprised. In my conversations over the years with Black youth workers in Pleasant Ridge, they expressed how nothing they read about the racial disparities in the city surprised them. The shock and surprise of white residents they encountered were upsetting or comical to many of them. In their view, Black residents, including Black youth, had spoken about racism in Pleasant Ridge for years, but their suffering was ignored. Sam, a longtime Black youth worker in Pleasant Ridge, articulated this frustration most passionately.

When I met Sam, he was in his late twenties and among the Westside Community Center's most recognized staff members. He was born and raised in the Midwest, adopted by a white family, but grew up in what some might term a "Black city" ninety miles from Pleasant Ridge. Sam came to Pleasant Ridge to attend college and has lived there for nearly two decades. Sam stands over six feet tall, has a light brown complexion, and could easily be characterized as a big teddy bear with sweet kindness that emanates when he smiles. Sam has incredible connections with the youth at his center. When I meet youth workers for interviews at their program sites, it is common for interruptions from coworkers and young people needing a question answered. These distractions are expected and, frankly, welcomed. These interactions demonstrate youth workers' many roles and how much they are needed. One pleasant interruption was from former students, two young Black men, whom Sam greeted with elation. As they dapped and hugged, Sam let them know when he would be finished so that they could catch up. When he returned to me, he beamed brightly with a smile. He shared that the young men were alum of the program and visiting from college. After this interaction, Sam seemed even more excited to talk about his work at the center.

The report about racial disparities in Pleasant Ridge caused an uproar of shock and disbelief. Sam was angered by the need for the report and the subsequent surprise and disbelief from white residents he encountered. "That thing is kind of a joke to me. Black people know this. Black people have been [saying] how white people didn't believe [them] . . . And so, with that being just the common knowledge, the time and money [that] has been spent towards putting [the report] together and putting it out there is just ridiculous, right?" Sam's frustration about how white residents frequently minimized or dismissed the Black community's cries of racism, police brutality, and other forms of physical or emotional violence experienced by Black youth in schools was palpable during our conversation. Scholars of race have consistently pointed to this kind of interaction; the experiences of Black people and People of Color are routinely ignored, dismissed, or told from the position of the white gaze, rendering their experiences invalid.[9] Not believing Black people about their encounters with anti-Black racism, through overt or subtle acts, is a typical tactic to ignore or evade the realities of white supremacy and anti-Black racism.[10]

In Pleasant Ridge, while many white residents acknowledged that racism and disparities exist, it took a report that garnered national attention for people to notice the severity of the situation. Black organizers and youth workers had long expressed anger about the violent treatment of Black youth in schools and the hypersurveillance they experience in the city. Black youth in Pleasant Ridge were often surveilled in public places, including libraries, malls, and downtown areas. On far too many occasions, news reports surfaced about Black children and youth being removed from spaces where white residents freely roamed. The anti-Black violence ranged from ordinary and mundane to humiliating and vicious.[11] In 2018, a middle-school Black girl was physically assaulted by a white male administrator. According to reports, this young girl was asked to leave a classroom after spraying perfume. While there are various accounts of what happened when she left the classroom and entered the hallway, what is not in dispute is that a white male administrator pushed, kicked, and yanked several braids out of her head. These incidents were not unusual—from police shootings of unarmed Black teenagers, disproportionate school suspensions, and restaurants and bars in downtown Pleasant Ridge that banned "hip hop music," "baggy clothing," or "durags," which consistently signaled to Black youth that they did not belong.

The concern expressed by white residents in Pleasant Ridge during local forums felt disingenuous to the youth workers I spoke with. "Again, nothing at all surprising, and when people react to it in a very shocked way, I feel like that's just telling, right? It's you showing me your cards because how the hell did you guys not know that this is going on?" During our interview, Sam's frustration with the shock, or what sociologist Eduardo Bonilla-Silva describes as "structured ignorance" on the part of whites, was palpable.[12] This frustration was shared by other Black youth workers in Pleasant Ridge, like Gia, a youth worker committed to encouraging and uplifting Black girls. Gia is originally from the Midwest and is a dedicated organizer and youth worker who provides safe spaces for Black girls and nonbinary youth. She was reluctant to move to Pleasant Ridge but wanted to pursue a graduate program in African American studies at a local university. Gia leads a group of Black middle and high school girls at a self-defined political education community program for Black and Southeast Asian youth. Although Sam and Gia work for independent youth organizations operating on philanthropic dollars and small city and state grants, their leadership structures differ vastly. While the leadership in Sam's organization is predominantly white, including the board of directors, Gia's program is intentionally led by Black and Hmong women and nonbinary leaders.

Much like Sam, Gia expressed that Black folks in the city knew the reality of racism there and didn't need the statistics from the report to communicate what they had been saying for years. "[Black] people didn't have statistics and didn't necessarily need them." According to Gia, youth in her organization regularly told the staff that " 'these are our experiences, and we've been saying things for a long time!' But I'm happy this is making other people upset, but for us, it wasn't." In some ways, Gia's explanation of the statistics provided a measure and data for what her organization had been saying for years. "This is what we've been saying around arrest rates in schools, around homelessness, around poverty for a long time."

Like Sam and Gia, Ellis also shared his frustration with how white residents of Pleasant Ridge appeared shocked by the documented racism in the city and across the state. Unlike many youth workers I interviewed who lived and worked in Pleasant Ridge, Ellis was not a transplant; he was born and raised in the city. He has worked in many youth work organizations, including a national after-school program, for over two decades. At the time of our interview, Ellis had recently started directing a school-based program for the Pleasant Ridge School District. This position gave Ellis a leadership role in a program focused on college preparation and youth development. Although the program for high school students takes place in the school, the school district pays youth workers, and classroom teachers support the program during designated class periods and after-school courses. While discussing the public events about racism in the city, Ellis expressed that many of those events were "powerful for, I think, largely white people who go and [say], 'Oh, I didn't know any of that.'" The first time I met Ellis was during our interview. He struck me as someone who seemed unsurprised by racism in the city or the reactions to it. He spoke very matter-of-factly about Pleasant Ridge as a place steeped in denial of its whiteness and racism. Pleasant Ridge youth workers all provided critiques of Pleasant Ridge as a city and did their best to find the most accurate language to describe what the city feels like for Black people.

Wahid, originally from the Southwest, is a longtime youth worker with decades of experience engaging youth in educational spaces and the juvenile legal system and responded similarly to the supposed shock and denial among white residents. As a Black man and a longtime community-based educator who was pursuing a doctorate at the time of our interview, Wahid suggested that the city operated from a racial framework that prevented any structural change. As a consultant to one of the organizations that sponsored the report about racial disparities in Pleasant Ridge, Wahid suggested the popularity of the report embarrassed white people because it contradicted the notion that Pleasant Ridge was a liberal place that was livable for everyone. He explains that the report was a "mirror to Pleasant Ridge." The racial framework suggested by Wahid speaks to how many youth workers featured in this book working in Pleasant Ridge understand how anti-Black racism operates uniquely in this context. The contours of anti-Blackness are recognizable across various contexts but also hold specific characteristics and dimensions within particular contexts and spaces, like Pleasant Ridge. Lawrence, a local professor, longtime youth program creator, and leader, perfectly captured this point. In my formal interview and my conversations with Lawrence over the years, he always captures the uniqueness of Pleasant Ridge, how white supremacy is sustained, and how anti-Black racism flourishes in such a context.

My research assistant and I met Lawrence at his office. As I expected, our conversation was raw and honest. Lawrence never held back, and he did not during our interview. Once we finished our conversation, I expressed my gratitude for his time and headed toward his office door. As we gathered our things, he stopped us with another observation about living and working in Pleasant Ridge. "[Pleasant Ridge] is like a dead zone. There's no oxygen." Lawrence's comment stopped me in my tracks. I turned to face him with my hand on his office doorknob. The words, *there's no oxygen*, hit me emotionally. A lack of oxygen means that one cannot breathe. Throughout my fieldwork, I repeatedly heard Black youth workers describe the whiteness of Pleasant Ridge as "suffocating," "overwhelming," and "relentless." To be clear, it is not just that most of the population in the city is made up of white people; instead, it is the reality that Black people find themselves at the bottom of the social ladder across almost every indicator of social success. The structural anti-Blackness embedded within Pleasant Ridge's institutions locks Black people out of opportunities for education, wellness, employment, and political power.

I respect Lawrence's work and his knowledge of Pleasant Ridge. Lawrence arrived in the city as a new assistant professor in his mid-thirties. Now, in his early to mid-fifties, he has spent decades establishing rich connections between the local universities and Pleasant Ridge schools. He gained praise for establishing peace circles in local elementary schools, where youth work volunteers and part-time workers engage mostly Black boys around issues they face at school or home during lunch, a class period, and sometimes after school. Lawrence's engagement in youth work represents the rich connections that schools can make with youth development programs. I often crossed paths with Lawrence and appreciated his insights about race and education in Pleasant Ridge. During our conversation, he shared his opinions on the racial and economic disparities in the city. At times, he was quite critical of the university's approach to engaging with the local community and their refusal to acknowledge their role in perpetuating racial disparities. For as long as I've known Lawrence, he has always been excited to speak about his program. Lawrence said the program made students feel more connected to their schools and reduced conflict and suspensions. Because of these outcomes, Lawrence was often disillusioned with *how* Black youth were spoken about in Pleasant Ridge.

Lawrence travels around the state and believes that Pleasant Ridge's school district and the city are the most resistant to change. "They won't admit there is such a denial among the white people in power, and that's across the board . . . But I can't think of any work I've done . . . I've been here seventeen years, where I haven't bumped heads with someone. Two things: there's this sort of smug arrogance . . . You know we're liberal, progressive, smart, and all that, whatever. And so, you're not prepared to learn." As Lawrence's comment about Pleasant Ridge suggests, its reputation as a liberal bastion operates as a shield from the anti-Black racist reality of the city, and it rejects evidence that it is a space of deep suffering for Black people, especially young people.

Ignoring and Shutting Down Racial Dialogue

Michael Dumas, an education theorist and scholar of anti-Blackness in education, frequently writes about schooling as a site of suffering for Black children.[13] Black students' school experiences range from routine and mundane acts of violence to rituals of humiliation and violent encounters with school administrators, school resource officers, and teachers.[14] In the face of this, community-based educational spaces that intentionally engage Black youth in conversations about this violence, anti-Black racism, and other sociopolitical issues that shape their schooling experiences and other areas of their lives have long been necessary for the academic and social development of Black youth.[15] Conversations and structured activities to discuss sociopolitical issues are important to youth programming. These approaches allow youth to unpack this kind of violence and suffering through discussion groups, structured curriculum, book clubs, and organizing efforts. These efforts are often led by youth workers who guide young people through exercises that allow them to unpack their experiences in schools and neighborhoods.[16] More specifically, community-based educational spaces—and other spaces outside of school—have been vital sites of critical consciousness-raising and youth organizing for racial justice and education reform.[17] However, it is important to underscore that having conversations about racism in this country is not a new practice within Black educational spaces. Educators—classroom and community-based activists, scholars, and community members working to support the development of Black youth—have, for generations, recognized the necessity of discussing with youth the realities of anti-Blackness. Within Black educational spaces and independent institutions, including Black schools, Black religious spaces, and civil society organizations, conversations about white supremacy and strategies to combat it (including the power of education and learning) are central to the history of Black education in this country.[18] These conversations and tools to navigate racialized and anti-Black racism were and are essential to the educational, social, and political development of Black youth.

The approach to youth development varies, especially regarding unpacking racism and other sociopolitical problems. Some Black youth workers who value youth work with a social justice approach sometimes struggle to have these conversations with youth or among their colleagues in organizations led by white leaders. Specifically, within Pleasant Ridge, conversations with Black youth workers there revealed that youth organizations run by white leaders in the city sometimes avoided conversations and programming about racism with youth. Yet, no matter the politics of the leaders of these organizations, it is important to note that any decision to avoid explicit discussions about racism within an organization is not made in a vacuum. Local and national politics play a powerful role as well. In Pleasant Ridge, citywide discourses about racism and education—including the debates about solutions to combat racism—consistently framed educational and personal success through the lens of individual responsibility rather than advocating for structural changes. This kind of framing of youth is directly informed by major strands of American political and economic thought, including classical liberalism and neoliberalism, that place blame for an individual's or group's plight on their own shoulders.[19] In Pleasant Ridge, many examples highlight this influence. For instance, Wahid and other youth workers described how Pleasant Ridge had a particular way of talking about Black youth and education in ways that blamed them for underachievement. Wahid voiced his objection to this framing: "[Instead of] saying, oh, Black kids aren't achieving, people [need] to be more upfront and just [go] straight there and [say] no: The reason Black kids aren't achieving is because of white supremacy because the system is broken." Wahid had strong feelings about the way corporate funding for nonprofits in Pleasant Ridge perpetuates these problems:

> Corporations have a vested interest in making Pleasant Ridge look a certain way. And because of that, they give money, and if the [large funding group] gives money to these organizations that are being radical or being pro-Black, it's like, what are you doing? It's the status quo; that's what it is. Status quo is: We're in [Pleasant Ridge]. It's this great place to live. There's no conflict. Race is minimalized, meaning that yeah, we may have some racial incidents, but it's not like Chicago or [Detroit] . . . But racism [and] white supremacy is played out in other ways, not just in violence. It's in racial inequities, schools, police harassment, [and] Black folks not having opportunities.

Wahid's assertion that some of the city's largest and most powerful funding entities would not fund organizations perceived as "too radical" or "pro-Black" was shared by other youth workers. Gia, for instance, was candid about the varying levels of support from community members and donors her organization receives. At the time of our conversation, Gia was in the middle of an ongoing battle with the local district to remove police officers from schools and engage young people in dialogue around police violence. "There [are] a lot of people that support our work in different ways. Some people are like, 'oh my gosh, it's so great that you're doing this [reading program]; I want to donate books.' Or . . . 'I have some kids at my church that would love to come,' but then when we're talking about police violence, they're like, 'Well, I don't know about that because my uncle is an ex-police chief, so I'm not with you there.'"

Gia's comment about the politics of funding demonstrates the uncertainty and precarity of funding, which are often predicated on donors' comfort and discomfort. Funding demands in youth programming bring with them pressure to appease donors and align organizational programming with the political and cultural views of the funder (perspectives that are often racialized, gendered, and classed). Gia spoke honestly about the financial support her organization is willing and unwilling to accept. The political education youth acquire in her program and the rhetoric of anti-Black violence and white supremacy that she incorporated startled many people outside the organization and created a perception of Gia's organization as much more "radical" than other youth programs in the area. The influence of racial capitalism shapes the political economy of community-based education and youth work, causing a delicate and tension-filled relationship between philanthropy, race, and paternalism.[20] Youth-serving organizations engaging youth of color are often beholden to wealthy and often white funders with their own agendas and values that may not align with those of the organization.[21]

Influential community leaders and major funders in the city often pitted Gia's organization against other organizations in the area. Yet, these same people often lauded her program's work even as they kept a distance from it and positioned it as "too radical." Nearby universities, schools, and organizations in Pleasant Ridge frequently asked youth leaders in Gia's organization to provide workshops or speak on panels about racial and gender justice in the city and state. Sometimes, these educational organizations would give youth in the program a platform to talk about their organizing work on panels at conferences, meetings, and events at local universities. I observed young people from the program speaking about their work and concerns about living and being educated in Pleasant Ridge. When they would speak on panels at universities, the discomfort among faculty was always visible. During one workshop led by youth workers in the program featuring some high school–aged students, participants wore buttons that said, "No Cops in School"; *school* was written in blocked white lettering, circled in red with a line crossing out *cops*. Some young people spoke about schools being inherently violent, especially considering how school resource officers harm students. The program encouraged students to be themselves, show up as they are, and speak in ways they were most comfortable with—often using slang or African American Vernacular English (AAVE). Gia and her coworkers saw this approach to Black youth development as a form of resistance against anti-Black racism that ignores the humanity of Black people and where Black youth are often policed for their forms of expression and styles.

Each Black youth worker I spoke with in Pleasant Ridge believed that engaging Black youth in conversations and programming about racism in community-based spaces was paramount. Black youth workers understood the value of engaging Black youth in deep conversations about racism (and its intersections) and the importance of unpacking how it is sustained in their schools and the city. (This approach to youth work is rooted in the historical traditions of Black educational spaces including schools, homes, and communities, preparing Black youth to understand the world as it is.) Yet many expressed challenges, tensions, and conflict in trying to do so, depending on their program's structure or organizational status. Ellis, who once held a leadership position at a national youth organization in Pleasant Ridge, explains that although his center strived to be "culturally responsive," they "didn't have too many explicit things on race." Ellis noted that in this organization, the direct engagement around race only occurred when prompted by acts of police violence in Pleasant Ridge schools, the larger community, or when national headlines were made. Wahid suggested that for educational programs in Pleasant Ridge to engage Black youth in meaningful conversations about how racism shapes their lives, program leaders, directors, and youth workers must understand what "justice" is:

> When you are having conversations about race and politics, you have to have youth leaders, workers, and directors who understand what justice is. But you have to have folks who aren't scared to call things for what it is, to use the word *white supremacy*, to use the word *racism*, to use those words without anyone getting mad . . . Let's use that same language when we're talking to kids . . . So when youth are able to recognize white supremacy, they can call it what it is.

How Black people come to make sense of how anti-Black racism shapes their lives and the world more broadly varies. Black people are not a monolith. Social identity markers like class status, ability, age, political orientation, gender, sexuality, or the context in which people grew up are factors in how they understand their racial identities, how they make sense of their Blackness, and their responses to acts of anti-Black violence.[22] One's social identity or ability to think about social conditions can be shaped by the organizational context they are within.[23] For instance, Sasha, a Black woman and development director for one of the city's largest youth-serving organizations and a local chapter of a national organization, also believed that Pleasant Ridge's racial disparities were appalling. However, Sasha felt that within her organization (which primarily served Black elementary and middle school students), Black youth had "other things to focus on," like food and housing insecurity. When asked if staff members received guidance on how to have conversations about anti-Black racism with youth—even when linked to the issues Sasha named—she responded "no" and, while knocking on her wood desk, shared that they had been "lucky" not to have had any "incidents." Her assertion that there had been "no incidents" referred to overt acts of racism enacted by staff onto students within the program. I wondered if Sasha's role in fundraising—away from direct engagement with youth— played a role in her analysis. Although Sasha's perspective differs from most of the other youth workers interviewed in Pleasant Ridge, it confirms that anti-Black racism is not conceptualized or understood in the same way— including among Black educators and youth workers—even as these issues deeply inform their approach to engaging with youth. Sasha's perspectives on social issues like the food and housing insecurity Black youth faced were absent of an analysis of structural racism or poverty. Sasha's reflections speak to how youth workers and organizations exist and work within a paradoxical landscape—one where they can acknowledge that structural inequality exists but may not name it or always recognize how it shapes their understanding of Black youth or organizations.[24]

In contrast to Sasha's perspective, other youth workers like Ellis, Wahid, and Sam felt it was essential for community-based programs to provide space for Black youth to react to and process racist violence in their schools and communities. As Sam explained, his organization strives to have conversations about incidents that happen in the city and students' schools: "So, being able to talk about [the police murder of a local Black teenage boy] and . . . to be able to get the kids down to the protest." As someone who spends much time with students, Sam holds deep knowledge of students' personal and academic challenges. Students will often come to Sam to complain about the racist actions of teachers or administrators in their schools. "While [students] may not know exactly how to articulate that there's something there . . . we explore [it]," Sam shared. In the context of the organization, Sam encouraged a space where it was okay for youth to be "pissed off" about the racism they experience in schools. "Like it's okay to be pissed off over shit. You should be . . . and you don't have to sit back and be quiet and raise your hand and speak quietly about it. You can kick a fucking desk over about it, and that's okay," Sam passionately explained.

Sam's message to youth captures an important function of community-based educational spaces; they are necessary spaces for youth to process their feelings without fear of the punitive policies found in schools. Certainly, especially in today's educational policy context, a student who flips over a desk frustrated with mistreatment would be cited, suspended, expelled, and likely arrested. As schools are inherently punitive, community-based educational spaces are celebrated for the second, third, and fourth chances they can provide youth.[25]

Community-based programs offer Black youth a much-needed space to express their emotions. However, specific factors help create the conditions for this, including the views of the organizational leadership and the presence of Black staff or volunteers. For example, when I asked Sam if his conversations with students about racism would likely occur if he were not present as one of the two Black people on staff, he suggested that this was a critical factor. He also suggested the leadership in the organization made a difference and that he was grateful for the executive director and the level of "freedom" and "latitude" he was given to lead youth in the best direction. He noted that the director, a white man with a background in community organizing, was comfortable pushing funders and the board of directors on certain issues. However, Sam believed that his director was sometimes uncomfortable with aspects of race programming, and consequently, some conversations were shut down. "I do think that [the center where I work] is uniquely different than the other centers, and now [at my center] there is at the very least an . . . expressed willingness to go there. I think that we talk about wanting to foster that kind of environment and encourage those kinds of conversations, and a lot of the time, we do good in that, and there are sometimes when things start to get shut down because people get uncomfortable." The discomfort Sam references is important to unpack. As a "liberal bastion," Pleasant Ridge is perceived to be a place of openness and acceptance, a community that claims to seek equity and fairness for all residents. But white community-based leaders with relative power can shut down programming, reinforcing whiteness as a credential in organizations.[25] According to Sam, conversations regarding racism were sometimes shut down even within a program that achieved high levels of analysis of other structural issues. From Sam's point of view, this programming disruption rested on the level of control and power leaders within the organization held. Because of Sam's position as a youth worker, he had some control over how he engaged youth, but he had to follow the director's leadership and decision-making.

Lawrence echoed Sam's sentiments about his supervisors' discomfort with specific issues. "There's lots of ways [that] white liberal progressive people just avoid situations that would force them to confront their discomfort. I mean, you know racism," he tells me. Avoiding conversations, denying promotions, and shutting down conversations that prove to be too "stressful" trigger specific emotional responses that can further harm Black youth workers. Within some organizations, opportunities for Black youth to unpack the specificity of the anti-Black racism they experience in schools and within the broader community may be stifled, disrupted, or may not even occur because of white discomfort. For most Black youth workers featured in this book, their dedication to engaging youth rests on their desire for Black liberation and the well-being of Black youth; thus, acknowledging, unpacking, processing, and finding ways to disrupt anti-Black racism and other forms of oppression is essential to their youth development practice. These moments and other moments of shutdown left many Black youth workers feeling undervalued and disregarded. Yet, many of them were often asked to handle specific race-related or "Black-related" issues, which led to feelings of resentment and exploitation.

Navigating Exploitation in Pleasant Ridge

Black youth workers face tremendous obstacles to professional advancement in their organizations, and many of the youth workers in Pleasant Ridge highlighted their difficulty in earning promotions to leadership roles. This difficulty intersects with various personal and professional challenges that Black youth workers face—it is both a cause and a consequence of the broader structural problems inherent in youth work today. Sam had worked at Westside Community Center for six years at the time of our interview. He held a full-time position, had an amazing rapport with students, and sought a promotion with additional responsibility and higher pay. After four years in the organization, an assistant director position became available, and several board members approached Sam about applying. "So, when the assistant director position came open, three or four board members talked to me about applying, and I did. I went to talk to [the executive director] and was told that I'm just not ready for it right now, and I got really pissed." Sam was disappointed and felt led on. After asking for more explanation on his understanding of what happened, Sam believed that it was the director's discomfort in supervising him as a Black man: "And what that totally was about was him not being able . . . him feeling like he couldn't supervise me." Sam continued, "[the executive director] talked in the past about recognizing this feeling [of being] uncomfortable that it's all white people [who are] assistant directors. And a handful of years ago, when I was in [the] position to step into new shit, bro, it was like strong pushback." Sam was finally promoted to a leadership position about three years later, and the executive director retired after decades of service. Sam stayed with the Westside Community Center while the board searched for a new director and eventually hired someone new. Not too long after, Sam left the program. Since leaving, the center has seen a lot of turnover in its leadership and has experienced conflict about the direction of leadership, as many are calling for the center's leadership to be Black or Latine—a reflection of the youth attending and the community surrounding the center, which is a historically Black neighborhood.

The Pleasant Ridge Black youth workers I interviewed often raised concerns that many of the youth-serving organizations engaging Black youth were led by white people. They highlighted several reasons for this concern, including the negative impact they saw on opportunities for professional advancement for Black workers and the influence that white leadership can have on the nature of their engagement with Black youth. However, their views on this were clearly informed by their awareness of the more positive impact that Black leaders can have on these issues. Gia, for example, who had lived in Pleasant Ridge for four years at the time of our interview and who runs a small organization dedicated to the liberation of Black youth through community-building and organizing, describes the loving environment at the organization where youth can always come for food, conversation, and supportive adults who will listen to them. Because Gia has a leadership role in her organization, coordinating programming, she has quite a bit of autonomy and freedom to design and explore conversations with youth about race, gender, violence, and systems of oppression in ways she deems fit if they align with the program's mission. When asked about the autonomy her friends and colleagues have working at different organizations across the city, Gia claimed they do not have the same flexibility as she does. When asked why, Gia replied that it is because "white leadership hires Black people to do the work." Gia means that Black people, mainly front-facing staff members, do most of the labor but do not have the power to make decisions because they lack power and positions of leadership in the organization. Alexis, a lifelong youth worker who spent many years working in social services and for city and county youth service providers and was now a scholar of youth work and regularly worked with organizations in Pleasant Ridge, shares Gia's observation. "So, you have this professional white core of leadership running these organizations. They'll say, 'We've been doing this work in the community and in partnership with the community for decades' . . . And then they'll have some frontline staff from the community," she explains. By "from the community," Alexis means that those engaging directly with youth are Black and other workers of color, and those leading organizations are outsiders to the community.

Alexis's and Gia's perspectives on the impact of white leadership in organizations focused on engaging Black youth were backed up by comments from other Black youth workers. It is also worth pointing out, however, that white leaders in these organizations are also aware of this issue. Wahid and Sam, for example, recounted conversations with white organization leaders who acknowledged the lack of Black leadership in Pleasant Ridge. Nevertheless, awareness of this issue among white leadership does not necessarily improve the situation without any action, and Black youth workers who try to speak about it have felt threatened. Sam mentioned that he has friends who pushed for Black youth workers in positions of power in organizations in Pleasant Ridge, and many were "completely cut off [or] cut out—even fired from organizations [for] talking about [it]." The "it" is race and challenging organizations to have staff members that racially and culturally match Black youth participants. There are a handful of prominent youth organizations where Black leadership is present, and Black youth workers highlighted this impact. Sasha, for instance, firmly believed that her organization was successful because of the predominantly Black leadership. Research has shown that Black youth have better academic performance and self-esteem outcomes in youth-serving organizations led by Black leaders.[27]

The lack of power among Black youth workers in organizations leads to contradictions that impact both youth workers and the Black youth they work with. For example, Black youth workers consistently discussed the contradictions and gatekeeping processes that kept them out of important positions within specific organizations in Pleasant Ridge. Hiring in youth work varies according to each organization's policies, politics, and traditions.[28] Black youth workers explained that not holding college or advanced degrees often disqualified them from certain leadership positions. During an event that celebrates the liberal traditions of Pleasant Ridge, Gina, a prominent Black organizer in the city, spoke on a panel about navigating police violence. She spoke very candidly about how she feels exploited for her knowledge and expertise in engaging Black youth. With great power in her voice, Gina said to attendees: "Most of us get up every day to help ourselves. [You want to 'help'], but when you go out to apply for a job and need a degree, which I don't have, they say no. Yet, [they] call me every day and ask me about the kids. What kind of sense does that make? Because I don't have a degree?" Gina shared these comments in a predominantly white room at an event celebrating the liberal and progressive traditions of Pleasant Ridge.

Embedded in her statements is the description of the landscape of youth work in the city as paternalistic in that community organizations and educational "interventions" are celebrated as efforts that can "help" Black youth in the city as though the issues they face are not structural. Gina's poignant comment about being rejected from jobs because of her lack of a degree, while she is simultaneously asked to speak about her organizing work with Black youth, often without proper compensation, speaks to the exploitation Black youth workers feel in Pleasant Ridge. While it may be easy to look at Gina's circumstances as just a function of one program's policy for hiring, the exploitation is evident as she and other Black youth workers in Pleasant Ridge are called upon, as Wahid says, to "have their brains picked" about how to best work with Black youth by organizations that will not hire them or pay them for the knowledge they share. Unlike other professions, the credentials needed to be a youth worker vary by program type and organization. Some people enter the field through programs like social work or psychology or work for state agencies that may require an advanced degree or licensing.[29] Some have college degrees, while others only have high school diplomas but have been in the profession for decades. The broader ecology of the youth work sector demonstrates that leadership and youth workers' comfort or challenges depend on their organization, how it is funded and led, and the sociopolitical conditions shaping the organization. Debates about credentialing and professionalization have long existed in the field.[30] I cautiously enter these debates because stratification and inequities will undoubtedly emerge with standard professionalization, but I recognize the field's instability without it.[31]

The exploitation of Black youth workers discussed also included how, even without having a role in decision-making or without monetary compensation, they felt poked or prodded for their expertise about issues related to Black youth or racism in the city. For instance, during the same panel discussion, Gina also shared how leaders from other programs, city officials, or university researchers constantly approached her with questions. "You have all these programs, they don't work together, they have silos, and what they do is, they will come and pick your brain about what needs to happen or what should happen. But at the end of the day, you're not a part of the ending conversation." Like Gina's experience, Wahid discussed his many hours with white people in Pleasant Ridge while working for different agencies, local universities, or local government, trying to create equitable educational opportunities for Black and other marginalized young people. Wahid explained that he often feels like white people come to him as an "academic exercise" to learn about his experiences in Pleasant Ridge as a Black man. These types of requests often triggered Wahid. "I had several times where I had to tell people who wanted to have coffee to talk about my experiences, my Black experience in Pleasant Ridge . . . 'I wanna hear your story, Wahid. And then also, tell me about how you got here" . . . like there's only a few of us, and they wanna know how we were able to beat the odds," Wahid explained. Often annoyed by the implication that he was an "exceptional" Black man, Wahid pushed back on these types of questions and attempted to center the legacy of "Black excellence." It is a typical move in neoliberal discourses of achievement and progress that mirrors my own journey to youth work to highlight Black exceptionalism that reinforces narratives that celebrate "beating the odds," as though Black people are meant to suffer.[32] But this framing reinforces anti-Blackness by obscuring structural oppression impacting Black youth in educational spaces. Wahid's experience is a good example of what this looks like and shows what it means to face this in a city that purports to be progressive. It is no surprise then that many Black youth workers, like Sam and Wahid, found the city to be "paternalistic" and "oppressively white" in a way that hinders structural change across education, employment, and other avenues toward social mobility.

The city of Pleasant Ridge and its racial and economic disparities are not an anomaly. A predominantly white city that expresses an ethos of equity but has immense racial and economic disparities disproportionately impacts those who are most vulnerable—Black, Indigenous, Latine, immigrants, and other marginalized folks—is common.[33] The racial and economic context of Pleasant Ridge creates challenges for Black youth and the youth workers who work with them. While the release of reports documenting the racism experienced by Black residents and additional data about the city of Pleasant Ridge and the state "shocked" some white residents who claimed not to be aware, Black youth workers I spoke with remained unsurprised and felt like the suffering of Black youth was ignored. Because youth workers hold a specific position in the lives of youth as non-parental adults that allows them to understand the educational and social lives of youth, they are aware of the racism Black youth experience in their schools and within the city. In addition to feeling like their voices and experiences are dismissed, Black youth workers must contend with how community-based educational spaces are racialized organizations,[34] and how this affects their professional opportunities, influences the decision-making of organizational leadership, and how this shapes programming with youth. Discussions about racism with youth and staff, hiring decisions, and Black youth workers' labor within these spaces were raised as critical issues for youth workers I spoke with.

———

I began this chapter by sharing Brandon's experiences living and working in Pleasant Ridge. For Brandon, struggling for employment, finding employment, and then struggling financially doing work that he loves was challenging to hear. However, Brandon's story of economic precarity and housing instability as a youth worker and his organization's empty promises of promotion were heartbreaking. Brandon's experiences and those of other youth workers reveal the precarious conditions youth workers face; how they piece together various forms of employment inside and outside of youth work to support themselves is inspiring. But they should not have to do this—they should be structurally supported in the field and by their organizations to engage in this work.

It is a frustrating challenge for Black youth workers to battle the same structural forces in the very organizations they work for. Black youth workers are important influencers in the lives of youth. Still, depending on their positions of power, many Black youth workers in front-facing roles do not always have much power to make consequential decisions for the organization. Scholars studying organizational leadership, philanthropy, and race have repeatedly shown how race, capital, and power work hand in hand throughout the nonprofit sector.[35] In cities like Pleasant Ridge, where white people are in leadership roles in many of the programs serving Black youth, if structured ignorance, denial, and discomfort abound, it prevents Black youth from sociopolitical development and can reproduce the racism and psychic and cultural violence youth experience in schools.

The stories in this chapter demonstrate that the sociopolitical context and landscape of youth work shape *how* youth work is provided and received. Broader sociopolitical forces like anti-Black racism, capitalism, lack of employment opportunities, spatial inequality, city politics, organizational funding, and leadership play a significant role in the experiences of Black youth work professionals, and these forces induce the layers of precarity they experience within their organizations. Despite their struggle for power and respect for their value to their respective organizations, youth workers in Pleasant Ridge spoke fondly of their engagement with young people. The structure of youth work as a field, like many other precarious employment situations, creates a circumstance whereby youth workers can feel taken advantage of while still feeling fulfilled by their engagement with youth.

THREE

Mourning to Movement

> In the midst of so much death and the fact of Black life as proxi-
> mate to death, how do we attend to physical, social, and figurative
> death and also to the largeness that is Black life, Black life insisted
> from death? I want to suggest that might look like wake work.
>
> CHRISTINA SHARPE, *In the Wake: On Blackness and Being*

> The catalyst for political engagement has never been misery, pov-
> erty, and oppression but the promise of constructing a new world.
>
> ROBIN D. G. KELLEY, *Freedom Dreams: The Black Radical
> Imagination*

I did not finish the entire video. I could not bring myself to watch a Black
man suffocate because of the full weight of a white man's body on his neck
for over eight minutes. Watching a Black man murdered while officers looked
on with indifference, ignoring the screams and cries of distraught onlookers
and those of George Floyd, was enraging. I was enraged and heartbroken. I
was in disbelief but also not surprised. George Floyd was murdered on May
25, 2020. Two months earlier, Breonna Taylor was killed in her own home
when officers executed a no-knock warrant. A month before Taylor, Ahmaud
Arbery was murdered by two white vigilantes while jogging in his neighborhood. Floyd was indeed an inflection point, but there were others before
and after Floyd. Tony McDade, Rayshard Brooks, Andre Hill, Daniel Prude,
Manuel Ellis, and the list, sadly, continues.

The uprisings against police violence in the spring and summer of 2020,
or what scholar and activist Robin D. G. Kelley calls *Black Spring*, captures

the uprisings that took place across the country (and the world) to demand justice for George Floyd and other victims of police violence.[1] *The New York Times* reported that protests on June 6, 2020, took place in over five hundred locations throughout the US.[2] It is estimated that fifteen to twenty-five million people participated in these protests. Accountability only came after Black Spring protesters demanded arrests, indictments, and the release of police video footage to prove that the harassment or killing of a Black person was unjust (a sad reality in an anti-Black world where the pain and suffering of Black people are not believed or when there is a presumption of guilt or a sense that we deserved our murders). These protests led institutions of all kinds to release statements, develop new policies for increasing racial diversity, and fund the Black Lives Matter Movement.[3]

Having social media at our fingertips meant that camera footage of state-sanctioned violence was on constant display. To make matters worse, shelter-in-place orders took effect nationwide to protect against the COVID-19 virus. And yet, despite the fear of contracting the virus, Black youth workers, side by side with Black youth, joined the movement to protest state violence, continuing the legacy of Black resistance, demanding justice, accountability, and asserting humanity. Movements such as Black Spring are born from cultivated Black space[4]—Independent Black Institutions (IBI)[5] and Black community-based educational spaces.[6] As Kelley proclaims, freedom dreaming is grounded in the radical Black imagination and captures the visioning, strategies, and dedication of those who dare to change the world.[7] Young people are often at the forefront of change-making and world-building.[8] This is also true for Black Spring. Black Spring, like the emergence of the Black Lives Matter Movement in 2014, are not new fights or struggles, but rather these moments are part of an ongoing movement for justice, self-determination, and freedom; they are manifestations of collective outrage dating back to earlier movements for justice, including the Civil Rights Movement and the longer commitment to Black freedom in the US and beyond.[9]

Today, Black community-based institutions, including churches, advocacy groups, Black schools, and community centers, remain as they have always been: key sites of identity affirmation, protection, nurturing, political education, and organizing. Black youth workers, like those discussed in this book, continue to play a central role in this work, helping to support Black youth in their personal and academic lives while also helping them navigate the unique violence and marginalization they experience in a society shaped by anti-Blackness. As a field, youth work, as we understand it today, is profoundly shaped by the historical legacy of this struggle and by the impact of current events and contemporary culture and politics, including pervasive state violence. Previous chapters have explored how Black youth workers manage financial and housing precarity, as well as leadership ceilings in youth-serving organizations—including those which are part of national networks of after-school programs and independent local programs run by leaders with roots and long-term commitments to Black communities, as well as outsiders.

Youth work and all educational experiences occur within a larger sociopolitical and historical context,[10] including the structural and unfolding violence that Black youth faced before, during, and beyond Black Spring. Black Spring is not an exceptional moment. It is an inflection point. Yet these moments of violence, reactions, and resistance to that violence are not new. This chapter turns to how Black youth workers and the political sanctuaries they create support Black youth in their sensemaking of anti-Black violence and Black death via state violence to ensure they feel safe, and receive emotional support and political education that can lead to resistance, engaging in what Christina Sharpe describes as "wake work."[11] I suggest that Black Spring and other moments of societal rupture and reckoning shape and reshape Black youth work through the sobering reality, possibility, and inevitability of Black death. As Black youth workers I spoke with struggled to protect Black youth from the threat of white supremacist violence, they confronted their own mortality. I detail how they carefully craft physical and emotional space to care for Black youth and make quick decisions to protect them while oscillating between exhibiting care for youth and themselves.

––––––

When Hippolyta was not at school, she was at church. The church served as her after-school, weekend, and summer program. For young people like Hippolyta growing up in faith-based households, religious institutions can offer vital spaces for academic, social, and spiritual guidance. "I grew up in church," she recalled fondly, reminiscing about her childhood. "I always tell people that's really the only program I was in . . . we had Tuesday night Bible study. We were in church every Sunday. Fun Out Fridays. I was in church heavy. And that was my program." Faith-based spaces have consistently been part of the youth work landscape to various extents. Beyond spiritual development and teachings, these spaces hold significant cultural importance and are deeply rooted in community care, particularly within Black communities. They have served as sites for formal education, organizing and activism, academic support, recreational opportunities, and more.[12] Hippolyta spent her early years in the Midwest, but her family relocated to a city in the Southeast when she was in first grade. Adjusting to new parts of the country was a significant challenge for her. From navigating new neighborhoods to acclimating to different accents and slang, Hippolyta had to adapt quickly. As a first grader, she quickly learned she could no longer call "soda" by its previous name, "pop." She described herself as a "country girl" adjusting to the big city.

Pregnant at seventeen, Hippolyta went to serve in the military while her mother cared for her young daughter. While in the Air Force, one of Hippolyta's duties was to organize funerals, which made her somewhat comfortable dealing with death. But nothing could have prepared her for the news she received on the day of her graduation from the military when she found out that her uncle had just been killed. He was shot in the face by a teenager, who then later shot himself. Hippolyta would later channel the impact of this tragedy into her future work with young people as a violence interrupter.

When Hippolyta returned from the military, she came back to a neighborhood in deep conflict. Plagued with gang violence and funeral homes exploiting families, Hippolyta used her experience in the military, where she became comfortable with death, to support families in burying their loved ones. She wanted to work with young people to prevent violence while also teaching the community to support itself as city services often neglected her neighborhood—from hypersurveillance by police to a lack of adequate health care. Hippolyta helped cofound a program allowing the community to "heal themselves" as the nearest hospital was too far away to treat people. "I realized, you know, it takes a while to get to the nearest hospital . . . So, this program teaches children and communities . . . what to do when someone is shot. As I'm talking, I think about one of the kids in our program; his brother took our [Heal the Wound] class. And a few weeks ago, he called me, and he said, 'Miss, I was shot.' I'm like, 'Oh my gosh, what hospital are you at?' 'Oh, I didn't go to the hospital,'" he replied. Hippolyta takes a long pause, makes a quizzical face, laughs, and responds, "You got to go to the hospital." Though she would have preferred that he go to the hospital, the wound was not severe, and she was happy that he was able to "heal himself and stop the wound." Hippolyta's program works with youth from three different neighborhoods. She refers youth from these neighborhoods to mental health services and provides exposure to civic engagement and higher education opportunities like college tours and support with college applications.

Hippolyta's mission is to create the conditions for safety zones and places for young people to feel secure in spaces where their voices can be heard. In this role, Hippolyta forges strong relationships with young people, many of whom have conflicts with each other that emerge from school, gang violence, and other neighborhood circumstances. Beloved by young people in her program, Hippolyta's nurturing energy shined through during her interview.[13] Hippolyta describes how her program "takes the roughest of the toughest kids. We pour resources, we pour love. And we just do all we can for that group to, you know, encourage the entire community."

Her work does not come with fixed hours. Instead, like others featured in this book, she is on call, receiving phone calls and text messages from students at all times of the day with requests for guidance, transportation, or information about a needed resource. Youth workers like Hippolyta establish relationships with students and choose to be available for young people who may be facing serious challenges outside the context of school, particularly in their families and neighborhoods, such as homelessness, abuse, threats of violence, or other safety concerns.

Hippolyta's work with young people encapsulates the role of youth workers engaging young people in disinvested neighborhoods where structural oppression shapes the infrastructure of the city, its schools, hospitals, and employment systems. For example, there is a lack of adequate public transportation, and school systems are unsympathetic or apathetic about what young people are navigating, according to Hippolyta. She clearly understands the importance of her role in this context. She is acutely aware of the stress on families and the struggles young people are navigating, and she knows about the vital refuge that the physical space of youth programs provides. "So, everybody just has these expectations for families that's unrealistic. [One of my kids] lost two of his friends to gun violence, so he missed some days because he was at the funerals. And sometimes, he couldn't get rides . . . and his other summer program cut him. They cut him!" Ms. Clara, Hippolyta's mother, who sat it on her interview, interjected, "And [these programs] keep them safe. Keep them out the neighborhood for those couple of hours so that they don't have to deal with all of it." Hippolyta adds, "[One of my kids] was with these two kids I said were shot. One was shot in the neck and the shoulder; the other one was shot in the back. And my kid was sitting right there watching. So, when I go tell the school that, if they're not sympathetic to that fact, I will run straight to the news!" Hippolyta laughs after commenting on the news, but it signals her savviness and political astuteness to work on behalf of young people to get them what they need. Her commitment to Black youth is inspiring, and this commitment was shared by other youth workers featured in this book.

Compelled to Act: Political Sanctuaries in Black Youth Work

Black Spring was a defining moment for Hippolyta and other youth workers' engagement and commitment to Black youth. As news of police killings of Black people captured a rare level of national media attention, and being amid the COVID-19 pandemic, Black youth, alongside Black youth workers, took to the streets to be in solidarity with others.[14] Being in solidarity with others against injustice is a cathartic process during immense anguish and uncertainty. Many youth workers I spoke with said their students were eager to protest despite the fear of getting sick. They longed to be in solidarity with others. And, given the onslaught of violence and the routine witnessing of Black death over and over again, standing side by side was healing. For Hippolyta, who was there protesting alongside her students, it was a powerful experience. "You know," she said. "I had the kids out there protesting . . . Oh, it was wonderful! It was lovely for them because they could go out there and yell and scream at the police. Like, it was just, you know, it was just LIFE, for us."

Police violence is a national crisis in the United States; it is a relentless and deeply rooted expression of America's anti-Black racist history.[15] Amid this violence, youth workers across the US play a critical role in the lives of Black youth. Black youth workers and youth have a shared understanding of the fear of and maneuvering around police surveillance and violence.[16] Robeson, like Hippolyta, has dedicated himself to supporting Black youth in the face of this violence. He has worked in cities in the Northeast and

Southeast, where his engagement with young people often involves conversations about processing and navigating police violence. Robeson is viewed as
a father figure by the young people he works with and has been recognized
locally for supporting young people in his city. Robeson's primary concern
during Black Spring was students' safety. "Protests," he said, "sometimes go
in [different] directions . . . People get hurt. I just wanted our kids to be safe.
I wanted our kids to be in the best positions to have great experiences, and if
they wanted to participate . . . I wanted them to be safe." Robeson's concerns
about young people's safety during the protests are understandable, as we all
were witnesses to police assaults on peaceful protesters.[17]

Much like the youth that Hippolyta worked with, Robeson's youth were no
strangers to witnessing or experiencing police violence. Amid the summer 2020
uprisings, the young people he worked with suffered the loss of a peer at the
hands of the police, and protests became "cathartic" for his youth. "This isn't
like an amorphous, theoretical thing for us," Robeson shared and continues:

> And I think they'd had enough, as a general rule, they'd had enough in-
> teractions, or enough interactions by proxy, with police that had gone in
> really, really dangerous, or difficult, or disrespectful directions, that they
> didn't need this particular wake up call. The benefit, however, was that
> it gave them what I saw as a cathartic opportunity to express how they
> felt about it. Like it opened up the conversation, whereas otherwise, they
> might have just kept it to themselves, it gave them a venue and a vehicle,
> and it, I don't want to say a reason, but it gave them an opportunity to
> really deal with the processing that they needed to do because a lot of
> them were dealing with primary or secondary trauma that was directly
> related to these issues, and so they understandably were very emotionally
> reactive.

Police violence and the threat of death is not a theoretical idea for most Black
people. João Costa Vargas and Joy James, in a meditation on the killing of
Trayvon Martin at the hands of George Zimmerman, contend that Black
death at the hands of the state and white violence and subsequent mourning
are a "predictable and constitutive aspect"[18] of US democracy—necessary
even. According to Costa Vargas and James, the need for Black death is a
sobering statement but one that could be freeing. They write: "The ongoing
state-sanctioned legal and extralegal murders of Black people are normative

and, for this so-called democracy, necessary; it is the ground we walk on. And that it *is* [original emphasis] the ground that lays out that, and perhaps how, we might begin to live in relation to this requirement for our death. What kinds of possibilities for rupture might be opened up?" Possibility in anti-Blackness may seem doubtful, but with history as a guide, it is in the face of anti-Blackness and despair that envisioning a new world through mobilization and collective action is what Sharpe calls "wake work."[19] The relationship Black people in America have with death and dying, while also holding a commitment to collective care, joy, and beauty, through slavery, humiliation, and dehumanization, encapsulates the wake work that is necessary for survival.[20] Black youth work, in essence, is the process of wake work.

Robeson and Hippolyta's engagement with youth requires them to confront that which may harm the young people they work with—including anti-Black violence at the hands of law enforcement, school systems, and other systems that may harm them. They both enter their work with a deep commitment to the safety and well-being of young people. Robeson makes clear that youth have firsthand experiences with police violence or know other young people or members of their families who have been victims of police brutality. When recalling the protests of 2020, youth workers reflected on the challenge of protecting themselves emotionally while also holding space for young people. They had to find ways to hold space for young people (and their families) and guide them through their sensemaking about what they were experiencing and feeling while also trying to do the same for themselves.

Black youth workers we spoke with, especially men, are constantly faced with the impending threat of police interactions.[21] Ruben, a youth worker from the East Coast in his mid-to-late thirties, has family in the deep South. Because of the time he spent with his family down South, Ruben felt prepared for the racist encounters he might face in the world. "Where my family comes from is different, so it's like, they come from the deep, deep, deep, South, so it's like, you're going to hear this, you're going to hear that." Growing up in the South, Ruben witnessed overt forms of racism that shaped his disposition toward racism and law enforcement; "you do develop, uh, I'm not going to say a 'hate,' but you develop a kind of despise or anger towards the situation because it's like . . ." Ruben pauses, his eyes look upward, and he continues, "[As] a matter of fact, I just got pulled over yesterday, like, a traffic stop, and that could've just been different."

Indeed, it could have been different. Chris, who was introduced in chapter 1, is also no stranger to witnessing and experiencing police violence. I asked Chris about the unique challenges that Black youth workers might face. He pulled back from his desk, just slightly moving out of the video frame, struggling to figure out how to respond. "I mean, there are so many ways I can talk about this; how am I going to talk about this?" he asks himself aloud. He then begins to speak about his white colleagues and their inability to really understand the fear and danger of police interactions as a Black man:

> I had a coworker who got pulled over on his way to work. And, you know, for other people in the [organization] it was like, oh, he'll be here twenty, thirty minutes late, and they didn't check on him, right? For me, I was like, okay, this is a dark-skinned Black man on his way to work. I'm not only going to call, I'm going to try to figure out where he's at. I'm going to figure out where you're at. I'm going to show up. I'm going to leave where I am to make sure that he's okay. That's just part of the way that we live and work, right? That, you know, everybody doesn't understand.

Ruben, Chris, and Robeson, as three Black men, understand that navigating police interaction is sometimes a daily part of life and, therefore, imperative to address with Black youth, particularly the racialized and gendered dynamics of police violence.[22] Preparing them for their likely interactions is important and, quite literally, a matter of life and death.

At the time of Black Spring, many youth workers struggled to cope with and process everything happening but tried to appear strong for students in their programs. Harriet, a longtime youth worker from the Northeast with family roots in the Caribbean, has worked with young children for decades. Exasperated by the state violence and subsequent protests, she needed to shut out the world to cope. "As for George Floyd, I just turned off my TV for a while. It was very overwhelming to hear about it over and over and over and over again." Similarly, Zora, a youth worker from the Southeast committed to the development of Black girls, was also emotionally overwhelmed. She created space for girls in her program to discuss their feelings, nurtured their desire to be engaged, and released tension through activism. Zora also had to confront how she was feeling. "[I was] creating space but also dealing with how I was emotionally dealing with it myself was, was difficult." The routine display of violence and torture of Black people on many forms of media took a toll on many youth workers, as it did for me. Witnessing the horror of someone's breath leaving their body is traumatic—witnessing it on a constant loop can be destructive to the mind and body.[23] Decades-long social psychology and mental health research has shown that racism can have psychological and physiological impacts that can harmfully shape one's mental and physical health.[24] The youth workers I spoke with were concerned with their own psyches and their management of all that was happening in the world, and they did so the best they could while also trying to support Black youths' understanding of the moment.

Zora has worked with Black girls for over two decades. Now, in her midforties, Zora and her colleagues work fiercely to support and protect Black girls. At the height of Black Spring, Zora held space for her girls, but fear of imminent danger was always present. She vividly describes how the protests impacted her students' lives and the challenge of managing the pandemic and protests. "There were more things piling on top of the already horrible things that had happened. Anyway, we held space for girls in those days. And because I have a social work degree and have done some therapeutic work with people before, I was able to facilitate those. But even that, I was not prepared for the amount of sharing that was happening." After a long reflective pause, Zora continues, "I didn't really have the support of, like, my coworkers in this way because they really didn't have any kind of experience in this realm. So, I kind of had to just push through on my own . . . I would have liked to have a co-facilitator to help because it was a hard topic to get into." While managing her own emotions and helping her students without much support, Zora was conflicted about how she helped her students make sense of the protests and police violence. She shared that it was "interesting to hear some of their perspectives" about how people were protesting, especially after a popular fast-food chain restaurant was set on fire in a neighborhood where many of Zora's students lived. Zora then began mimicking the voices of the young people who were parroting media narratives about being more upset that property was destroyed than the killing of Black people. "Oh, they're destroying property," students might say. Zora would reply, "Yes, *and* they are killing people." Zora struggled to focus on questions from students about property. "Why are they messing up the [fast food restaurant] in our neighborhood?" the girls would say. She then would respond, "Yeah, why are they messing up the [fast food restaurant] in your neighborhood?" And, while pounding the table, she proclaimed, "Also, why did they kill that man?!?"

There is an art to teaching, guiding, and mentoring youth through many of the world's most complex and challenging moments—and creating political sanctuaries of sorts in the context of youth work allows youth space and time to ask questions and unpack all they are witnessing in society. Engaging with what some scholars term "sociopolitical development"[25] or what the Black Panther Party for Self-Defense called "political education,"[26] working with young people to get them to understand political and social problems is necessary for political education. Some approaches to political education within youth development allow young people to observe and process the world around them, including the systems and spaces they engage within, like schools, neighborhoods, and employment systems.[27] Asking critical questions regarding relevant history or popular historical narratives through dialogue is an important practice within youth work.

Other traditions of political education can include more direct teaching about structural oppression and social institutions in this country that shape the lives of young people marginalized by systems of oppression. These different approaches have been debated within educational and organizing spaces for a long time. Educational historian Daniel Perlstein writes about the shifts in the philosophical and pedagogical approaches to political education for youth within the Civil Rights Movement and the Black Freedom Struggle more broadly. His analysis of the Student Nonviolent Coordinating Committee's (SNCC) early Freedom Schools and the Black Panther Party's political education and Liberation Schools captures the diversity, conflict, and changes in the approach to political education for Black youth. In the early Freedom Schools organized by SNCC, teaching allowed students to draw comparisons between their educational experience and that of white students. Questions were asked to get students to think critically about their lives, the country, and how they could create change. Perlstein and others note that as Stokely Carmichael's ideology shifted on the heels of the Black Power Movement, less questioning occurred in favor of more direct teaching about oppressive forces that shape Black life.[28] Within Freedom Schools, one major shift was the deliberate effort to recruit Black teachers from Black colleges in the South instead of white volunteers from the North who had previously participated in SNCC's Freedom Schools.[29]

Approaches to engaging young people in political education shifted as the broader sociopolitical landscape within the country shifted, and new strategies and approaches to education and liberation were required. Even though changes in pedagogy and philosophy shifted over time, what remained true is that the transmission of knowledge and the raising of consciousness are the foundations of education and have the power to lead to social change.[30] Given the ongoing attacks on race-centered initiatives across school districts and institutions throughout the country,[31] community-based spaces become vital for political education and critical consciousness-raising—existing as political sanctuaries to support Black youth. Community-based educational spaces as political sanctuaries become even more necessary for young people in the face of state violence, political corruption, and societal collapse. For Zora and others, finding a balance between allowing space and time for young people to process their feelings, make observations, and draw their own conclusions after learning new knowledge is vital to youth work and the sociopolitical development process.[32]

Zora's passion for supporting, encouraging, and protecting Black girls and young women was evident in her work and approach to engaging them. Helping them make sense of complex and often nuanced social and political problems while also trying to validate their lived experiences was sometimes a challenge. She wanted to ensure that her girls were not "distracted by the policing of protests, as opposed to the killing of people" while still honoring the voices of youth who were distraught that their neighborhood institutions were being destroyed. This balance can be difficult for youth workers who want young people to think for themselves but also critically. Research about engaging youth in political education does not always have the same outcomes, and the critiques that describe youth as "indoctrinated" by political education can limit adolescents' agency and free thinking.[33] In many ways, early adolescent research shapes how we understand their capacity.

Initially dominated by developmental research that perpetuated paternalistic kid-fixing discourse, adolescents are framed as being ruled by their hormones and depicted as not having any agency.[34] Education researcher Ben Kirshner provides a helpful discussion about how developmental research created a dominant narrative of teenagers as immature, apathetic, and emotionally incapable in his scholarship on youth activism against educational inequality. He writes that framing teenagers in paternalistic ways has "destructive consequences for their opportunities for participation in the public square."[35] In other words, treating young people as incapable and vulnerable objects to be acted upon diminishes their agency and capacity for change-making. Rooted in critical theory, seeing youth as agents of change is at the core of youth activism in community-based educational spaces. An expansion of positive youth development—seeing young peoples' assets and strengths and moving away from deficit discourses—is the desire for social justice and critical approaches to youth development, which center youths' agency, critical consciousness, connection with adult allies, and their capacity to create change.[36] These approaches offer young people language and ways to understand the world and their own experiences—and allow them to question, think for themselves, and gain an understanding of the tools needed to push back if desired.[37]

Movement Backlash

Black youth workers consistently wrestle with the reality that a student they have worked with might become a victim of police violence. Hippolyta, like Robeson, revealed in her interview that they both had students who were shot and killed by the police before and during the summer of 2020. The safety of students was a priority for many youth workers, as was their well-being during the height of the pandemic. Jamea, the cofounder and director of an innovative local organization in the Midwest, where youth in the program, ranging from age fifteen to twenty-two, are leaders within the organization, was careful not to speak for youth but shared what she saw students go through during that time,

> They was going through it, and they couldn't understand why it kept happening, you know? Why is it on the news every day? Why? What do we do? Why are we being blamed for it? Because it generally comes down to people saying, "Oh, it's the younger generation," with most things. It wasn't. To me, it just compounded what they were already going through, having to be displaced and put into such a digital space so quickly. And then to see yourselves in these images on the news and on the TV while also trying to figure out what the world is gonna look like on the other side of this happening. It just added to the negative narrative for that time.

Black Spring, alongside the COVID-19 pandemic, induced precarity especially among those most marginalized.[38] While educational policy discourse was overly focused on the perceived dangers of academic "learning loss,"[39] I, along with many other youth workers, program leaders, and scholars of education and youth work, were concerned with the collective trauma young people were witnessing.[40] While the fear of increased educational inequities is an important concern, there seemed to be more focus on the potential failure of future standardized testing than on young people's well-being. In a 2021 *New York Times* article, the voices of high school students from the New York area were highlighted as they spoke about what they were losing during the pandemic.[41] Deep friendships and after-school activities, including sports and arts programs in their schools and community-based organizations, were the things young people mourned. Students talked about the depression they felt not being able to connect with their peers and mentors in community-based organizations and after-school clubs. The loss of connection to others, mental and emotional health struggles, and the inability to hone their crafts are the losses that should have been discussed more. There have been over a million COVID-related deaths in the United States, according to the World Health Organization.[42] Indeed, academic milestones are essential in child development, but the socioemotional well-being of a young person also matters— and often matters more.[43] A constant loop of media announcements of Black people being violently assaulted, humiliated, or killed at the hands of the state and of COVID-related deaths profoundly shaped the world, and the impact on our bodies, minds, and hearts is still surfacing.

The compounding impact of the uprisings and COVID-19 demanded action. For those featured in this book, action took on many forms. Youth programs are diverse, with various focuses and functions for youth. Programs that intentionally engage young people in organizing and activism for social and educational change are important to the critical youth work landscape.[44] About a third of the youth workers interviewed for this book came to youth work through activist spaces. Activism and organizing are essential elements of many youth organizations.[45] Youth programs that explicitly engage young people in strategies for organizing and activism to make their schools and communities better hold an important role in the youth work landscape.[46]

For those whose organization did not explicitly engage youth in activism, they were still committed to fostering a space for students to continue their activism. Zora even suggested that there was a push from youth development funders to encourage activism: "There seems to be a push even in the grant community now of, like, holding space for children to be able to do activism type of work," shared Zora. However, Zora acknowledges that many of the girls she works with are active on their own and that her program is likely their "igniter." Whether programs function as "igniters" for activism, as does Zora's program, many organizations, frequently those with Black leadership committed to justice, aim to provide a space for youth to unpack social and political problems and transform them. Youth work professionals with deep roots in activism found their work in this area to be even more critical during Black Spring.

Waverly, a Black woman in her mid-twenties, was born and raised in the Northeast and has been part of youth programs all her life. Waverly has a strong, quiet presence, and when we met to talk, she had just returned from a long day of coursework as she was pursuing a master's degree. Her fatigue was palpable. She was balancing a master's program, working with youth organizers in nonprofit organizations, and carrying the weight of the world. With deep roots in youth activism, Waverly is a proud community organizer and appeared in many public and televised protests in 2020. In the spring of 2020, Waverly was offered a job on the West Coast but was forced to decline due to the pandemic. Ultimately, staying on the East Coast renewed her commitment to young people and organizing. However, her protesting and rising profile garnered the kind of attention she did not want nor expect. This negatively impacted her emotional well-being. Waverly was also concerned for her physical safety as she received hate mail often. "I had the media hounding me. But then I also had white supremacists in my DMs. I had like hate DMs." Waverly described walking down the street one day in her home city when she was aggressively approached by someone who threw cash at her and said, "You are the reason the city burned down." At one point during the summer, Waverly began to carry a knife with her everywhere she went to protect herself. "I didn't even recognize that I was carrying a knife in my pocket, and I didn't realize it until like the fall of that year . . . There are so many people in my messages in my DM. On Twitter, on Instagram, saying like, oh, like we're gonna kill you," Waverly shared.

Hate mail and death threats became part of Waverly's daily life for about a year. The intensity of violence during this time weighed heavily on her, but she was steadfast. She continued getting involved with campaigns to resist police violence and supported as many youth activist organizations as possible by planning collective actions across organizations. Political attempts to roll back civil rights legislation, from book banning to punitive consequences for standing up against police violence, hate speech, or genocide around the globe, are relentless.[47] At every moment throughout history, as gains are made, efforts to thwart these gains surface;[48] they become more powerful and unyielding, making organizing against these efforts a constant struggle. Waverly understands this and has been deeply committed to activist work within her community and beyond. Even though youth workers like Chris, Robeson, Zora, and Hippolyta do not work for programs that have missions related to activism and organizing at the time of their interviews, their programming and engagement with youth lean toward sociopolitical development and supporting young people's desire to organize. The precursor to organizing and activism is critical consciousness and sociopolitical development.[49] Neighborhoods and suffering around the world are now even more prevalent with the viral nature of our global and ever-changing world. Young people see these conditions in their own lives and those of their families and friends—and they have questions. They seek to understand and make sense of their worlds, and youth workers play a critical role in holding space for them to process and add language to their sensemaking or affirm the language they create to define their own experience. Raising youths' social awareness and engaging them in social action occurs within Black homes, faith-based spaces, and community-based and advocacy organizations.[50] It is a critical component of Black education and youth development and has always been necessary for survival.[51]

Youth Activism and the Constraints of Nonprofit Youth Work

The landscape of youth-organizing programs exists within a complicated space within the nonprofit sector. It lands directly in the shadow of the shadow state, as Ruth Gilmore describes, and it is most impacted by the nonprofit industrial complex, which is inherently racialized.[52] In her ethnography of Pan Asian youth-organizing programs in California, anthropologist Soo Ah Kwon discusses the complicated dynamics between philanthropic entities, youth development, and youth-organizing programs. She argues that an inherent tension exists in the funding landscape of youth organizations, as funders prefer providing money that will support young people's academic development but not their political organizing for change.[53]

Within community-based youth programs engaging youth in social action, a paradox exists at the core of the work that shows up organizationally. It manifests in power struggles between board members, philanthropic entities, and program staff.[54] Staff members, including youth workers, who do not hold leadership positions or positions of power find themselves on the losing end of the power tug-of-war. The external political landscape of philanthropy must include a discussion of racial capitalism.[55] These external realities, like racism and capitalism and how they function together, shape large movements for social change, as the history of social movements has shown us, particularly those fueled by Black self-determination.[56] Still, for organizations committed to social justice–oriented work, these forces are deeply embedded in the structure of the nonprofit industrial complex.[57]

Contending with policy change, state violence, and deeply racist and anti-Black narratives that penetrate youth development and care work can weigh heavily on youth workers and program leaders.[58] Broader structures of power and sociopolitical events and forces shape organizations—how they are constructed and experienced. Amid the uprisings of 2020, many companies and organizations, including corporate entities, colleges and universities, and national and local businesses, wrote statements or made financial or cultural commitments to Black Lives Matter and antiracist practices within their organizations. The sales of books on race, diversity, and inclusion increased. People overwhelmingly donated to groups like Black Lives Matter. Yet, these commitments eventually dwindled (and at the time I am writing this book, executive orders are being issued to legally prevent companies and institutions, including colleges and universities, from being able to take stands against racism or publicly advocate for inclusive policies and practices).[59] For organizations, some Black youth workers involved in organizations that either had predominantly white leadership or boards of directors experienced frustration and disappointment with how their organizations' leadership did little to understand the gravity of what Black students were experiencing.

For example, with deep frustration and anger, Zora exclaimed that company and institutional displays of solidarity were performative and a lie, including her own board of directors: "To know for *sure* that it was all, it was all a lie, it was all a lie. All these companies, even the money that was like, [mimics voice] 'Oh, let's give these Black-led organizations money,' even that, like all of it, was just publicity and PR, and the work was never going to be done. And we're back to where we were when we started." Zora, alongside her executive director, also a Black woman, often battled their board of directors to ensure that young people had a space to process what was happening and to support them through COVID-19 and attending school online. Throughout her interview, Zora referenced the ways she and her executive director felt dismissed and disregarded as Black women by a predominantly white board of directors. The specific experiences of Black women leading youth-serving nonprofits reflect the sexism and misogynoir Black women experience in the workplace,[60] shaping how they can raise funds and make power moves in the field.[61]

Zora is painfully aware of the ways that an alignment and misalignment between young people and organizational leaders can impact the opportunities for listening to the concerns of Black community members fighting for police accountability and reckoning with the ways racism shows up in youth work practice. She was relieved and motivated by the energy from Black Spring. Since then, however, she feels like there has been a "backlash of everything." "I think about George Floyd," she said, "and I just don't know a better way to even categorize that summer, but I keep thinking about how, [long pause] not how good it felt, but how, like, it was like, 'Finally! People are listening to what we're experiencing! Like, okay! Let's open dialogue!' And then to just, like, go *completely* in the reverse of that . . . with our board." Zora's anger is understandable and unsurprising, as indicated by the next thing she said: "Like, we're still going to do the work again because we were already doing the work. Like, we'll continue doing the important things while y'all continue to make money." I was struck by Zora's resolve and her knowing that the power structure within her organization had no intention of staying true to their commitment to support Black Lives Matter or racial justice more broadly, despite the reality that the program serves Black girls. Zora plans to continue to "do the work" of organizing, guiding, and preparing young people for the world as it is, strategizing to achieve and maintain human rights, despite what those with power and wealth claim they will do. Zora's response here demonstrates a long-standing sentiment within organizing spaces in which oppressed and marginalized communities understand that the powers that be, so to speak, will always be fickle and that the relinquishing of power by those who have it is not likely to occur. Instead, being steadfast in pursuing justice, liberation, education, and freedom continues to be the focus and the goal.[62]

Grief and Disappointment into Action

Scholars have argued that there was a very broad backlash to the uprisings in the early 2020s—one that went well beyond the drop in support for Black-led organizations—and that includes newly energized efforts to ban books in schools, the removal of diversity-related initiatives, the dismantling of affirmative action and abortion rights, anti-gay and anti-trans legislation, mass deportations, thwarting elections, attacks on critical race theory, and a host of other attacks on efforts to understand and dismantle structural racism, homophobia, transphobia, and sexism.[63] Deliberate disinformation is at a peak, and the truth appears uninteresting and irrelevant to many.[64]

This political and cultural backlash has led to frustration and anger among Black youth and adults alike, something that youth workers—at the same time as they also feel this anger—are also helping youth to cope with and understand. Jamea witnessed her young people with excitement and hope in their eyes as they protested against police violence, wanting to hold the state accountable for the terror it causes. They hoped for change, and Jamea had to help them process their disappointment when things ultimately did not change. Jamea looks to history for guidance and inspiration from ancestors who fought for freedom. "What can we do differently? Where can we find our niche in this to continue to live, as many generations have before, beyond the traumatic experience," she reflects. This comment also illustrates Jamea's belief that her work is tied to a deeper legacy of supporting Black communities, and that is reflected in her hope and desire to continue fighting as our ancestors did, despite profound disappointment and betrayal by a country that Black people helped build.

Jamea's point about inspiration from ancestors and the fight to continue "beyond the traumatic experience" made me think about success. The definition of success is often wrapped into a neoliberal logic rooted in competition with others or quantifiable measures; however, in youth work, "success" operates on multiple levels. Within organizing frameworks, if the stated goal of a particular action is attained—change in a policy or practice—that is indeed a success.[65]

Personal growth, raising consciousness and awareness, and relationship-building among young people are also successes. For decades, Toussaint, a long-time activist, youth-organizing program leader, and scholar from the West Coast, has organized alongside Black and Latino middle and high school boys and young men. In his work with multiple organizations, Toussaint supports youth as they speak to city officials, organizing campaigns to protest, boycott, or raise awareness specifically about the racial and gender-based violence they might experience within their schools and neighborhoods at the hands of law enforcement. For Toussaint, growth in young people's leadership and their participation is a strong indicator of success: "When they start coming to committee meetings, right, those are the smaller ones where things are more focused and, you know, we're trying to target, more specific things that's just like our research reports that we conduct, or like the media and columns that we engage in . . . that's when we know they're starting to grow in their leadership." Toussaint believes that success occurs when young people participate in campaigns, lead meetings, and attend programming that is not structured or prompted, where they are motivated to implement the skills they have learned and feel empowered to take the lead:

> When they start to lead these . . . meetings and now they're meeting with us outside of . . . anything structured that we have planned or they're taking the lead in facilitating larger movement conversations, you know, they're volunteering for panels or, you know, they're able to . . . bring their friends in for phone banking, you know, or canvassing or any of those things, that's how we know that their leadership has affected the ground and they've gone from being a participant to now being an organizer . . . So. when we see young people when they first come in, they're just participants, right, like but then as they grow, they're not just being a part of strategy, now they're driving strategy. When they drive strategy, that's when we know, right, that they've effectively, right, like gained from this particular, from this particular programming.

Toussaint shares that when a young person can apply what they have learned in his organization to other organizations, that is his personal indicator of success. During Toussaint's interview via Zoom, he spoke fondly of a teen named Ahmad. Toussaint recruited Ahmad as an eighth grader. He refers to Ahmad as his "little homie" while reaching his arm up to point out a photo he is using as a virtual background. With a broad smile and a sense of pride in his voice, Toussaint says that Ahmad began working with him in one organization and then continued to other organizations, eventually leading to involvement with the larger Black Lives Matter Movement. "All of the skills he had learned in one organization, he began to apply to others." Toussaint then pauses and reaches for a copy of *USA Today* to show that Ahmad's work has been featured in a national media outlet. "His engagement in that space led to another space . . . this young person . . . just had good ideas [and] facilitate[ed] a statewide camp for boys and men of color across [the state] right, you know, and he did all of this before his eighteenth birthday." The levels of growth, leadership development, greater sense of self, and awareness of the world were transformative for Ahmad. Toussaint reiterates that Ahmad's work as an eighth grader contributed to change in local and state policy.

Toussaint's sense of pride mirrors that of many youth workers who have witnessed the power of young people who are inspired, fearless, and equipped with the necessary skills and tools to create meaningful change: "Yeah, to have young people lead that, participate in that, and help to drive that conversation and what that looks like was amazing. It was absolutely amazing, you know? So, those are the two greatest parts of doing this type of youth organizing work. One is right, like again, that aha moment, and the second is the policy win, the victory that these young people get to bring to their communities." The policy win and the growth or coming into consciousness is important to Toussaint. However, Toussaint has organized alongside young people in different types of organizations and among young people navigating precarious circumstances or captivity. Toussaint once worked with incarcerated young Black men where indicators of success had to be measurable and tangible to ensure these young men would not return to jail. Toussaint explained that his program measured success by ensuring students met the state's high school course requirements. It was also important that students did not return to incarceration. "We wanted to make sure that our students, if they had been arrested, that they didn't rearrest; if they had been suspended, that they didn't get suspended again; if they had, you know, had a frequency of being kicked out of class that frequency went down or stopped altogether, and that they had, you know, greater attendance at school." Toussaint is situated within programs in the youth work landscape that engage systems-impacted youth, organizing and activism, and academic and youth development.

These outcomes were important to the organization. But for Toussaint, there were many successes he felt could not be quantified. "I think other indicators of success, right, that we had that didn't necessarily, that couldn't necessarily be quantified, but these are things where we knew our model was successful, was that young people will begin stepping up into leadership roles, then people would begin to attend more activities outside of what was man-dated in their program, as well as, you know, young people would also start to recruit for this program, right? We knew that the program was effective if they wanted their friends to be a part of it."

For many youth workers featured in this book, Black Spring is a moment of global and national unrest that shifted how they were able to do their work with youth. Again, however, there are always Black Springs. Black youth workers are constantly faced with a similar reckoning in their work as they support young people in navigating racist and gender-based violence in their schools, cities, and neighborhoods. In many cases, the activism and organiz-ing among young people within community-based organizations are guided by young people themselves. Chris recalls an incident when students in his program frequently complained about a local corner store and the racist in-teractions they had with the owner:

> So there was another time [when] a kid came in and said that they went to the corner store and had a racist interaction. I'm not sure. It was [a] long time ago. So I'm not sure of the specifics, but we actually did a podcast. We recorded it. And at the end of the podcast, they were like, okay, this has apparently been a pattern. And they came to me and we're like, okay, so what can we do? So we wrote a letter to the entire organization [that] went out to all the members. And we asked the organization to, instead of going to this corner store, go to [another] corner store . . . And yeah, that corner store is no longer in business. So, it's important that we treat these things as serious. We take them seriously. We also want to ensure that kids realize their own power in these situations.

This incident was not an anomaly. According to Chris, he and other youth workers always take students' concerns seriously, which means that youth workers provide the context needed for students to understand why and how an incident occurred, draw their own conclusions, which may lead to support with social action if students desire. Chris points out that in taking students' experiences and concerns seriously, youth workers provide opportunities for deeper understanding and action. He also makes clear that young people hold him and his fellow youth workers accountable for how they promised to support youth:

> So, like kids come in all the time and say it and say, "this teacher was racist toward me." We have a conversation. We figure out what happened, and we've gone so far as to write letters to the administration in the schools before. Not much has happened. But it is important that kids see action happening when they come to you with things that are hard like this . . . And I mean, we've done that a couple of times, and they always come in, and they're like, "Yo, so what's happened? Have we talked to any-body? Has there been any movement? Should I send an email?" And then sometimes parents get involved, too, because I hear these stories, too. So, I really love moments like that because advocacy becomes such a lived thing in those sorts of rooms.

Chris's reflection that the letters of discontent from students to school administrators, protesting local stores because of racial profiling, or raising awareness about racial discrimination in their schools are all important ex-amples of how youth workers create sanctuaries for students to be heard, to feel safe, and engage in social action if they so choose. In a moment like Black Spring, which, for many, compounded forms of suffering due to the threat of COVID-19 and other forms of societal suffering, I asked Chris how he and his program handled conversations about George Floyd and the uprisings. "It's something we talked about," he said. "We talked a lot about resistance." Chris then said something that really struck me: "We talked a lot about love . . . I was trying to tell kids, like 'yo, we can change the world!' But part of the trouble . . . is that they want to immediately go down and go in and tear down the systems that exist." I appreciate Chris's commitment and shared desire with young people to change the conditions around them and tear down the systems that seek to destroy them. But Chris also said something that made me pause. "But like, part of changing the world," he continued, "has to start with changing the way that we are with one another." After hearing Chris say this, I wondered if his comments here reflected a common response to protests and large demonstrations against police brutality that avoids calls for police accountability because of "Black on Black crime." To some, Chris's comments might land that way—as a deflection of structural and systemic oppression to address intraracial community tensions. But hearing Chris say this made me think about his relationship with Mr. Rashad. Mr. Rashad showed unconditional love for young people and encouraged them to do that with each other. The gentle and loving leadership he modeled profoundly impacted Chris. Chris is a beautiful reflection of Mr. Rashad, and their relationship reflects the love Chris speaks of. Chris explained that Mr. Rashad's style of engagement was rooted in a sense of family, respect, and love. Love and familial feelings are consistent findings in research on youth experiences within community-based organizations.[66] Chris is unwavering in his commitment to Black liberation and justice; he is also a protector, a nurturer, and leads with a gentleness that Black children and youth rarely experience in this world.[67] Chris displays an intentional love or a love in action that is necessary for liberatory youth work.

The youth Chris worked with, who knew all about his commitment to Black liberation and justice, had questions about his response to their desire to go out and join the protests during Black Spring. Chris continues to reflect on this: "To them," he said, "it seemed like a cop-out at the time. Like, 'you gonna tell us we need anti-capitalism, anti-imperialism, all the isms. You say you want to get rid of all of them. But then you're also telling me to be nice to my mom, you know, it's not equating.' During that time, this is still something I struggle with, but making the macro micro, like turning world-changing moments into ways that we talk to one another, into ways that we dream for one another." Chris's reflection here is a powerful meditation on the forcefulness of love and care in community building and within youth worker–youth relationships. I see Chris's reflection here not as a "cop-out" or a deflection of systemic issues. Rather, he suggests that in the face of the distortions of Blackness amid white supremacy, the adultification of Black youth where they are not afforded the same innocence as white youth, and where their humanity is constantly questioned and disregarded, he is fully conscious of what danger may come their way. Still, he fights for Black life and wants his young people to do the same by starting with their love for one another. As Kelley tells us, this is the process of freedom dreaming and

"wake work," as Sharpe reminds us, and has always been part of Black education and youth development.

Crucial to our *freedom dreams* is our understanding of the world as it is,
and our desire to push back is rooted in how we envision and imagine a new
world.[68] Seismic shifts in our social worlds, such as the inflection point of
Black Spring, forced a moment of reckoning.[69] As horrific as it was, it was
not exceptional. Sure, it was shocking and catalyzed a global movement for
Black lives, racial justice, and greater accountability for law enforcement.
However, it is not exceptional in the long and ongoing fight for liberation
within Black communities. To call on Christina Sharpe, there is something
ordinary about Black death in America at the hands of the state, emboldened
by white supremacy.[70] The violence inflicted upon Black people is routine
and ordinary—a somber reality, but a reality.[71] Cultivating political sanctuaries within Black community-based institutions signifies freedom dreaming
or wake work.[72] Community-based educational spaces created within Black
communities or established with Black youth in mind have long been vital for
sensemaking of the world, affirmation of Black identity, protection from anti-
Black racist harm, and as a space to learn how to dream and resist. Youth
workers who are also organizers, like Toussaint and Waverly, engage young
people in resistance as a core part of their engagement with youth. Zora,
Jamea, Robeson, Chris, and Hippolyta guide youth in processing social and
political problems and support their efforts to organize. Both approaches to
youth work in Black space are vital and critical to Black youth development.

———

This chapter detailed how Black youth workers comforted Black youth during
tense times, great uncertainty, and the constant circulation of police violence
enacted on Black people. It also captures how Black youth workers understood their vulnerabilities as they tried to make sense of their witnessing of
Black people being victims of police violence. They, too, needed space to shut
out the world and sit with and in their grief. As Black youth workers were
mourning alongside youth, they also saw possibility from their resistance
through protest and action. Given the precarity in the youth work profession,
not all youth workers had coworkers or supervisors they could process with or
worked in organizations where they could process anti-Black police violence.
Black youth workers strived to allow Black youth to process, vent, and create

ways to resist and create change—even amid their fears, grief, and heartbreak watching the murders of George Floyd or hearing the cries of Ezekiel Ford or pleas from Tony McDade and others who called for parents, mercy, and implored their attackers to see their humanity to no avail. The presumption that Black youth are threats and problems to be detained and repressed is a logic tethered to anti-Blackness. Much like Jamea, I, too, look to the past for inspiration and to remember what is possible through the achievements, strength, and relentless efforts of Black educators, organizers, and leaders who knew they were laying a foundation for future generations. The ongoing nature of movement work through organizing within Black spaces is always powerful; the resistance and an unwavering determination to improve Black youths' conditions and educational experiences, with young people at the center, capture organizing in Black youth work.

Black youth workers fought hard to make sense of Black Spring's weight and terror, and the beauty of collective action and power building through much grief and mourning. For many youth workers featured in this book, their efforts to resist, dream, and imagine another world are deeply connected to their motivations for entering the profession. Their motivations are rooted in their commitment to Black liberation despite the inevitability of physical and psychological anti-Black violence. This chapter shows how, in contending with the many afterlives of slavery,[73] including routine and mundane acts of violence, Black youth workers continue to offer respite for Black youth—fostering dream spaces and opportunities for resistance. In the next chapter, I look more deeply at how Black youth workers seek respite and joy for themselves as they work to protect youth and themselves from the harms that emerge from the racialized nonprofit structure in which youth work is embedded.

FOUR

Protecting Youth, Protecting Ourselves

I had to examine, in my dreams as well as in my immune-function tests, the devastating effects of overextension. Overextending myself is not stretching myself. I had to accept how difficult it is to monitor the difference . . . Caring for myself is not self-indulgence, it is self-preservation, and that is an act of political warfare.

–AUDRE LORDE, *A Burst of Light and Other Essays*

We have to take care of ourselves, take care of each other, honor memories, and honor legacies that just don't exist in the same way for other people.

–CHRIS, youth worker

Chris became emotional when he told me about Bobby, a former student he worked with at his youth center. Bobby was tragically killed by gun violence. Shortly after Bobby's passing, Chris and another Black male colleague, who also knew Bobby, were leading a workshop for a class at a local university with which their organization partners. In the weeks following Bobby's death, there was much discussion in the local media about this tragic event. The students knew that Chris and his colleague had worked with Bobby and wanted to discuss what happened. Most students in this class were white, creating a complicated dynamic for Chris and his coinstructor. In the end, Chris's coinstructor did not feel ready or comfortable discussing what had happened. "It's always my job to process my grief as a Black man in front of a roomful of white people," he said to Chris. "And this time, I can't do it." Chris appreciated this stance, but it left him wondering how to handle class that day.

Although Chris was willing to speak with the students about what happened, he decided to approach the subject of Bobby's passing differently than he assumed students expected. Instead of talking about what led to the violence that took Bobby's life, he decided to "talk about [Bobby's] life" and the activities that brought Bobby joy and how he brought joy to others. He shared fond memories and talked about Bobby's elation after taking a woodworking class during a summer program. Bobby felt immense pride about what he created in this class, and Chris explained to the students how whenever he ran into him in the neighborhood, Bobby would talk about everything he made there. They would also talk about Bobby's family and his younger cousins who were planning to participate in the program, which excited Bobby because he wanted them to have the same great experiences he had.

In the United States, events like Bobby's tragic death due to gun violence are consistently presented through a pathological racial lens by popular media and in politics in ways that reinforce "cultural depravity" among Black communities and Black boys and men in particular.[1] For youth workers like Chris, who, as discussed in previous chapters, will sometimes interact with youth whose lives have been touched by gun violence, this can lead to frustration—particularly when dominant narratives ignore the structural conditions that shape the lives and decisions of Black youth.[2] It also directly influences how youth workers approach their work, motivating them to find ways to reject culturally pathological explanations for violence among Black youth as a way of protecting their humanity—and for Chris and his coinstructor, they wanted to protect their emotions from engaging in this kind of discourse. After Bobby's death, the local media ran several reports, and Chris felt a responsibility to "intervene on perceptions about this kid that [he] loved." He wanted to disrupt stereotypical anti-Black narratives that followed Black male youth in urban contexts. "I felt a responsibility to also say to the room that this feels icky in a lot of ways. To make them aware of, like, y'all are white, I'm talking about this Black kid that died, who y'all already had feelings about, y'all don't know anything about. And now I'm protective of his memory and sad for the future that was cut off here in a way that nobody else is, except for this other Black man, who is deliberately choosing not to engage in this conversation." As Chris shared this story with me, I was struck by his and his coinstructor's protection of Bobby's memory *and* their emotions. They engaged in a politics of refusal[3]—a refusal to play into what education scholar Kevin Lawrence Henry terms the "feasting" upon Blackness in which the suffering, harm, and violence of Black folks are consumed and made a spectacle by whiteness.[4] They wanted to protect the memory and legacy of this Black boy and protect themselves from the white gaze and the harmful assumptions undergirding this tragic situation.

As the youth workers featured in this book consistently demonstrate, they strongly desire to protect Black youth: their minds, spirits, legacies, and futures. They are determined to support young people as they navigate hostile school systems and society while they manage to support themselves in a profession plagued by deep precarity. Black educational institutions and the workers within them always carefully craft spaces of protection and affirmation for Black youth.[5] Black youth workers today, like their predecessors, see the development of critical consciousness and sociopolitical development as a form of protection for Black youth. Like Black educators of previous generations, they continue guiding students through challenging school environments, which is central to youth workers' protection of Black youth by cultivating spaces to decompress, process, and make sense of their experiences. But this work, which comes with great personal investment, can be taxing physically, emotionally, and mentally. As they work to protect Black youth, youth workers must also find ways to protect themselves and to create balance in their lives and avoid burnout.[6] They develop ways to show up for young people while striving to take care of themselves in the face of significant precarity like housing insecurity, low wages, inadequate health care, and anti-Black racism in their workplaces. Through their strategies for teaching, mentoring, and guiding students, youth workers also create opportunities for joy and play for themselves and students as a form of protection and resistance against a racialized nonprofit industrial complex.[7] The subtle and overt acts of resistance and refusal, joy and play, discussed in this chapter, highlight both the urgency and complexity of Black youth work today.

Knowing the World as a Form of Protection

The potential threat of white supremacist violence and terror is part of Black life.[8] In the United States and elsewhere, this has been the case for centuries, and working with Black youth has always been tied to this threat. From SNCC's Freedom Schools to the Black Panther's political education and Liberation Schools in the twentieth century, to youth uprisings in Soweto in 1979, to the global demands against state violence and the groundswell of the Black Lives Matter Movement, Black educators have always had to prepare Black youth for the potential violence they might be subjected to, and provide them with the knowledge and skills to navigate the world. However, being hyperfixated on the threat of white supremacy is not, nor has it ever been, the entire focus of Black life.[9] As the stories in this book highlight, Black youth workers consistently seek ways to make space for Black students to process the realities of the anti-Black racism they witness and experience. This is fundamental to critical youth development[10] and social justice youth development practice—fostering critical consciousness and engaging in social action.[11] Having gone through the education system themselves, Black youth workers have an intimate knowledge of what it means to be a Black student in this country and the significant risk of internalizing anti-Blackness through formal schooling.[12] Their personal experiences help youth workers understand what their students are experiencing, how it differs from their experiences and the many ways it is the same. The capacity to relate to youths' experiences creates an essential knowledge that allows youth workers to offer social and emotional protection to Black youth living in a world where anti-Black racism is constant.

One of the essential aspects of this work of protection is supporting and teaching Black youth as they confront the realities of anti-Blackness in American society. Following the 2020 murders of George Floyd, Ahmaud Arbery, and Breonna Taylor, Black youth workers across the country engaged in conversations with Black youth about the horrors of anti-Black violence that these killings highlighted for the public en masse, but it was hardly the first time Black youth workers engaged with Black youth about the horrors of anti-Blackness. "Kids come in all the time," Chris told me, "and they say that this teacher is racist, or [they] had a racist interaction at the store." Supporting students as they process racist incidents that happen nationally or in their schools is important to Chris. Chris is the type of youth worker who does whatever is in his power to support students, even if that means dropping whatever he is doing at the moment to protect them. One day, a young man in his program told him he wished he had "been born white." Chris was floored and wanted to talk with the student immediately. "What we've learned to do is take every situation like this seriously, right? . . . We take every situation like this seriously and build safe places to have these sorts of conversations. So, when the kid came in and said, 'I want to be white,' I stopped everything that we were doing that day."

Chris had students leave their classes and activities to discuss "blackness and whiteness, what it means and what it could mean . . . So, part of engaging these conversations is having knowledge around critical race theory, knowledge around who you are, who the people around you are, and the people you love are, but in ways that connect with kids." Chris's actions at this moment characterize how many quick decisions are made in youth-serving organizations. Crises in the world or in the lives of young people require immediate engagement and the creation of space for youth to process and obtain resources and other forms of support. Youth workers often must be nimble and adapt to young people's needs at any moment. Holding this conversation with students was necessary for Chris. The young man who made the comment about wanting to be white understood that to be white was to be afforded opportunities, privilege, and power that he did not have. Chris knew there needed to be an opportunity to analyze and make sense of the construction of Blackness and unpack how this young man was feeling. This incident opened a dialogue for the student and others in the program—without judgment but with love and a great opportunity to hold space for someone who had internalized anti-Blackness.

For youth workers like Chris and others featured in this book, this kind of engagement is seen as necessary to engage, teach, and intervene on attitudes that may be a sign of internalized racism or anti-Blackness. Community-based educational spaces and youth workers committed to social justice approaches to youth development value these conversations.[13] However, given the dynamics of power and leadership within organizations, these conversations may not always be possible.[14]

Although the threat of white supremacy is still relevant due to funding structures, the nonprofit industrial complex and instances of internalized oppression rooted in intergenerational, class, and religious differences can have a profound impact on how youth are engaged, how curricula get created, and ways that coworkers and supervisors interact with each other. For example, Ruben, introduced in the previous chapter, is about ten years older than Chris and shares Chris's perspective on the urgency of teaching. "The only thing you can do is teach," Ruben stated. "Teach. Because if you don't teach, what's going to happen to them?" But Ruben's refrain "to teach" means something slightly different than Chris's. Ruben works with incarcerated youth in the Northeast and has worked with young people for more than fifteen years. Ruben believes that his trips down South prepared him for the racism he would experience in life. He was confronted with the realities of the hostility of racial segregation and understands the dangers of white supremacy but believes that there should be certain "guidelines" and ways to go about speaking out against injustice in a "respectable manner." This tension is a familiar one. This perspective tends to be the source of strife between Black youth workers occupying multiple generations with different class backgrounds and political leanings. Squabbles over modes of expression or how to address injustice is a long-standing tension within movements for Black liberation.[15] I see these tensions as part of the reality that Black people are not a monolith despite the shared reality of living in a society with anti-Black racism. The prevailing sentiment is that these youth development spaces operate and feel like family.[16] While these dynamics can be true, they do not mean conflict-free or that those involved are always politically aligned. Intergenerational, class, political, and gender-based conflicts arise within Black youth-serving organizations like any organization.[17] Conflicts also arise causing disagreements about the approach to pedagogy. Youth work does not have one standard pedagogy but one that constantly adapts to new currents of unsettled moments in society and social justice discourse while also integrating people's life experiences and doing so within widely differing organizational structures.

Jamea and Ruben have different opinions on how to respond to instances of anti-Blackness, but their support of Black youth is unquestioned. Approaches to engaging youth and these issues do not follow one standard process. Jamea speaks sternly about the disconnect between adults and young people's desires for justice: "The ideologies that we've been passed down through religion, you know, turn the other cheek, you know, God got your back kind of thing. Yeah, the kids ain't working with that no more! They kind of tired of that." Jamea's comments reflect what she perceives as a passiveness among older generations in the face of oppression. While I may not characterize past actions as passive, activists and educators have often differed in their strategies and approaches.[18] What I hear reflected in Jamea's comments is a desire to ensure that Black youth understand the historical underpinnings of their current conditions. "We teach them about Black history as it relates to your identity, who you are, and how there is a rich history that you're not aware of that you have around you, that you can seek out . . . So we open that up for exploration for the youth so that they can understand, you know, look at history. How did you define white? . . . So we go into those things so that they can understand how they've been identified. And they can then determine their own identity and be comfortable in it." This approach connects to Chris's approach in supporting students' understanding of race and identity; social identity development is central to sociopolitical development and subsequent social action among young people.[19] It is an aspect of youth work that has, for generations of youth workers, been understood as an essential part of helping Black youth understand and navigate injustice in their schools and more broadly.

Although differences exist among youth workers in the way they might approach their support and protection of Black youth today, there is still a fundamentally shared motivation aimed at preparing youth for the realities of the world, and this motivation is directly linked to the same core motivation of the activists and educators during the Black Freedom Struggle in the 1960s. A clear throughline exists between contemporary Black youth-serving organizations and independent Black institutions during the Civil Rights, Black Arts, and Black Power Movements, where political education and organizing for young people, publications, and creative arts was imperative.[20] Olivia, a classroom educator and youth development practitioner, embodies this throughline. Olivia and I met when she came to a workshop I was leading for youth workers of color on the West Coast about navigating racism and self-care. Olivia's strength is palpable and can be felt as she speaks. She is confident and comfortable in her skin and in her power. She is Black (of Nigerian descent) and Samoan and spent her formative years in an all-Black Afrocentric school. She attributes the foundation for who she is as a Black person to loving Black educators who led her to teaching and youth development. Olivia's school was a church-led education academy and was a "99.9 percent Black school. All the students, all the staff, our church staff. We had one Latinx educator, one white educator, and that one white educator was married to one of our Black members of the church. Even his kids were Black!" she recalls fondly while smiling. When Olivia's parents could not afford tuition, she had to switch to attending her home public school. "And

every time I went to the public school, something would happen . . . something racist," Olivia said in a matter-of-fact tone. As Olivia reflects, she tells
me that her all-Black school is the foundation for who she is. "My foundation
was really strong in who I was as a Black girl. Not as strong as in who I was as
a Samoan girl or Pacific Islander. But my Blackness or being in a Black space,
a Black church, Black elders." When she experienced what she called "she-
nanigans" and "foolishness" in her public school, she was able to navigate it
more easily than her Black friends. "I was able to, I think, navigate a little
bit easier than maybe some of my friends" because of the foundation she had
in her all-Black academy. The warmth of her Black school and the embrace
of impactful Black educators nurtured her curiosity about the world, her creativity in the arts, her intellect, and her reverence for Black communities.
"That school was the safest place on Earth," Olivia declares as she reflects
on her childhood and education. For Olivia, that experience directly informs
her motivation as a youth worker, former classroom teacher, and performing
artist to provide that same kind of safe space for the youth in her life.

Jamea, Chris, Hippolyta, Olivia, and other youth workers interviewed
understood that while Black youth require the kind of patience, support,
structure, and grace *all* young people deserve, Black youth must also be for-
tified with a sense of history and purpose connected to Black liberation and
a strong sense of self in a world that would rather they not exist. This protection youth workers sought to provide from societal harms and hostile schools
occurred with very little resources, reflecting the variation in funding and
support among youth development organizations. For instance, Hippolyta is
audacious in her protection of young people. She is unafraid to hold anyone in
authority accountable for the harm they cause Black students. She is forceful
in her efforts to ensure that schools, law enforcement, and city leaders recognize her students' humanity and lived experiences. The protection provided
by community programs and youth workers also alleviates food insecurity
and ensures that neighborhood, housing, and school conditions that could
be harmful are quickly addressed. Hippolyta frequently called out school
administrators and local politicians and provided resources to advocate for
students whenever she could. Ms. Clara, Hippolyta's mother, sat in her interview with immense pride and appreciation for her daughter's work. She
raved about her daughter's work that protects students from food insecurity
and other societal harms.

She set up giving away clothes, giving away food . . . she used to have this truck . . . It was an ice cream truck. She pulled up in the neighborhood. It was free. Free ice cream, Oodles of Noodles, anything. She would go on Fridays and pass this food out into different neighborhoods. You know, because we know in some homes, kids don't eat on the weekends. So, she would go to these neighborhoods on the weekend . . . and give out food. And one thing they had to do when they got the food, they had to get a book. So not only did they get the food, they also got the books.

Ms. Clara is proud of her daughter's work in the neighborhood. She recognizes that some students go without food when not in school and also navigate complicated neighborhood dynamics. Hippolyta did this work with modest donations and her personal money.

Youth workers and program coordinators like Zora wanted to do more, especially during the pandemic, but they had limited resources. Zora, who works with Black girls, desired to do more to protect students from neighborhood and societal harms like financial insecurity but lacked the resources.

I wish we would have been able to give parents more, like, families, more money, more financial support. But not having the kind of infrastructure to do some of that type of work . . . I know that we've tried to connect families with resources in other organizations . . . seeing how hard it is to get rental assistance . . . I wish we would have been able to do more of that. We were primarily doing gift cards for, like, food and, like, household items, not necessarily utilities. We did a few utilities for a few families, but not on a grand scale. So, that's something I wish we would have, could have done more of.

The theme of wanting to "do more" became a pattern as my team and I spoke with youth workers and program leaders, whether they wanted to do more to mitigate the violence young people experience in their schools or the societal harms caused by things like poverty, neighborhood and school disinvestment, or racial discrimination. Young people also relied on their youth programs and youth workers for protection and support beyond academic needs. If students needed anything, they knew to call Hippolyta. "And you know, her phone rings all day!" Ms. Clara says. "I was in the car with her the other day. We were driving, and a little boy called." The boy was trying to get food, and upon hearing this, Hippolyta wanted to send the boy money. Hippolyta laughs lovingly and says, "They know who to call!" Indeed, they know who to call. When young people experience roadblocks in schools, home life, neighborhoods, or negative interactions with law enforcement, they depend on Hippolyta and youth workers. They understand that, as a non-parental adult not attached to the school system, youth workers and their organizations will do what is in their power to intervene, support, and protect students as best they can. This understanding is cultivated through deep relationships and trust building between youth and youth workers in community-based organizations.[21] It is a feature of youth work that is celebrated in research but that needs greater societal understanding, celebration, and respect for the level of skill it takes to connect with youth in genuine and authentic ways—and perhaps more importantly, greater respect for the entire ecosystem of support young people can have which can include schools and out-of-school youth-serving organizations facilitated by youth workers that are vital for youth development.

Protecting Youth at a Cost

Youth workers strived to safeguard students from the physical and psychic violence they experienced in schools and cities. They also worked to protect youth from harm within the very organizations where they work. An organizational paradox exists within the youth work landscape where programs can simultaneously disrupt and perpetuate racial harm.[22] This paradox can be most central in the quest for funding, as donor control and racial hierarchies in philanthropy have a long history in Black organizations, especially those centered on liberation and justice.[23] Nonprofit funders often make demands in the organizations they fund—including demands regarding the organization's programming, internal and external communications, and pedagogy—that may impose deficit framing and performativity of poverty that feeds into white savior narratives and perpetuates anti-Black stereotypes.[24] Youth workers will often work to protect the humanity of Black youth from these kinds of demands. For example, Gia, who lives and works in Pleasant Ridge in an organization committed to racial and gender justice, describes the need to be constantly attentive to this common tension and contradiction that emerges in youth work committed to affirming Black youth. While she and her co-workers are cautious about the money they take from philanthropic groups, they remain committed to avoiding the kinds of stereotypes and damage-centered narratives[25] that funders often expect but that feel exploitative of young people. In other work, I have described funders' demands of this kind as perpetuating narratives of damage and struggle to maintain funding,[26] or what sociologist Gregory Wilson terms "racial finesse,"[27] to tug at the heartstrings of funders or tap into their limited understanding of Blackness.[28] Kid-fixing discourses that position Black, Latine, and low-income students as needing to be fixed or saved by an organization are dominant in youth development discourse and practice.[29]

Gia, who was introduced in chapter 2, was open and candid about her disappointment in Pleasant Ridge's Black youth program leaders, who she felt were less cautious about how they talked about their students or the policies at their organizations, as they sometimes did so in ways she believed were harmful to Black youth by depicting them in deficit ways. "I do think when you're the CEO or whatever of an organization, and you're perpetuating negative stereotypes of Black kids in order to get funding, I think that's really fucked up, right?" Gia's comment was in reference to a local chapter of a national youth program and the executive director, who often shared space with local politicians, media outlets, and corporate donors. The layers of the organizational paradox are evident; Gia's comments point to how the paradox functions through the sociopolitical landscape that shapes organizational decisions about money, their content, and leaders' and youth workers' actions. These decisions can heighten the financial precarity for organizations and reflect their larger precarity and fragility within the nonprofit system.[30] This landscape includes the political climate and the nonprofit industrial complex—a cycle between state power, philanthropic wealth and power, and nonprofit organizations—that creates a dependency that ultimately benefits the power structure and not organizations or their members, especially those that are most vulnerable.[31] This industrial complex itself is racialized,[32] and these broader social structures enacted by the state (particularly surveillance) and philanthropy ultimately shape how programs *can* do their work. Youth workers like Gia question the way some program leaders, for example, capitulate to the worst anti-Black stereotypes about violence, poverty, and underachievement to appease donors. Or when Chris refused to talk about the killing of a former student, he refused to play into others' preconceived notions about Black youth, which is commonly expected in nonprofit youth work and expected by many donors. Still, decisions about funding and the narratives about youth and what the program does on their behalf are not always simple. They reflect a complex set of issues that reinforce the nonprofit industrial complex.[33] The broader structures of racist paternalism that feed on anti-Blackness and the hoarding of wealth due to capitalism create a dependency on philanthropy that creates the need for youth workers to navigate the white savior complex of funders and the deficit-framing of Black youth used to appeal to them.[34]

Olivia provides an important analysis of how this complex stifles Black agency in nonprofit organizations. Olivia has worked with young people as a classroom theater teacher, youth worker, and nonprofit leader. She understands the challenge of working in both settings. She explains that "trying to figure out how to dismantle the nonprofit industrial complex" has consequences for Black leadership in nonprofit settings. "The system is not making it easy on Black creatives or start-ups to thrive in the way that they need to and, and then at some point in the longevity or legacy of an org, stuff starts getting weird because you're working hard trying to navigate this, this nonprofit system. But it was never meant for us to do things the way we in our guts and in all of our ancestry know how to do." Here, Olivia powerfully points to what many youth workers from racially minoritized backgrounds engaging in organizations led by and funded by people outside of their communities have experienced.[35] Those in leadership positions constantly negotiate program values and goals with the intentions and priorities of donors in mind. Black program leaders make tough decisions that may lead them away from their missions or values to ensure their programs stay financially afloat.[36]

In the face of this, Black youth workers consistently seek ways to protect young people's humanity, as Chris and his colleague tried to do for Bobby. It is, as the comments from Gia, Hippolyta, and Chris above make clear, one of the most essential and urgent roles youth workers can take on today. The decisions to protect Black youth from the deficit framings rampant in youth work or resisting the decisions of leadership that play into the complex web of paternalistic philanthropy and the nonprofit industrial complex can have consequences for youth workers who are already vulnerable within their organizations. When program leadership and front-facing staff resist board decisions they find harmful or youth workers with limited power push back on leadership who reinforce deficit depictions of youth, it does not always go without consequence.

RETALIATION

In speaking with youth workers who currently hold front-facing roles in their organizations or those now in leadership positions, they reflected on moments they experienced retaliation in their programs. As Black and other youth workers of color—or those who are in allyship—seek to protect Black youth, many find themselves facing forms of retaliation for their efforts. This retaliation can result in demotions, less face time with students, or a lack of leadership and decision-making opportunities. It is a part of the harsh reality of the precarity that youth workers of color face, especially within organizations where they do not hold power. Working within a system that one must critique can create layers of conflict and contradictions, and youth workers often face this reality in their work.[37] An organizational paradox surfaces in myriad ways; funding structures create a dynamic of dependency on philanthropy that may not be aligned with an organization's values, resulting in mission drift. Organizations that work hard to protect Black youth from deficit framing rooted in anti-Black stereotypes or poverty tropes navigate this paradox constantly. In previous work, I have discussed how organizations appease donors by relying on deficit, stereotypical, and paternalistic language or by attempting to capitalize on stories of damage and struggle to secure funding.[38] The deficit-oriented language, which frames Black and other racially minoritized youth from a position of lack, leads to the positioning of them as broken and in need of fixing.[39] Many organizations try to disrupt this language in their marketing materials and their programming in general and opt for more asset-based framing—language that seeks to present young people in their whole humanity as people who possess many strengths and talents that need to be nurtured.[40] As I have explored in other work, program leaders who understand how philanthropy relies on racist and class tropes understand that racialized and deficit framing has long been used to encourage donors to reach into their pockets to support youth programs financially.[41] The framing of programs shapes how youth are engaged and treated within these spaces; it narrows the quality of programming, dismisses the agency and strengths of youth, and perpetuates hierarchies of deficit thinking and practice.[42] Steep challenges for youth workers arise in programs that struggle to resist the deficit framing in their work.

In some cases, youth workers' acknowledgment and disruption of anti-Black racism and the treatment of Black youth participants, particularly in white-led organizations, can have consequences. For example, Carlos, a youth worker at an organization on the West Coast, believed he was demoted when he tried to push back against this kind of deficit framing. One day, he noticed that his organization's website framed Black students in deficit ways. But when he shared his concerns with program leadership and encouraged them to reconsider their framing, he was soon demoted to translating materials from the organization into Spanish behind the scenes and away from engaging with youth. Carlos believed he was retaliated against for his attempt to protect Black students in the program. Carlos is not alone in understanding the risks of speaking truth to power. Darren, a youth worker from the East Coast, had a similar experience as a youth worker in a school. He had a question about a new curriculum being offered and asked the principal about it, and he says he was "dismissed" the following year. "I didn't do anything. I didn't do anything wrong. I didn't like disrespect anybody. I didn't scream about it. I just asked a question about it." Reflecting on this incident, Darren continued, "I literally was not offered a job to come back. But I wasn't like mad. I knew that there was a possibility. But that's what happens when you speak up, right? You get punched in the face sometimes, but you got to be able to deal with it. You know, and I dealt with it." Darren's reflections echo Sam's in chapter 2, who told me about youth workers he knew at other organizations who were let go after raising questions about race.

Even the fear of the possibility of retaliation concerned youth workers we spoke with. Zora, for example, described her concern about speaking out against how her board of directors talked about Black girls in the program. For some time, Zora had been frustrated with the board of directors for her program, specifically with the board's lack of racial and cultural competency and what seemed like their disregard for the Black girls served in the organization. When Zora spoke about her experiences working in her organization, she was concerned that should her board learn that she was critical of their decisions, they would retaliate against her. The fear of retaliation among youth workers was more common than I had originally thought. The fear was palpable; Zora wanted to ensure that my research team and I would protect her identity. Fear of boards of directors was not the only concern for youth workers. Some youth workers were fearful of how they were perceived by other youth workers and fellow staff members when they stood up for Black students by disrupting deficit language or harmful attitudes in their organizations.

In chapter 1 we met Gabi, an Afro-Indigenous youth worker on the East Coast at a lauded program serving Black and Latino boys. This program has a long history in her city, and while she has a front-facing role with youth, she coordinates programming, which makes her part of the program leadership. She is mindful of how being Black is perceived, judged, and considered a threat in her role at this popular youth program. Gabi has a no-nonsense demeanor, which I appreciate, but she shared that her demeanor was a source of tension between her colleagues, as they labeled her "aggressive." "I'm not aggressive. I'm assertive. I speak my mind, and I'm not afraid to do so . . . if I disagree with you. I'm gonna let you know I disagree with you," Gabi declares. Gabi joined her organization ten months before her interview, so she was still relatively new and was still adapting to the culture of the program. Despite her short time at the organization, she is unapologetic about not liking to "put on a mask." She is who she is and doesn't apologize for it. Gabi's love and dedication to boys in her youth development work directly reflect her commitment to the Black boys in her personal life, like her brother and other family members. Gabi shared that one day she was in a meeting with her colleagues, and someone made a joke about students in the program being "dumb" for not participating in a particular activity. Everyone laughed, but Gabi was not amused. She did not find the joke to be appropriate and shared that feedback with her colleagues in the moment:

> I remember a colleague made a comment in a meeting one time referencing our boys as like dummies or something. And it was in a joking off the cuff way, but I call them out. And I was like, I don't think that's funny. I don't think that's funny at all. Because you're talking about Black and Brown boys, and you're referring to them as dummies because they didn't take a chance on an opportunity or didn't accept the opportunity. And I didn't think it was cute . . . And another colleague was like, "oh, she didn't mean it that way" . . . I . . . had to let it be known in that space that you can't make jokes about these kids like that around me. And I was only, like, six months into the job. But I had to say something . . . I do feel it's my responsibility to let them know about it, you know . . . I didn't call them out. I didn't disrespect them. I just said I don't think that's funny. And I meant [it] when I said it.

Gabi's respect and advocacy for her students are paramount despite the fear of retribution from her coworkers or supervisors. Fearless and determined, Gabi's perspective on supporting young people is embedded in who she is as an educator: "I told myself a long time ago that being an advocate means speaking up with [and] for these youth in these spaces, in these behind the scenes, you know, conversations where things are being planned and done. I'm gonna speak up for these youth and speak up for them in a way that's respectful and with integrity."

Access to power and control in organizations varies among Black leaders, coordinators, and youth workers and is based on the organizational hierarchy they work within. Those with front-facing roles with youth—part-time or full-time status—tend to hold the least decision-making power, making them more susceptible to retaliation, demotion, and hostility within their organizations. However, Gabi was unafraid and stood in her power and commitment to the boys she worked with. But the need for this kind of willingness to stand up to protect the youth they work with reflects how, for Gabi, like for other youth workers, organizational dynamics, including leadership—including this kind of threat of retaliation—shape their work. These dynamics create the conditions in which youth workers enact this effort to protect Black youth, often forcing them to push back and resist harmful narratives or actions against Black youth while adding to the complexity of their efforts to protect the youth they work with from the harms they may face inside and outside of their organizations.

The day-to-day engagement in youth organizations can be taxing for youth workers. For youth workers and program leaders who are constantly navigating the dynamics of a racialized nonprofit industrial complex, challenging funders, boards of directors, and, in some cases, program leaders who may not fully understand the conditions that shape the educational and social lives of Black youth, this work can be exhausting. To do this in the face of potential retaliation, long hours, little pay, and lack of structural support, youth workers consistently struggle to care of themselves.

Youth Worker Well-Being

The protection of Black youths' legacies and futures through preparation for the world and the education system—as they are—has long been a central and urgent part of the youth work process in Black communities.[43] But this kind of critically oriented youth work is emotionally and physically taxing work. This kind of engagement, coupled with the day-to-day counseling and guidance of young people through their various stages of development, can be challenging, and many youth workers in nonprofit organizations struggle to care for themselves, too. Many organizations are aware of this issue, and the wellness of the "youth fields" workforce has been a significant concern for prominent funders and foundations supporting youth work, especially at the height of the pandemic and the uprisings of 2020.[44]

Today, one can find advertisements for the importance of self-care everywhere. Self-care is promoted by social media influencers, popular companies, and references in popular culture—encouraging people to slow down, take care of themselves, and indulge in pampering, naps, and other wellness routines. These conversations mean well; caring for one's health, mind, body, and spirit is important. Still, these conversations can miss structural conditions that do not allow some of us to engage in popular wellness routines, take vacations, or indulge in self-care practices that require taking time off or abandoning caregiving responsibilities. These things can feel like a luxury for some. Absent from these conversations about self-care and wellness is the role of capitalism and exploitation in the labor market[45]—and how labor exploitation intersects with racism, patriarchy, and economic injustice that, especially, leave women and nonbinary folks of color unable to take part in the "self-care" movement.[46] Angela Rose Black, scholar, integrative health practitioner, and founder of Mindfulness for the People, a creative healing house committed to disrupting white supremacy in the mindfulness movement, often asks, "Who *gets* to be well?"[47] In the context of education and nonprofit youth-serving work and the reality of structural anti-Black and cis-heteropatriarchal violence, who gets to be well? Writers and activists like Tricia Hersey have declared that to *rest is to resist*. Following grind culture rooted in capitalism leaves those most marginalized physically and emotionally exhausted.[48] Black feminist scholars have long discussed self-care for Black women as a radical act or an act of renewal and reclamation precisely because of the structural anti-Blackness and patriarchy that shape the lives of Black women[49] or misogynoir to be more precise, a concept coined by scholar and activist Moya Bailey.[50] In a society in which Black folks' humanity is contested, the opportunities for rest and wellness are not always afforded to them. In care and helping professions like education, social work, and health care, the expectation of overworking and overfunctioning in the name of the cause is rampant.[51] For Black youth workers, who are consistently overworked, overfunctioning, underpaid, and lacking benefits, opportunities for wellness and self-care are few and far between. While the youth workers I met during my research strive for wellness and demand space and time to care for themselves, there is also a structural and organizational responsibility to ensure that these workers are supported. Reminders to take care of themselves come from within the networks they have established as they try to evade burnout. Burnout in youth development nonprofit work is a massive challenge for many organizations struggling to maintain consistency for young people.[52] In addition to low wages, the physical and emotional toll it takes on workers to care for youth who are navigating systemic violence in their schools and larger society can be daunting. As a result of this, burnout and turnover in the profession are common.[53]

Centering wellness and self-care is challenging for Chris and the other youth workers I spoke with. Chris gives everything he can to the youth in his program, but this work takes an emotional and psychological toll. Processing the issues youth are going through can also help him process those same issues in his own life. But he was also very candid about how he could take better care of himself: "I'm not quite sure how well I hold space for myself in those moments . . . but I think that's also because, in those moments, I'm not the priority." Chris captures a nuanced understanding of what it means to create spaces that affirm Black youth by providing a physical and emotional space to be seen and of how the profession often requires a deprioritizing of oneself to support and protect young people. Youth workers with backgrounds in counseling have tools to support young people's healing from compounding trauma. Harriet, a youth worker from the Southeast, has taken college courses in counseling, which "taught [her] a lot [about] how to deal with kids' trauma and people with trauma." Like Chris, Harriet can prioritize students, sometimes over her own needs. "[I know] how to step back, remove myself from the situation, and don't take a lot of things personally. Because we deal with a lot of people with severe trauma, sometimes you can trigger some behavior you don't expect yourself." Youth workers, especially during perilous times, must move quickly to respond to crises and the demands of funders and colleagues while supporting students through many domains of their lives.

But this instinct to take care of others, to invest emotionally while at the same time trying to maintain a professional distance, reveals both how essential and complex the issue of wellness can be for Black youth workers. Unlike full-time equivalent (FTE) teachers, as discussed in earlier chapters, who may have more secure employment benefits, youth workers are particularly vulnerable, and the impact on their health and well-being is something we must pay attention to. Due to the potential for dealing with severe trauma, in addition to the day-to-day flow of working with youth, youth workers rarely have a moment for themselves. Youth workers can quickly face burnout—the hours can be long, the pay can be low, and the energy it takes to guide multiple young people at once can be difficult to sustain.[54] Mason, a program leader and author from the South, discusses the difficulty in overcommitting and burnout in the profession: "It is very difficult to do the work, because you're drawn to the work often from a place of trauma and a desire to transform. But . . . it's very easy to kind of overcommit, because there's so much work to be done. And if funding isn't there, then you end up kind of taking on all of these jobs and these hats and burnout is huge, particularly if you have never had experience outside of the sector." In a similar conversation with Chris about burnout in the profession, he reflected honestly about his struggles to be well in the work: " I have been called a workaholic, to be fair. It helps that I have an art to lean on when I'm overwhelmed; I lean on writing. It helps a lot to even me up." Chris has been with his organization for ten years and took his first one-week vacation a few weeks before our meeting. "I was uncomfortable the whole time," Chris said through laughter. After we finished laughing, Chris told us, "Burnout is a real thing. And it took me a long time to realize that I was getting burned out because I was the only Black person in the room solving all the Black kid problems, right? Other people were hanging out having a break, going on vacation, and I was in the trenches with the kids figuring out things with families, figuring out things . . . like, how they were with each other, breaking up fights."

For Black youth workers who are one of few Black staff members in organizations, much like Black classroom teachers, they become the de facto go-to person or "discipline stop,"[55] as education researcher Ed Brockenbrough argues, in which educational spaces send Black students to be guided and disciplined only by Black educators, especially Black male teachers when

it comes to disciplinary action for Black boys. This kind of labor disproportionately impacts Black youth workers, as Chris highlights. "Burnout is a real
thing" and has been the focus of growing research on the experiences of youth
workers, especially racially minoritized and undocumented youth workers.[56]

Given the stressful and precarious nature of this profession, in conversations with youth workers, I wanted to understand how they took care of themselves in the face of burnout and how they sought to take care of themselves
while caring for young people at the same time. Their responses to this were
notable for what they had in common with workers in other professions—
relying on family, for example or, for those with benefits, taking vacations.
But they were also notable for what was specific to their field, including relying on other youth workers who understood what they were going through
and the need to find ways to set physical and emotional boundaries. Hippolyta, introduced in chapter 3, for example, who engages in violence interruption in her organization, pointed out how essential it was for her to have
the close support of a family member in her work—specifically her mother.
Even during Hippolyta's conversation with us, her mother sat alongside her.
It was clear that she was a consistent supporter who regularly reminds her
daughter to take care of her mental health. During a sincere moment of care,
Ms. Clara, Hippolyta's mother, turned to her daughter to say, "I need to make
sure you're okay;" she then turns to us and says, "I know she's okay, but mentally! That's the thing, the mental part. Physically, she's okay, but the mental
part." Hippolyta jumps in to explain, "And she [her mom] gets worried about
my health." Hippolyta paused and turned to her mom to reveal that she had
recently gotten COVID again. She then went on to describe how, when she's
sick, her mother supplies her with ample water, green smoothies, and other
"concoctions." Hippolyta chuckled and pointed to her mother when asked
about the practical ways she takes care of herself. "If my mother goes out
of town, I'm frustrated all week," Hippolyta shared through laughter. This
exchange between Ms. Clara and Hippolyta was humorous and relatable; it
highlights how the role that family members and loved ones can play in supporting youth workers and other workers engaged in precarious fields. Ms.
Clara supports her daughter's work and knows how dedicated she is to her
community and the young people she works with. But it is also an example of
the awareness among youth workers, and in this case, a family member, of the
urgency of this support and protection from burnout for a youth worker like

Hippolyta, whose unpredictable and all-consuming work can quickly lead to overextension.

Other youth workers also described reliance on family. But they also described other approaches they found essential for wellness within such a demanding—albeit rewarding—and precarious field. Jamea, for example, emphasized the need for boundaries, something that took her a long time to pay more attention to. After years of working with youth, Jamea said, she finally feels she knows how to care for herself. But in Jamea's case, learning how to do this came from struggling with the toll of her work and the impact of a personal tragedy. A few months before the COVID-19 pandemic hit and forced us all to shelter in place, Jamea suffered the traumatic loss of her daughter. "It was like everybody else had joined me in my little devasting situation," she said, referring to her daughter's passing and the tragic deaths resulting from the pandemic. While grieving the painful loss of her child and navigating the pandemic, she became more conscious of what impact her work was having on her, and she became more proactive about the need for self-care. "Because I was going through that tragedy, while also support- ing youth and community [while they] were going through a whole different tragedy, I learned a lot about boundaries, self-care, [saying] no, and really, really being honest about personal time management. And, so self-care, you know, for me had to go beyond spa days to mental health therapy, to . . . vacations are necessary to get away from the everyday of every day." Jamea's personal loss, coupled with the stress of the pandemic and the uprisings, was overwhelming. It's easy to work "sixteen-hour days," she told me, and this was true for many other youth workers I spoke with. Jamea's tragedy, com- pounded by the tragedy of police violence and the pandemic, took an emo- tional toll.

Workers in many professions struggle with finding a balance between home and work.[57] But in youth work, where workers engage in profoundly personal ways with youth, this balance is particularly difficult.[58] This is the case not only because of the emotional and mental demands of the work but also because of the lack of time on the job to process things. Chris, for exam- ple, believes youth workers need built-in time and space to "take a break," especially after hearing something triggering from a young person. Much like therapists, who are always encouraged to find their own therapists to support the information they hear, youth workers, too, need time to "take a minute, recollect, and come back," according to Chris. In addition to turning to family members, as Hippolyta described above, youth workers consistently turn to other youth workers to help with this. Reflecting on how organizations can support youth worker wellness and combat burnout, Chris suggested it's vital to have "allies to talk to." He continued, "Having allies in your organization that you can talk to . . . I feel like one of the core pieces to having kids acknowledge their weight as a political actor is teaching kids how to build advocacy, and a huge piece of that is identifying your people . . . identifying your community . . . youth workers need to be specific and intentional about identifying your people, identifying your community . . . I have a lot of trouble asking for help. I have a lot of trouble delegating."

Although Chris acknowledges that he needs to be better at delegating and asking for help, his intentionality around building a support community is imperative for this work. For Hippolyta, it was Ms. Clara; for Jamea, it was putting up boundaries, being intentional about stepping away, and engaging in talk therapy to help process everything she had going on in her life, including running her organization. For Chris, he had to establish "healthy relationships" with his coworkers so that they could "hold each other accountable [so] that [they] can notice when people are being pulled a certain way and encourage them to . . . take a minute." Chris's comments highlight the importance of support, care, and accountability relationships in youth work organizations. The relationships cultivated between youth and youth workers are the essence of the youth work process.[59] Simply put, youth work does not happen without youth workers. The relationships between youth workers are critical to their flourishing in the field and have been understudied.[60] As Chris said, "Identifying good people, making sure that those good people are around . . . by paying them and learning how to lean [on others]" is necessary to provide emotional safety for youth workers. Paying them a living wage can undoubtedly reduce a layer of financial precarity many youth workers endure. Financial support is imperative, as Chris says, and he also shares that learning how to lean on others and the emotional support needed for youth workers to help manage the precarity they may face is also important.

Community building, accountability, and opportunities to learn with and from other youth workers are essential to thriving in a rewarding profession but, at times, it is challenging to manage their wellness while supporting youth who are made vulnerable and lead precarious lives. There is a structural level of support needed for youth worker wellness, including paid time off, living wages, and health care. At the organization level, some programs practice wellness days or wellness weeks, where youth workers have time off for self-care, or "staff appreciation" days that may be centered on wellness. However, as discussed in previous chapters, precarity is built into youth work—a precarity perpetuated by organizations, their funding structures, and the neoliberal logic underpinning nonprofit work in the US today. As a result, much of the burden of managing the psychological and emotional weight of youth work is turned back onto the shoulders of youth workers. Some of the Black nonprofit leaders of youth-serving organizations I spoke with highlighted how this burden is placed on the youth workers and emphasized the consequences of this.

Kim, introduced in chapter 1, is a longtime youth worker and founder of an organization that provides after-school programs centered on creativity, music-making, and joy for all grade levels. Kim's programs run in multiple schools in major cities in California, Chicago, Washington, DC, and the Caribbean. As an organizational leader, Kim strives to sustain her organization financially. Kim sees opportunities for wellness, or the lack thereof, as a structural issue connected to the dismissal and neglect of the youth work profession. At the time of her interview, Kim was participating in a summer social impact fellowship program for nonprofit leaders of color. The fellowship provided Kim with a couple hundred thousand dollars to sustain her work—the largest amount she had ever received: "[It's] the biggest fellowship I've gotten . . . They, from the start, said, what should we do to be different? And I'm like, if you centered our wellness as social impact leaders, that could be game-changing. Because if I am my healthiest self . . . the game would be so revolutionary, and I wouldn't be out here, like, I'm tired . . . I would have the things that I needed."

Kim and others who led programs strongly believe they would have more time to care for themselves and their staff if they had more financial support. Kim then shared an adage I have heard many times growing up and throughout my career: "You can't pour from an empty cup." This familiar phrase rings true for Kim and other leaders struggling to make ends meet to ensure their programs stay afloat. Youth workers, especially program leaders, carry the weight of sustaining their organizations while also trying to support the young people they serve. Kim reflects, "And so, we as youth workers are constantly pouring from, I'll say, a half-full cup. I mean, the work that we do, the way that it's funded, and all the work, [I've] realized we live in a world where scarcity is a mindset. And so, people don't always prioritize this work. But this work is the work [with] possibilities that exist." Kim believes in and envisions a world where it is possible for some school districts and foundations to provide health care for youth workers. Her reflection captures the paradox in the arrangement of the nonprofit youth development system. The youth work sector is relied upon by school districts, cities, families, and society at large, yet those who hold up this sector are an afterthought.[61] Their labor and commitment to guiding and supporting young people is overlooked, which impacts their professional and personal stability, including their wellness.[62] Kim asks, "How do we make this a living? Because it's important work." Indeed, it is important work, and the lack of financial investment *and* respect for the work and the workers perpetuates precarity. Material precarity, like the impact of a lack of adequate financial support, or symbolic precarity, like a disregard or dismissal of their expertise and the skill it takes to engage in youth work practice, leads to youth workers being unable to take care of themselves. Kim believes that she could do much more if she had more funding. "As a Black woman, I'm tired. And, like, I'm trying to think about my exit strategy right now because I can't do it for much longer, honestly, not this way." The reality of potential burnout and physical and mental health challenges looms closely for Kim and others featured in this book. These realities of the profession, coupled with broader sociopolitical issues like Black Spring, COVID-19, and other social problems, left some youth workers unable to function in the same way. Gabi had to take a total break from her work with youth. "I spent most of 2020 engaging in radical self-care to return to working with youth in a healthy, intentional matter," Gabi shared. Taking time away is not always an option for some people. Gabi had family members she could rely on. Ensuring that youth workers are protected, healthy, paid a living wage, and provided the resources they need to do their jobs is essential for their engagement with young people, and this should be a priority for a society that claims to care for young people and their education.

Chris, Gabi, Hippolyta, and Kim all mentioned various strategies to protect youth workers from precarity at the structural, organizational, and professional levels. From a living wage to organizational staff support through wellness days, manageable hours, professional development opportunities, and opportunities to connect with other youth workers to talk through challenges and find ways to support each other are all critical. In the face of societal unsettled moments,[63] Black youth workers also strived to safeguard their joy and used joy as a form of protection for Black youth in their programs.

Joy as Protection

> More than a method to endure, however, black joy allows us the space to stretch our imaginations beyond what we previously thought possible and allows us to theorize a world in which white supremacy does not dictate our everyday lives. House parties, backyard cookouts, and other spaces where black bodies gather in celebration produce rich and profound moments in which black love and laughter "lifts everyone slightly above the present" and allows to feel, to know in our bones, what black utopia might be like. I firmly believe in that our bodies harbor knowledge, and in these moments, every smile, head nod, hip shake, and high five is an exchange of embodied truths that black joy is phenomenally transformational. In this way, black joy provides another set of political tactics to "make do" and use the in/visibility and in/audibility of black joy as a site with which to operate outside of white supremacy.
>
> JAVON JOHNSON, "Black Joy in the Time of Ferguson"[64]

Joy is a central tool for youth workers' protection both for youth and for themselves. Joy is a shield. Joy is respite. Joy is sustaining. And, for the Black youth workers who shared their stories with us, the joy they cultivated for youth and the joy they experienced from their relationships with young people helped them to endure the precarious nature of the field and the stress of the world. As a former youth work professional, I know firsthand the joy, laughter, and excitement of witnessing young people's brilliance, creativity, and humor. Engaging in a profession saturated by uncertainty, Black youth workers struggle to care for themselves without structural support and financial resources amid the day-to-day grind of a physically and emotionally taxing field. Still, Black youth workers have the ability to foster and experience joy in their work, which is important to elevate. I don't mean to replicate narratives that suffering should come with following one's passion[65] or fighting for a cause that furthers the exploitation of nonprofit care workers[66]—rather I wish to demonstrate that creating pathways to and for joy in youth work can be a form of resistance against the structural harms in the field.

For example, Kim's organization is rooted in music and creativity, and she and the youth workers she hires center joy whenever possible, despite the funding constraints they face. During her interview, Kim pulled up documents and videos showing her work and process for youth engagement. "There's equity-centered design. If we're talking about sociopolitical awareness, this is holistic wellness thinking." Short on time, Kim ended her display by saying that "building joy, fun . . . becoming leaders in a joyful way" is central to her organization's values and her integrity as a leader and youth worker. As a pre-pandemic and post-pandemic strategy, Kim used gift cards, food and fellowship, and music to keep participation among youth and engage the broader community. Kim shares,

> We are in food insecure communities . . . So when we say we got food, they show up, and that's a very big thing. And you ask them . . . "What would make you come?" [They say] "What kind of food have you got?" Okay, we'll get you some food. Music creates a vibe . . . we use music throughout. We ask them what they like, and so we blend in music all the time . . . I would say, in terms of mentorship and connection, like we want the space to feel like family; we want it to feel like home.

Like others featured in this book, Kim is intentional about creating welcoming and "fun" spaces that center joy. "I don't have them call me Dr. Carter . . . but I have them call me by my first name. I think removing this power dynamic is what we try to do to create a better, more fun space." The power dynamics within youth development organizations, especially youth-adult partnerships, are important dynamics to consider in the field.[67] Even if unintended, the construction of youth and adults as social categories perpetuates a hierarchical power dynamic between youth and adults that surfaces in myriad ways.[68]

Later in the conversation, Kim reflected on her organization as predominantly Black and acknowledged the importance of thinking through the traumas youth are experiencing and what they are experiencing as Black youth work professionals. In professional development spaces with her staff, Kim finds any moment to spark joy and laughter for her team. "We just named each other Marvel characters. And so, one of them got named T'Challa, and he was so excited, and they're referring to each other in our meetings, like 'what T'Challa said.' And so, it's the authenticity of this; it is just how we get to be because we don't have to perform for others or even necessarily consider others who don't understand where we're coming from." Her staff jokes around and sees each other as family. She characterizes these moments as "authentic . . . we're just engaging in and being family. This is what family does, and [it's not] hurtful." From joking and creating nicknames to creating music playlists and engaging in movement work like yoga, experiential learning exercises are used by both youth workers and young people so that they can learn by doing, feeling, and engaging with their peers—ultimately strengthening the connection among youth workers and between youth and youth workers.

In contrast to Kim's experiences, some youth workers managed daily racist slights or microaggressions from white colleagues. Bria, who works with young people as a care coordinator for their mental health needs in the Midwest, shared that despite professional learning opportunities about race and culture, she still faced anti-Black comments in her organization from a coworker. "So, for example, like, there's been certain comments she's made. I went out in the rain to like, help somebody bring in something. She's like, 'Oh, God, you better like, cover up your hair,' implying that, like, I would be upset with my hair getting wet," Bria shared through a little laughter and annoyance. Bria was annoyed and talked about the limits of professional learning about "cultural competency" that fail to "change the mindsets" of her coworkers. Morris provides helpful analysis about the field that speaks to Bria's frustration. "Historically, youth work and teaching have been a vocation of, or for white women," Morris explains. "And so, the value of the work of youth work is through the lens of often middle-class white women and what they believe. Particularly young People of Color who tend to be the benefactors or the attendees of after-school and out-of-school programs and at least urban communities, what gets measured, what gets funded, what gets tracked, and what's valued," Morris continues. Morris's perspective here captures the tension that arises from what he names as the field's reliance on "white middle-class values" that shows up in programming and relationships with philanthropic donors.

Kim and other organizations that rely on philanthropy, donations, and grants have different constraints than youth workers in schools or school districts dependent on public funding. Olivia, for example, started an after-school program engaging students in theater production while she was a classroom teacher. As a classroom teacher and after-school program leader engaging predominantly Black and Latine youth, Olivia experienced joy in watching young people be free and creative in the space she designed for them. According to Olivia, she created the program "in direct response to what we were dealing with at the school at the time," which included queerphobia, xenophobia, and anti-Blackness. Olivia's students were already creating music and writing plays and wanted to "produce plays that dealt with issues that were important to them, that represented who they were." Olivia wanted to fully support their goals and facilitate a process for them to be creative but ran into opposition from the district's superintendent at the time. I watched and listened to Olivia beam with excitement and joy as she highlighted her students' brilliance and boldness. After one culturally specific play celebrating Mexican culture, the superintendent deemed it racist and inappropriate. Olivia assumed she would get fired after the production since the superintendent left halfway through the show. Afterward, Olivia's funding was cut, and "a lot of our materials had gotten taken from us, like our equipment and things. And so, then he comes at me real wrong. And I was like, I don't think you understand my philosophy. This isn't my theater program. I've already done theater. I've already gone to school and studied; I've already worked professionally in theater. I am here to facilitate my students' process and journey. And so, they are the directors; they decide, and I support them."

The students and Olivia met with the superintendent, where they shared that their next play would be a production of Shakespeare's *A Midsummer Night's Dream*. He approved. But what he didn't know was that it was a reimagining of the Shakespeare play—a queer reimagining. "My students had decided they wanted to redo *Midsummer*, and it was going to be a 'Midsummer's Queer Dream,' something like that . . . my students were like, well, in response to the Club Pulse shooting, we want to dedicate this performance to those lives lost. And there's a real transphobic issue on our campus that we feel we have a responsibility to address." Olivia went on for a while about the students' beautiful costumes and stage designs and reinterpretations of pivotal scenes in the play that captured joy, queerness, and freedom. "I thought it was brilliant. And I absolutely wanted to support their vision," Olivia told me. The superintendent, however, eventually banned this production. Students asked for another opportunity, and because they still wanted to address queerphobia, the students wanted to pick the Laramie Project about the murder of Matthew Shepherd in Laramie, Wyoming. He was unaware of the project and the preceding case, so he approved. Olivia laughs as she remembers this incident, but sadly, she continues to share how she and her program were targeted by the district and her superintendent. Olivia respected and affirmed the brilliance of the young people she worked with and encouraged them to follow their passion and joy. Following passion and joy are things Olivia's former students continue to do today as college students and graduates entering their careers. Olivia's smile widens as she talks about student after student who are designing theater sets, using their skills in architecture and passion for social justice to create inclusive spaces for all, budding fashion designers, architects, actors, and artists who are committed to just, free, queer Black, and People of Color spaces.

Creating spaces of joy in programming for youth is central to the pedagogical practices of the youth workers I met. Black youth workers featured in this book find immense joy in their work despite its challenges. Whenever youth workers were asked what excited them or brought them joy about being a youth worker, the response was always "young people." The way youth experience "aha moments" and begin understanding their power and capacity to dream and take action was exciting for youth workers. Tamir is a facilitator, youth advocate, and lecturer committed to fostering joy and progress for marginalized communities in the southern part of the US. Tamir, like others, is motivated to continue their work with young people because of the excitement they feel watching young people grow and step into their power.

> There's always the look that kids get when they create something that they didn't expect to be able to create. You know, when they started off early on with an idea that to them seemed crazy or, you know, even their friends laughed at or whatever the case may be, and still they received the kind of encouragement and support to keep trying and then they have this thing that they created and it's real. And that sort of recognition in their own eyes of having manifested something that was in their head that they can do that . . . those moments feel like triumph. Those moments feel like the seeds of self-efficacy. Those feel like the seeds of self-confidence, and you know, that's why I think that the community aspect, the belonging aspect of OST programs, is so important.

A sense of belonging, building self-confidence, and a young person's relationship to learning and the relationship to themselves as people who can go out into this world and accomplish something are some of the most compelling aspects of youth development organizations, and youth workers are essential to this process. Tamir continues to share that in comparison to other educators, youth workers can see "that little spark a little more frequently than some educators." This spark Tamir speaks of is connected to the many domains of life youth workers are privy to that go beyond youths' academic achievement. Youth work taps into who youth are as people and supports their journey to becoming who they wish to be. This spark, or the light that shines in young people's eyes when they connect the dots, where they accept and believe in their power and the possibilities in their future, motivates youth workers like Tamir to "keep pushing" and continue their work with youth despite some of the challenges facing the field or within their specific workplaces.

For many program leaders and youth workers, stressors arise from structural conditions that shape workplace dynamics and relationships with colleagues. Youth workers' attempt to create joy in their work for themselves and for the youth they work with is essential for protecting themselves against toxic workplace dynamics. For Whitney, a longtime youth worker who transitioned to an administrative role working in local government, connecting youth and families with out-of-school time programs, young people bring her joy. Whitney is a youth development systems worker, where she engages with intermediary organizations that have ties to local government and school districts to ensure that students have access to after-school care. When asked what brings Whitney joy in her work, she did not hesitate and responded, "Young people." She continues, "It's really like I've been in a funk. I feel like the adults . . . screwed this up royally." This doesn't mean that some interactions with youth or the circumstances they face may not be challenging—it does mean, however, that those engaged in youth work find the most difficulty with other adults, organizational dynamics, the politics of the work connected to funding, and leadership challenges.

Fostering joy among youth workers and young people in programs is crucial, especially for workers like Kim, who leads her organization by centering joy because of her experiences as a young person in after-school programs.

"I think specifically what's similar is a centering of choice, a centering of joy . . . I don't think academics is the center . . . I don't even like the word enrichment, but interest and passion is the key," Kim explains as she pulls up another video. This time, it's of the Black Panthers and how political education, food, music, and centering community were imperative for their liberation work. Kim infuses joy and play in her work with youth and professional development with her staff. Something as simple as playing music is important to her and her staff. "One of the things we also do in our programming is . . . we ask everybody what they are listening to, and then we play their songs throughout their session to say, *I see you*." Kim reminds us that joy, too, is part of liberation work, central to education and learning for young people, and essential to the struggle for social justice. To be truly seen is an extraordinary feeling. As a young person, being seen for who you are, feeling like you belong, and being accepted without conditions are things all young people should experience in educational spaces.

———

Black youth workers protect Black youth in myriad ways. By sharing vital social and political information about how the world works—and how social institutions work—they serve as institutional agents,[69] and guiding Black youth through complicated systems that may harm them is a form of protection that youth workers enact through community-based educational spaces. Because these spaces are not perfect, and paradoxes are inevitable, Black youth workers strive to disrupt harm whenever they see it surfacing—by pushing back against racist paternalistic framing rooted in anti-Black stereotypes that get reinforced through the nonprofit industrial complex and philanthropy. Some pay the price for their disruption and resistance and are retaliated against, resulting in demotions or poor treatment. Protection also looks like centering joy in the program for Black youth through music, food, and fellowship—giving young people a choice, fostering their passions, and affirming who they are as developing people.

Protection for youth workers is also rooted in the desire to be well and whole and continue serving youth in the way they need. In a profession with such great precarity and a lack of structural support for the well-being of youth workers, wellness and self-care are a challenge, but they must be a priority for organizations. As youth workers affirmed throughout this chapter, protection at the structural, organizational, and professional levels is crucial to overall youth worker well-being, respect, and regard for those who work tirelessly to protect children and youth. While holding on to youth workers' powerful stories of entry into the profession; their challenges with low pay, inadequate health care, or housing insecurity; and their modes of protection against forms of anti-Black violence youth might face as they strive to care for themselves without the structural or organizational support for their wellness, in the next chapter, I shift to how Black youth workers hold this precarity and complexity of the field while imagining new futures for Black youth and themselves.

FIVE

Shaping Black Futures amid Precarity

Fatalism is not a synonym for Blackness.

-YTASHA WOMACK, *Afrofuturism*

What would it look like to create a place where we have what we need?

-OLIVIA, youth worker

I have known Wynter for many decades. Her energy is infectious, and her commitment to Black youth development is palpable. She speaks with a power that demands you listen and has been this way since she was thirteen years old. Born and raised on the West Coast, Wynter took a West African dance class as a third grader at her local youth center. As a teen, she became a youth development intern at this same center, working with elementary students during summer and after-school programming. During college breaks, she would return to the center to support programming as a youth worker. After college, Wynter pursued a master's degree in organizational behavior and consulted with a firm after graduate study. After a few years, Wynter returned home and took a leadership position at the center, coordinating after-school programming. For the last three years, Wynter has served as the executive director and has been leading the organization she found refuge in as a child.

With the backdrop of change in the surrounding neighborhood, Wynter works tirelessly with other community-based leaders in many sectors, including education, workforce development, health care, and civic leadership, to preserve the Black neighborhood where her organization exists in the face of gentrification, subsequent displacement, and school restructuring. Wynter is not in this fight alone. She leads the center alongside a team of like-minded Black leaders and youth workers committed to young people and families in the neighborhood. Wynter's challenges as a director often come from her engagement with the city, trying to secure resources for the center's youth participants, their families, and the center's staff. For instance, she has been trying to get the city to agree to provide a "student-only bus" during certain hours so students can travel to and from school and then to youth programs after school. "Most of our young people . . . don't feel safe on transit." Wynter and her staff are particularly concerned about the students riding public transit as they go to the youth center from school and the youth center to home. As she reflects on the many reasons why a student-only bus would be helpful, she named the terrifying reality that there "was a string of Black girls who were almost abducted by traffickers." Wynter continues by sharing that in wealthier and predominantly white neighborhoods in the city, the Parents' Associations paid for student-only buses for after school. Yet, Wynter and her colleagues struggle to secure these protections for their students.

As a young person, youth worker, program director, and now executive director, Wynter has faced many battles in the nonprofit education sector. She deeply understands the complexity of the work and how to embrace its paradoxes—embracing the contradictions in a field that purports to center young people's humanity and consider their insights and voices but instead often relies on paternalistic racist and classist tropes rooted in deficit thinking about Black communities.[1] She is amazingly skilled at understanding how ongoing disregard and disinvestment in her neighborhood and city inform her work with Black youth. Sitting with and existing within the contradictions is common within youth work. Despite the paradoxes, youth workers and program leaders like Wynter still cultivate visions and dreams of a future where youth workers and young people can thrive and become the best versions of themselves.

Black youth workers are in a critical yet delicate position to cultivate opportunities for dreaming, allow youth to envision a future, and see that they are connected to a community of adult allies who can help guide them into the future. Beyond anti-Black racism and its permanency, understanding how

Black youth workers envision and dream alongside Black youth is something special to behold, understand, and affirm. As I write this book, a question continues to recur for me: How do Black youth workers foster dream spaces and places for imagination when the permanence of anti-Black racism is a reality, not a deterrent but a motivator to envision a different world? I began thinking about this question in the summer of 2020 when I organized a virtual convening, sponsored by the Spencer Foundation, for education scholars and youth workers to discuss what community-based education and critical youth work practice could offer us as we reimagined schooling considering the pandemic and how we fought to protect the hearts, minds, and bodies of vulnerable youth given the onslaught of racist police violence, xenophobia, and mass shootings.[2] Given the precarity youth workers face—particularly those vulnerable because of racial and economic forces—how do Black youth workers shape the futures of Black youth despite the hardships they face and the profession's instability? How do Black youth workers see themselves in the future? I make the case in this chapter that *Black youth work is the process of futuring.* Black youth workers wrestle with the contradictions and paradoxes within the youth work landscape that are caused by a precarity fueled by anti-Blackness, white supremacy, and racial capitalist structures that make their work, especially for education and care-based workers, precarious. Still, they teach and guide young people while fostering dream spaces and holding a powerful vision for themselves and for the Black youth they work alongside.

Confronting Both/And

Embracing the "both/and" is difficult for those who see the world in binaries. I have always been drawn to the gray areas. They have a way of forcing us to confront our complicities. Black youth workers consistently strategize and do their work embracing the "both/and," weeding out the harm whenever possible while nurturing what is beautiful. Chris and his colleagues have thought deeply about confronting contradictions and sitting within the paradoxes that emerge in their work. He speaks fondly of two former executive directors, both Black women who, he says, understood the complexity of the field and how to navigate the both/and. "My boss then was really adamant about the ways you move in the world being the way that you move with kids," Chris told me. The celebration of authenticity was at the core of his supervisors' values when engaging young people. Chris named "authenticity" necessary for relationship building and interactions with youth and youth workers. Authenticity in relationships helped him sort out when situations seemed contradictory or "weren't feeling right, or when things were complex, or when things were confusing." Chris could go to his director to discuss these issues and engage youth whenever possible to encourage them to think through them as well. Chris's organization even has a name for the paradoxes and the both/and: the "yucky and the beautiful."

Chris engages his students about his career as a spoken word artist. Even though Chris has gained so much from his experiences in spoken word communities, he is honest about the harmful parts. "It's also a very male-dominated, trauma-focused art form . . . we had conversations about how yuck and beauty can exist at the same time." For Chris, "remov[ing] a person or vilify[ing] a person" for bad moments when beauty is something that always has the potential to be present, is not something he is interested in, and encourages young people to think through the complexity of humanity in more critical ways. Chris believes naming these moments of contradiction is essential to excavating potential harm, repairing, and sustaining what is good.

As I have written elsewhere, community-based educational spaces can both disrupt and reproduce harm.[3] As Chris puts it, "I guess a couple of years ago, I would have said that the tough things and the beautiful things exist in two different spaces in my head. But now that's not true. They kind of intermingle . . . and it's part of my job to be really upfront about the yuck, to really uplift the beauty. But to also acknowledge, work with, and push and pull the gray area in between." Chris' articulation of the coexistence or intermingling of complex and beautiful things is vital to interrogate and wrestle with, especially within education and youth development spaces. In my conversations with youth workers and program leaders, I have learned that community-based youth workers are experts at sitting with and existing within what is messy, challenging, or complicated. They do so with immense skill and grace, wading through the complex waters of adolescent development and change.

The heterogeneous infrastructure of nonprofit youth work makes the landscape rich with different activities and programming that young people can participate in, but access and quality vary.[4] As discussed in chapter 1, the youth work landscape comprises many organizations, program types, and agencies with diverse leadership, funding, and pedagogical models. Because of the complexity of the field and its existence, material and symbolic paradoxes exist whereby the navigation of contradictions becomes inevitable and routine. The navigation of paradoxes that become further entrenched by precarity varies by the kind of organization youth workers engage with—their financial health, leadership, and organizational structure all matter. For example, programs tethered to national networks of youth organizations like Boys and Girls Clubs have visibility and resonance in our society, which is important for their financial stability.[5] In another example, youth workers in front-facing roles with young people may have limited power and opportunities to make decisions, are susceptible to leadership ceilings, and lack professional protections. Like schools, youth work organizations are also racialized. The field itself, like education, is dominated by white people, and whiteness is used as a credential for hiring, leadership, and funding. As established in chapters 2 and 4, a disconnect exists within organizations between established rules and the everyday routines enacted.[6] Some youth workers I spoke with deeply understand the flaws in the nonprofit system and how youth development and education nonprofits are treated within the larger nonprofit apparatus. However, their awareness of its racialization and its seemingly permanent flaws does not mean that program leaders and youth workers do not try to disrupt it.[7]

Rihanna, a vibrant and thoughtful lifelong youth worker, leads an independent local organization that centers and celebrates the voices and perspectives of young people. Located in the western part of the United States, Rihanna loves to disrupt the norms in nonprofit structures and culture. Shifting into a leadership position from a front-facing role with young people was a challenge Rihanna welcomed. She welcomed the opportunity to "fuck up the nonprofit model." Rihanna gleams with excitement as she talks about disrupting the norm in nonprofit structure as a joyful process. She bucks the so-called rules. "There's this implied association that if you choose the nonprofit industry, that if you're a person of color, right, or if you're a person coming from lower socioeconomic power, that you're entering a life of like hardship and poverty, right? . . . and that's bullshit to me," she explains. This sentiment was echoed in earlier chapters by youth workers like Chris and

Olivia, who critiqued the idea that noble work requires "martyrdom" for professions in the nonprofit sector which attempts to justify the exploitation of its workers.[8] Rihanna is excited to use her power to disrupt this logic and redistribute resources "to change the structure" of her program to "center equity and to actually promote a model for equitable pay for all nonprofit staff." Her approach to leadership radically differs from other models; part-time employees can get paid time off under her leadership. Her organization pays 90% of employee benefits to full-time employees. "My staff can access free mental health wellness resources for up to twice a month at no charge." These are examples of the possibilities that have come to fruition with Rihanna's leadership, things that she and others were told were not possible. "What people say you can't do, I'm doing it, and so, that's most exciting for me is like this opportunity to just demonstrate that you can do it differently."

Imagining and creating something different, despite the seemingly impenetrable structures that shape the nonprofit sector, is an attitude and skill that Rihanna has mastered in the face of minimal resources and, at times, sabotage. Rihanna's determination to create a different reality in nonprofits for her youth workers and youth participants in her program speaks to her tenacity to envision something more humane, where Black youth workers and young people can see themselves in the future.

Shaping Black Futures

Black communities and educators—formal and informal—have always faced precarity.[9] The labor on behalf of youth has always been done with transparency so that Black youth can know and understand the realities of the world and still envision a better future. Envisioning a better future requires that youth workers create opportunities and possibilities for Black youth, and it also means disrupting organizational structures within youth-serving organizations that can stifle youth workers' ingenuity and futuring for young people and themselves. Youth work and the nonprofit sector are filled with structural challenges that shape youth workers' personal and professional lives. Despite these challenges, youth workers cultivate experiences and opportunities for young people to thrive. Black youth workers create opportunities for youth to envision possibilities beyond what they could have imagined. Rihanna came to her organization first as a graduate research assistant and did the occasional workshop for high school students. She was initially drawn to the work because of her freedom; she "was not behold[en] to the stricter rules and regulations that teachers are . . . If I say something too radical, I'm not going to lose my job," she says confidently. During her visits to the program for research, "lights started going off about how out-of-school space can function" in supporting academic rigor. Aligned with previous scholarship about the benefits of community-based educational spaces, the "safe space" for dreaming, resistance, and creativity became appealing to Rihanna.[10] For Rihanna, the incubation of radical thought and action seemed more possible in community-based spaces where youth workers can control their pedagogical practices in ways they may not be able to within traditional school settings. To have "safe spaces in which you can incubate like more like radical or nontraditional thought, right? Where out-of-school time programs or nonprofit organizations are this alternative space for youth to develop skills or gain access to knowledge that is not compatible with the hidden curriculum of traditional school spaces," Rihanna passionately explains.

Radical thought, critical thinking, and exposure to what is possible for the future is vital to social justice youth development practice.[11] To envision a new world where young people can see themselves as part of social change, Black youth workers create opportunities for youth to understand the world around them and build confidence in their change-making possibilities. This process is sometimes a challenge for youth workers. As Chris explains, "It also took me a while to learn how not to be angry about the state of the world in front of kids, you know, like you don't want to tell them all these terrible things are happening and then just send them out into the world." Chris is channeling a common critique of political education—how not to leave young people in despair and unable to act. Chris and others firmly believe that youth workers are responsible for balancing teaching about the real harms in the world and cultivating and nurturing an imagination that allows young people to see a future that they can build and fight for. "You have a responsibility to have them imagine a future that is healthier for everyone, but it's a hard balance to have when things are happening in your face." Chris's vulnerability and sincerity were touching. As we spoke, I saw him grappling with finding balance in making sense of the world's reality while working toward a future.

Black youth workers have a deep understanding of the structural forces that shape their work and the lives of the youth they work with; they fight against these forces and see their work as a response to systemic oppression. Finding a balance between explaining how these systems shape youth's educational and social experiences and generating excitement among youth that shapes their agency and ability to fight back against these forces is not easy work. Still, youth workers love seeing young people connect dots and grow in their power. "I just love when I get to do . . . Getting to see the light bulbs go off and getting to see the shoulders straighten and like the confidence," Rihanna tells us. These moments keep Rihanna and other youth workers committed. Braylen, a long-time youth worker, teaching artist, and program leader, told us that the programs that excite him the most are the ones that "help young people see themselves as the brilliant lights they are—and the ones that are focusing on helping them understand how to make change." With a deep commitment to social justice, Braylen tells us that social justice begins with understanding "who you are and the beauty of value of where you come from." He then shares that structural forces "threaten" the value we have of ourselves and that it is incumbent upon educational spaces to help identify those threats and the "things that are put in place to make sure that [youth] don't see [their] value and the beauty in [their] community." Braylen believes that youth workers are instrumental in helping youth figure out how to push back against these threats and believes they can create change. In contrast to the belief that racially minoritized youth are being indoctrinated when engaging in sociopolitical development, Braylen, Rihanna, and Chris all carefully work with youth to ensure they understand the realities of the world they live in and are confident in their own power and ability to push for change.

Connecting the Past, Present, and Future

Black youth workers I spoke with articulated their vision for Black youth and the future of Black education. They understand what is sacred about community-based educational spaces. They understand how they should look, feel, and sound. For some, centering and affirming Blackness through community-based education and youth development opportunities mattered most. Gabi, for example, is steadfast in her belief that Black youth need to be in "safe spaces where they can be their authentic selves, feel seen, valued, heard, and exercise their agency while building skills." As Robeson similarly shared, Black youth "need cultural competence and familiarity. I think they need wrap-around services. I think they need robust, sincere, Black-centric programming." Robeson's feelings align with those of educators and activists of the past.[12] The same ideas and values about protecting the futures of Black youth have remained the same across time and space. This is a throughline that I want scholars and educators to keep at the center of their work. Anti-Black terror reorganizes and restructures itself; it does not dissipate.[13] And, while it is necessary to understand the shifts and contours of how racism and anti-Black racism permeate society, there are fundamental processes that we know "work" in sustaining liberatory educational spaces that affirm Black-ness and the humanity of Black people.[14] The threat of destruction is always present and does not matter; Black communities, families, educators, activ-ists, and young people build anyway.

What characterizes the struggle for Black educational freedom across time and space is the relationship between history and the future. Cultural anthropologist and education scholar Maisha T. Winn captures this in her conceptualization of Futuring Black Lives.[15] Futuring Black Lives entails a deep knowledge of history, which includes the structural violence and terror that have shaped Black life and educational opportunities, while simulta-neously holding on to what is possible for the future. With a deep belief in freedom dreaming,[16] imagination, creativity, building, and visioning, Black futuring has always been linked to social movements for Black education and liberation.[17] Building on scholars and activists like Robin D. G. Kelley and Ytasha Womack, Winn believes in future-oriented historiography—one that acknowledges the past, seeking to disrupt what is harmful while creating and sustaining a vision for the future. Multidisciplinary intellectual thinkers and artists draw on Afrofuturism to envision possibilities for Black people in the future. Coined by Mark Derby, who linked elements found across Black science fiction writers, Afrofuturism had been embedded within many do-mains of Black life and production before Derby's 1993 essay.[18] Afrofutur-ism provides a vital lens to ground Black youth work, from music to writing, to cultural aesthetics and Black interiority, to bridging history, present, and future.[19] In her book, *Futuring Black Lives: Independent Black Institutions and the Literary Imaginary*, a historical ethnography with influential scholars, ac-tivists, and architects of the Black Arts and Power Movement, Winn reflects on the creation of Independent Black Institutions (IBIs).[20] Akin to how we might understand community-based educational spaces today, IBIs include "cultural centers, publishing houses, food cooperatives, and schools focused on cultivating futures for black children and their families."[21] Together, Black educators, parents, and community members intentionally designed "futures for their children that included self-determination, economic independence, Black cultural pride, and creativity,"[22] writes Winn. Understanding the past and a resolute belief in the possibility of the future are paramount for youth work in Black space.[23]

Youth workers like Robeson understand the importance of the past and what can be learned from it while being future-oriented. Robeson speaks to the legacy Winn writes about by evoking "past models that have worked" to support Black youth today. In reflecting on Black youth development over time and the promise of Black youth work in the future, Robeson tells us, that he would "build a [space] that specifically engaged in education and advocacy around some of the more practical concerns the young people, especially Black young people, deal with. And that would help enhance their agency." Robeson envisions spaces where Black youth have "activity-driven" programming where "personal, community, and global advocacy" are centered. Together with these efforts, Robeson envisions wraparound services like academic support, mentorship, and even haircuts and meals to ensure that young people have everything they need to be fully supported. He uses a "Swiss army knife" analogy to describe the required multipronged approach in youth development. He concludes, "We're going to build this up so well that this is a place the kids come to because they like it and not because they're trying to stay out of trouble." I see Robeson's vision as a response to the typical nonprofit discourse that creates youth-serving organizations out of a structural or deficit-oriented perception of a cultural need.[24] Instead, Robeson's vision suggests that spaces with a wide range of services and resources for young people to grow and develop agency should exist for their enjoyment and edification—not because something is wrong with them. Robeson's futuring acknowledges systemic forces that create the need for supplemental learning and support spaces, but it is not limiting. It does not limit his vision for Black youths' educational futures.

It is infectious to witness youth workers' immense joy and excitement as they talk about Black youths' educational futures. The growth youth workers witness in young people is inspiring and is often what drives the field despite its challenges and precarity. Youth workers in this book engage in youth work with Black and other marginalized young people because they *are* future-oriented. Envisioning the future of Black education requires declaring what Black youth need now. Chris eloquently and passionately offers what Black youth need in this moment, and it is a beautiful articulation of futuring:

> They need people to care. They need to know that outside of the things that they achieve in school, they need to know that outside of [a] sport, they need to know that outside of all these ideas about what makes them worthy, that they are enough and they will continue to be enough and that love is free and everyone deserves it . . . Love is a thing that everyone holds and will continue to hold and deserves to be held . . . Black kids just need to know that . . . we love you all. We not gonna stop loving you all. And that's not tied to what we think you were capable of. Though we also think you all are capable of changing the world, you know?

Chris's reflection captures the importance of youth work operating in the current political moment and for the future. *Black youth work is the process of futuring.* Despite the threat of anti-Black violence which Black youth workers are patently aware of, their engagement with youth requires their belief in possibility and change. Black youth workers cultivate dream spaces for young people and for themselves. They foster joy and cultivate opportunities for young people to envision what is possible for themselves and the world. However, because of the complexity and precarity of the youth work landscape, including the pressure the field is under to address societal and educational problems, and the quick decisions youth workers are forced to make, the process of conscious futuring and dreaming does not always occur. Where Black youth workers will be in the future is a question that I have asked myself while writing this book. As I am writing this book, the current United States administration is making rapid changes that put our democracy and freedoms at risk while positioning those who are already vulnerable in even more precarious situations. Children and youth are among the most vulnerable groups—they have always been.[25] Youth who occupy multiply oppressed identities face specific challenges. Historically, Black educators, including Black youth workers, have been important to teaching and care during times of crisis. I see Black youth workers as essential to the current moment and our survival during challenging times.

Black Youth Workers in the Future

During Mr. Rashad's celebration of life, Chris learned that he was working on building another physical space for youth. This reveal was not a surprise to him: "One thing about Mr. Rashad was, he always set up off ramps and opportunities for us outside the walls of the program . . . I have no idea how he managed to make these connections and off-ramps happen, but he did it all the time. And this felt like a way that he was looking out for me in the same way across time and space," Chris reflects. Mr. Rashad practiced futuring. Looking for "off-ramps" or, said another way, building toward a future, he ensured that young people *and* organizations can flourish and thrive despite the systemic problems that face the field and that shape the lives of young people. When I spoke to youth workers in Pleasant Ridge, it was on the heels of national reports about the racial disparities between Black and white residents in the city. My engagement with other youth workers for this book occurred at the onset of the pandemic and when tension was most high following the murders of George Floyd and the subsequent uprisings to demand justice on his behalf and that of other Black people killed by law enforcement.

The realities of state violence, racial disparities, and social unrest required that organizations shift priorities and envision a future for their work that spoke to the needs of their communities. Gloria, for example, a dynamic former nonprofit leader and cofounder of a Black youth-serving organization on the West Coast, now coleads a national project focusing on healing-centered engagement for educational stakeholders, including school administrators, classroom teachers, youth development leaders, and practitioners. With an extraordinary lifetime career engaged in education and youth development, Gloria advocates for trauma-informed approaches to youth development that center on healing.[26] According to Gloria, healing-centered engagement is about "shaping who you are, like how do we shape who you are and give you opportunities to . . . rebuild yourself, reimagine yourself in the work, reestablish what your purpose is, do your own healing around your trauma." Gloria continues to acknowledge that her organization's work had to shift to a deeper understanding of the relationship between "race, gender identity, sexual orientation, class, [and] ability" to work more effectively. She explains that her organization spent most of their time examining how race shapes the work of educational stakeholders, but they had to pivot "to look more from an intersectional lens" to analyze the multiple and intersecting systems of oppression that shape the lives of youth and those that care for young people in formal and informal educational spaces.

In many ways, Gloria and other organizational leaders understood that the political moment demanded an intentional response to focus on healing, connection, and protection and a deep understanding of the social problems youth and youth workers would face. During the 2020 uprisings, many youth workers in front-facing roles had a different level of influence because of their lack of decision-making power. Still, they wanted to push their leaders, boards of directors, and the organization, as a whole, to consider how their programs and pedagogy would evolve, respond to the moment, and still resonate with youth. Zora, for instance, felt compelled to hold her board of directors to a high standard to respond to the moment and to be intentional with the girls in her program. "It's important that I do those basic social work skills that I learned . . . the importance of eye contact and reflection, like always meeting them where they are . . . they can *feel* how invested *everyone* is," Zora shares. She then laughs and quickly says as an aside, "with the exception of the board." In a humorously honest reflection on where Zora might be in the future, she articulates a vision where she and other Black youth workers and program leaders have the power and control they need to design programming in the way they deem necessary. "What else would I do?" Zora asked herself. "Um . . . never have a board again," she laughs but then shifts excitedly to envisioning a board that reflects the community she serves. "Or! Or have a board that is, like, parents and educators!" She pauses and then reluctantly mentions maybe having people on the board from companies, but they would have "training about race and power dynamics. And, like, really work with them, only have people that really are open to learning and growing in that space and finding a way to get rid of those that do not want to." As Zora giggles and blushes a little, she then says that "having some type of veto power," to have the authority to say to board members, "hmm, you got to go; you can't be here," is her vision of Black youth work in the future. While about half of the Black youth workers interviewed held some level of leadership, like coordinating specific programming, running departments of organizations, or being in leadership positions with decision-making power, those who held front-facing positions did not always have power, and struggled to assert themselves in the face of predominantly white leadership and boards of directors, and were regularly in fear of retaliation in the form of demotion or termination.

Youth workers envision young people returning to their programs to praise the program for their support; this is a prevalent finding in youth development research: youth participants in community-based programs tend to desire the roles of the youth workers who mentored them.[27] Jamea wants her program to be a "household name" and wants to build future leadership by sharing power with young people to make the program youth- and young-adult-led. Jamea's plan is rooted in her desire to step away from the program and move into a coaching or consulting role to allow young people to lead the organization. Jamea was one of the few youth workers I interviewed who knew precisely where she wanted to be in the future. Much too often, because of the fast-paced nature of youth work, the uncertainty and precarity of the nonprofit sector make it challenging for youth workers to reflect and dream of their futures as practitioners, especially for those in more intense roles where managing trauma is routine.

Because of the nature of her work, Hippolyta knows that one day, she'll need to stop the work she's doing. "I already know; I'm going to wake up one day and say, I do not want to do this no more . . . this work is heavy," Hippolyta says with a slight smile. She dreams of moving to Belize in ten years. Relying on her faith in God, Hippolyta feels she will know when it is time to move on to another line of work. "Whatever I do next is going to be totally opposite of gun violence prevention because that's just the type of person I am. I might just be a gardener or something . . . I really do this because I just love it, like, [I] don't have to." Hippolyta has witnessed so much in her career as a violence interrupter. "Heavy" is the word she uses to describe the work, but that may be an understatement. Hippolyta has suffered the loss of young people in her life; the youth she's worked with have experienced immense loss and trauma from neighborhood, school, and police violence. Looking toward the future, Hippolyta hopes to find rest—and she deserves it.

When asked where she saw herself or her work in the future, Zora loudly shouts, "No idea!" Although she says this laughing, she became serious as she reflected on what she calls her evolution. "With this kind of evolution that I'm having as a more seasoned professional, I am starting [to be] able to really recognize my worth and recognize that I have something to offer not just [the program] but the field of nonprofits or girls empowerment organizations."

This display of confidence from Zora is encouraging, considering her disappointment and fear of retaliation from the board. She has always dreamed of teaching a college course about youth development and girls' education in nonprofit organizations. Zora sees her purpose in the world as being able to play a role in empowering young women. She is also raising a little girl of her own, so her work is deeply personal.

For some engaged in youth work, front-facing roles with young people sometimes lead to leadership positions if the structure of their programs allows. Many youth workers deserve these promotions and choose to grow their management skills to take on more responsibility, aside from curricula development or guiding youth directly. Ruben, however, is not one of those people. He never intends to be in an office or "behind a desk." He prefers to be "hands-on with youth," so overseeing programs and leadership responsibilities that take him away from youth is not what he envisions for his future. "The more they see you, the more there is respect there," claims Ruben as he discusses the importance of being visible to young people.

In contrast, youth workers like Waverly and Darren seek leadership opportunities, not because they do not enjoy working directly with youth but because they want to do more for young people, which they feel comes with more decision-making power about the direction of organizations. Waverly is currently in a managerial role at a nonprofit on the East Coast. She is anxious to leave the East Coast, but she sees her next step as a leader. "My next step will definitely be . . . to go for a director-level role," she shares. Darren, who works at a citywide program serving boys and young men on the East Coast, has the goal of being a program director in the future. For Darren, "creating the narrative" is important to him, primarily because of the framing of Black boys in his work. In a field where narratives about Black boys and men are rooted in stereotypes and deficit ideas,[28] Darren sees an opportunity to shift narratives and build new ones about the youth he works with. Although he has done a lot of learning, he wants to learn more, "add to his resume," and continue to improve his skills in the profession. Joy holds a different perspective. Although she recognizes the leadership ceilings for youth workers of color exist in other predominantly white-led organizations, she believes her organization is different and does provide opportunities for youth workers to move into more long-term career pathways in the field.

Sometimes, they get stuck as youth workers, so it's like you started this job when you were eighteen. And now you're twenty-five, and you're still the youth worker, right? That's a challenge. Because my staff is very talented, very thoughtful. They work hard. They have lots to offer . . . So, they need a little bit more responsibility . . . Especially like with, you know, the Black and Brown workers . . . There are so many other things the [organization] offers like there are so many other groups that you can get connected to, but a lot of times they don't know, or you know their line of sight is just programs . . . I try to kind of interrupt that because before, the same folks have been in the same position with no movement.

Joy recognizes that educational attainment is a barrier as human resources requires advanced degrees for many director positions in her organization. Her program even offers some tuition remission for staff to receive additional training and degrees to strengthen their work, but she finds that some of her youth workers are "comfortable" only working with the kids. In the future, Joy wishes that other organizations can provide pathways and resources for youth workers to continue their professional learning and provide resources for them to pursue higher education, leading to higher wages and more stability in the field.

Chris intends to follow Mr. Rashad's wishes and complete his bachelor's degree. He plans to study education and then pursue his doctorate. Chris's organization has formed deep connections with local community-engaged university researchers who support professional learning opportunities for youth workers. Chris's interactions with them have been monumental for his development as a youth worker. They have "poured so much into me," Chris explains with sincere gratitude. He intends to use his doctorate to support youth workers and those seeking to engage in the profession. Chris combines his love for young people—including the lives he has touched—and his awareness that the precarity in the field makes it almost impossible for youth workers to build and sustain a future that is not economically precarious. Chris passionately describes his vision which includes young people thriving when youth workers can thrive by having the support they need. He desires to "build a collective future in ways that feels good for everyone." His vision captures the extraordinary role and significance of youth workers in society and how their labor is hidden and not compensated in the way it should be. "I feel like on college applications, you always hear about the coach, mentor, or person who affected the trajectory in a way that changed this kid's life. But how often do we ask how much was that coach paid? You know, how often do we ask how much? How can we ensure that this mentor keeps doing the work that is obviously important?" Chris hits the core of what I see as an intersection of the field's organizational and field-level paradox. There are moments when we, as a society, acknowledge and validate the importance of mentors, coaches, and others who are part of the youth work sector, yet Chris is right. After the praise, they return to the shadows.

Chris's freedom dreams include "build[ing] the capacity of organizations and people to change lives not only in the way that [his] has changed but also in ways that allow for the future to be brighter." As Chris prepares to return to school after a decade away, he's resolute on his purpose. "I'm trying to tear down all that is plaguing the world today. And I'm going to do that by teaching kids from two to six p.m." Chris' commitment to his personal growth and development, to his organization, and to the young people he supports is unbreakable. It reminds me of the time I spent with Olivia. Olivia's commitment to her healing and her commitment to the "deeply reflective, introspective, super difficult shadow parts are the bits that make [her] be able to show up in space, be in community and say the things even when [she's] terrified to say the things." Olivia turns to the poet and activist Audre Lorde as a point of reflection and reminder that she is engaged in necessary, brave, and courageous work. Her bravery and commitment to personal healing as an educator and advocate for youth, she hopes, can be a model to young people she works with:

> Audre Lorde, again, survival is better to say, even when I'm afraid, it's better to speak knowing I was never meant to survive. And that is, that's my approach that sums it up. Because in every space I'm in, my safety is not guaranteed. My visibility is not guaranteed, whether I'll be heard is not guaranteed. But I gotta show up and say it anyway. Because I know that my young folks I support may not be ready to do it themselves yet. And so, I'll keep doing it and keep modeling. So that when they're ready they can move up and take up space the way they feel is best.

Olivia's futuring here is happening on multiple levels and is instructive. It is a deeply personal reflection of her internal work, a meditation on how she hopes her modeling will shape her students' sense of self and ability to grow into the people they want to be. What I find so rich and powerful about

Olivia's reflection is her clear articulation of the inevitability of anti-Black violence and the disregard she experiences as a Black woman—and still she shows up, as a light and guide for young people. This demonstrates the precarity and promise of Black youth work. Olivia must be concerned about her safety and that of the young people she works with, and she sees youth development spaces as sites where Black and other vulnerable young people can be affirmed, feel safe, dream, and act.

————

Black youth workers featured in this book shared beautiful visions for what they desired for Black youth, their educational futures, and their futures in the youth work profession. However, this does not mean that they all had the same visions. As I have detailed, some want to remain connected to youth work through front-facing roles where they can guide and nurture Black youth. At the same time, others sought positions of power to be able to create a narrative of Black youth development and education that countered dominant discourses rooted in anti-Black tropes that viewed Black youth from a position of lack. In other conversations, Black scholars and youth-workers-turned-systems-level-workers advocating for youth development opportunities at local and state levels believed in creating structural and financial support for the youth work sector, especially during political and social crises, to lessen the material precarity they face. Black youth workers engage in the process of futuring, bringing together a deep sense of history and knowledge of the systems and structures that shape the lives of young people and their own. Black youth workers engage in futuring despite the anti-Black terror that awaits them. Despite the inevitability of anti-Black harm, Black youth workers deserve a structural shift in the field that will allow them to build organizational futures and create opportunities for Black youth to see themselves in the future.

The Promise and Future of Black Youth Work

Laboring in the Shadows continues previous discussions and begins a new one. It carries forward the critical dialogue in sociology regarding the precarious lives and dignity of vulnerable workers who are often made invisible but are central to how society functions,[1] and the significance of community-based youth work to the sociology of education landscape.[2] *Laboring in the Shadows* also initiates a new conversation that uncovers the invisible precarity within community-based education and its impact on the lives of Black youth workers. This book also situates Black youth workers today within a broader social, political, and historical context alongside committed Black classroom teachers, activists, organizers, and care workers advocating for educational freedom and dignity across time and space. Through the perspectives of dedicated Black youth work professionals from various sectors of the youth work landscape, *Laboring in the Shadows* offers an intimate portrayal of those who work on behalf of children and youth—individuals whom society professes to care about—yet these workers remain hidden from our view and consciousness.

Community-based educational spaces within the nonprofit landscape and the workers within them occupy a liminal space. Youth workers operate in a diverse and extensive field of youth-serving organizations and institutions, resulting in various forms of precarity that shape their personal and professional lives. This precarity is further intensified for those who are most vulnerable due to the social forces of racism, poverty, citizenship status, and other structural factors. In this book, I spotlight Black youth work professionals who have dedicated their lives to working with young people and assisting them in navigating a world that often disregards their humanity. In many ways, *Laboring in the Shadows* is a love letter to Black youth workers. Inspired by groundbreaking scholarship that honors the legacy and power of Black teaching and Black schooling and scholarship on youth work and after-school education, *Laboring in the Shadows* celebrates the tradition of Black educators who nurture the brilliance of Black children and guide them through liberatory educational experiences despite the forces of white supremacy that seek to destroy them.

Embracing the Paradox, Disrupting the Precarity in Shadow Work

Paradoxes are an inherent part of the complexity of social life, and many paradoxes exist within American education. Throughout history, Black students have faced violence and humiliation in their pursuit of education. At the same time, Black students have a rich history of learning in fugitivity[3] and asserting their humanity through the pursuit of educational freedom in the face of significant risk of violence in all forms.[4] Black educational spaces with rich diversity—from schoolhouses to church basements to community organizations—have shaped the opportunities for Black youth and have fought to assert Black dignity in the face of terror.

Paradoxes and contradictions are also embedded in youth work due to the precarity and instability of the field's existence, which then induces precarity in the lives of those who work in the field. These paradoxes manifest in significant ways. There is a paradox within the field itself. Society relies on youth work, but there is a profound lack of recognition and underinvestment compared to other expenditures. Another paradox emerges within youth workers' professional or occupational identities.[5] Their commitment to young people is deemed noble or a calling—but in a capitalist society, this framing leads to their exploitation. Labeling their work as "noble" justifies subjecting them to low wages, debt, food insecurity, and housing instability, among other challenges. Furthermore, at the organizational level, the paternalism and deficit-based framing of nonprofit and philanthropic models that sustain racist pathologies must be navigated by youth workers as they seek to support and engage with Black and other marginalized youth. Although youth work organizations can push back against this framing, they can also perpetuate it.[6] Because community-based educational spaces exist within a broader sociohistorical and sociopolitical context—encompassing structural forces, systems of oppression, histories, and ideologies—programs can produce contradictory actions and outcomes that shape the experiences of youth participants and workers within organizations. As this book demonstrates, the precarity in the field and the paradoxes it induces lie at the heart of youth work. To understand what youth work is, why it is so urgent, and the suffering it can soothe and create, one must understand these paradoxes.

CHALLENGING MATERIAL AND SYMBOLIC PRECARITY

As youth workers like Chris shared, navigating these contradictions is inherent in the practice of youth work. "The beautiful and the yuck," as he explained, can coexist in practice due to our complexity as humans engaging with young and developing people. But sitting with precarity is unacceptable—this is fundamentally a structural issue since the field is relied upon by school systems, cities, and families. The precarity and paradoxes reinforce each other, leading to challenging situations for youth workers, which I suggest is exacerbated for Black youth workers for whom life is already precarious.[7] There is a symbolic precarity[8] that exists for youth workers, which shapes their uncertainty, instability, and liminal social positioning as educators and care workers, yet they are not regarded or seen in the same way as classroom teachers in society. Black youth workers featured in this book reflect on this form of precarity as a lack of regard and respect for their work, and a fundamental lack of recognition for the lives they have touched and the sacrifices they make to support young people across various domains of their lives. The label of "youth worker" as a professional identity is sometimes only resonant for those working in the field. Youth workers constantly fight for respect, to be recognized, and to be valued for their essential roles in the educational, socioemotional, and cultural lives of children and youth.

This symbolic precarity—instability and the liminal social positioning further relegating youth workers into the shadows—considerably impacts the material precarity they face. As youth workers shared their stories, they discussed difficult moments of deep financial insecurity brought on by low wages and the inability to make a living wage that would allow them to take care of themselves and their loved ones. Low wages characterize the field of youth work and the nonprofit service sector in general. Black youth workers faced inadequate or nonexistent health care, food insecurity, and housing instability, forcing them to sleep on friends' couches and live in motels with the constant fear of eviction. Youth workers who had college and advanced degrees were burdened with loan debt that became impossible to repay on their wages as youth workers. Youth workers like Chris, Brandon, Bria, and others held multiple part-time jobs to make ends meet. As youth workers like Bria shared, everyone featured in the pages of this book had a strong desire to work with young people. They recognized the value of youth work as a complement and supplement to schools, particularly for Black youth and other young people marginalized by race, class, gender, ability, or sexuality. However, their passion for working with young people and their commitment should not be exploited to justify inadequate wages and a lack of health care or benefits. Structural protection is needed in the field that honors the skills and expertise of youth workers and the value they bring to the lives of youth. This requires the protection of federal funding in the form of 21st Century[9] grants and state and city commitments to support after-school education by supporting the workforce.

Youth workers are present in numerous educational institutions and non-profit organizations, including school districts, local government, nonprofit community organizations, faith-based spaces, and cultural institutions such as libraries and museums. As a result, certain constraints shape the experiences of youth workers that may not affect others. When asked to discuss the experiences of youth workers, I find that generalizing the field or the experiences of youth workers is not always feasible, as their experiences can be influenced by their specific locations. These experiences depend on the sociopolitical context of their organization, the organizational dynamics such as leadership and climate, and their relationship to power. However, additional scholarship that amplifies the voices of youth workers and those involved in the youth work landscape will assist the field in identifying and understanding specific needs. This will help create opportunities for structural and organizational support, fostering contexts where youth workers can organize, unionize, and resist their invisibility, precarity, and the challenges they face in the profession.

CONFRONTING PRECARITY IN BLACK YOUTH WORK

Labor scholarship demonstrates how precarity is induced and perpetuated by capitalism, as well as by anti-Blackness.[10] In an essay on the relationship between the enslaved and the worker, through a reconsideration of W.E.B. DuBois's classic text, *Black Reconstruction in America*, sociologist Moon-Kie Jung argues what it might mean for sociologists to consider an "underdiscipline of antisociology"—one that acknowledges how the historical reality of slavery, and its afterlives[11] shape social formations, including labor.[12] There is a fundamental contradiction for Black workers in the US as their labor is disconnected from their humanity.[13] While youth workers from all racial backgrounds can face precarity in the field due to the structure of the landscape and its paradoxes, this precarity is exacerbated for Black youth workers. They not only deal with common challenges in the field, such as low wages and inadequate health care, but these challenges are compounded for Black youth workers because of structural racism in society and at the organizational level.

Precarity in the workplace induces further harm for already vulnerable people who face precarity in all other forms of social life.[14] *Laboring in the Shadows* captures the experiences of Black youth workers who faced retaliation and harm, tokenization, microaggressions, or career ceilings that limited their decision-making power within their organizations. The experiences of Black youth workers varied based on their proximity to power in these organizations. Those who occupied leadership positions had control over their engagement with youth and a voice in the decision-making processes of their organizations. However, youth workers in front-facing roles had limited connection to this kind of power. Even those who led their organizations struggled with securing funding and articulated tension in overcoming the racialized nonprofit industrial complex.[15] Black youth workers saw themselves as crucial to the youth work landscape, and more specifically, they saw their presence as educators and mentors as essential for preparing Black youth for navigating school spaces and a society that views them as threats and problems to be contained.[16] Their precarity in the profession is not unique, as the labor of Black workers in other professions face similar challenges.[17] However, the voices of Black youth workers as valuable educators, caregivers, and activists are essential for our deeper understanding of their contributions of their labor.

Enduring Black Springs

Black youth workers spoke to me or to members of my team during pivotal moments of racial reckoning—deeply unsettling times marked by grotesque displays of anti-Black violence replayed incessantly in media outlets. In this book, Black youth workers created opportunities for young people in their programs to understand what they witnessed. They established political sanctuaries where youth could mourn and grieve the deaths they witnessed from multiple pandemics, process their emotions, envision a new world, and engage in social action to challenge structural oppression and build the future they imagined. The process of sociopolitical development, critical awareness, and social action are deeply rooted in Black educational experiences throughout history and are crucial to the process of social justice and critical youth development practice.[18] The ways Black youth workers navigated what Robin D. G. Kelley referred to as Black Spring—the powerful global uprisings demanding accountability for George Floyd—reinforced what research has shown us for decades: that building power among young people and allowing them to embrace their activist identities lead to significant social change in education and beyond.[19]

Black Spring, however, was not exceptional. It certainly marked what felt like a breaking point or an inflection point, but anti-Black violence is ordinary.[20] As Black youth workers shared, they supported youth in understanding and resisting the harm they encountered in their schools and neighborhoods. In many respects, their programming during Black Spring was routine. As Chris and Sam, both from midwestern cities, explained, they took seriously everything youth presented to them as a concern, from issues of racial discrimination in local neighborhood stores to unfair punishments imposed by teachers, school administrators, or school resource officers. Black youth workers have always filled the gap for Black students, aiding their understanding of their social worlds and empowering them to think critically about their experiences in pursuit of social action.

Although Black Spring was not exceptional, the grief was enormous. Through their heartache and fear, Black youth workers created and nurtured space (physical and virtual) for Black youth to grieve, process, and dream alongside them. They engaged in what Christina Sharpe terms "wake work." Black youth workers featured in this book answered, through their actions, the questions João Costa Vargas and Joy James raised in their essay, "Refusing Blackness-as-Victimization." That is, if we "accept that state-sanctioned legal and extralegal murders of Black people are normative," then "what kinds of possibilities for rupture might be opened up?"[21] Black youth workers entered the profession because they recognized the limits of democracy for Black people. They acknowledged the inevitability of racism, and more specifically, anti-Black racism as a system of structural oppression rooted in anti-Blackness, "the disdain, disregard, and disgust of [Black] existence,"[22] and the positioning of Black people as outside of humanness, as something "other than human."[23] With this understanding in mind, Black youth workers engaged in critical hope and a desire for Black youth to reach their full potential. Anti-Blackness was not viewed as constraining; rather, it instilled a specific determination in enacting Black youth work. Just as Black people are not monolithic, the Black youth workers interviewed shared diverse perspectives. They entered the field from diverse ethnic, class, and regional backgrounds that created divergences in how they might have done their work. Still, all Black youth workers understood the inevitability of anti-Black racism, the racial structures shaping youths' educational experiences, and the white supremacist terror Black youth may face. Rooted in a deep belief in the power of education, they still teach, guide, mentor, and prepare Black youth for the future.[24]

Black Youth Work and the Process of Futuring

Black youth work is a process of futuring. As Black youth workers expressed their dreams for Black youth and their visions for themselves, I heard echoes of the past in their words. It is impossible not to draw upon the history of fugitivity in Black educational experiences; Black schooling, Black teaching, and the movements for justice and freedom have informed how we freedom dream and envision a future. As I reflect in the introduction of this book, the legacy of Black youth work is rooted in history—from Black literary collectives to Mary McLeod Bethune's efforts in the Negro Division of the National Youth Administration to the Black Panthers' Free Breakfast programs, political education programming, and network of Liberation Schools. Despite the challenges and what Black youth workers understand about the world, they continue to engage in this work with critical hope and a desire for Black youth to reach their full potential. Black youth workers articulated visions of love and a desire for Black youth to know they are loved. They also expressed their vision for their work, which included safeguards, protections, and opportunities for them to engage in the work they love while earning a living wage to support themselves and their families. Black youth workers, such as Kim and others, passionately explained how the field should be more visible and structurally supported, considering that youth spend more time outside of schools. Youth workers who sought more power in their organizations through leadership roles conveyed powerful visions of development spaces for Black youth, led by Black youth workers and community members. Black youth workers like Rihanna and Olivia seized opportunities to challenge the nonprofit industrial complex, aware of how racial capitalism and paternalism are woven through the sector.

There is a long history of creating spaces for better educational experiences for Black youth, rooted in and sustained by community. Black community-based educational spaces have served the purposes of repair and redress. The enactment of educational fugitivity by Black students and educators in Black spaces was a direct response to anti-Black terror and violence.[25] The relative autonomy of community-based spaces has made them significant for educational and social redress, and Black youth workers have consistently played a crucial role in this process.

Efforts to Support Youth Work(ers)

So, how do we make visible the lived experiences of youth workers who are most vulnerable to systems of oppression that make the youth work profession precarious? Federal funding for youth work and after-school education through the 21st Century Community Learning Center grants is vital.[26] In response to COVID-19 (in which three out of four programs were expected to close),[27] states and cities used the American Rescue Plan and Secondary School Emergency Relief Act funds to support programs and the workforce.[28] Many city and state after-school networks, such as the Kalamazoo Youth Development Network, Chicago Learning Exchange, and Madison-area Out of School Time network, have used these funds to invest in youth workers by providing grants to create bonuses and establishing a fellowship program that facilitates professional learning opportunities while supporting their well-being. The Mott Foundation's 50 State Afterschool Network has been an important resource for the field, committed to ensuring access to quality youth programming and offering youth workers opportunities to enhance their skills and engage in antiracist practices. Similarly, groups like Grantmakers for Education, the National Academy of Science, Engineering, and Medicine, the Spencer Foundation, and the Wallace Foundation have been committed to cultivating research on youth workers and the workforce. A recent effort between the Wallace Foundation and the American Institutes for Research sought to better understand the field's workforce and distributed the Power of Us Survey.[29] Our data about the workforce, including race, gender, pay inequities, and other issues, remain insufficient and limited. Some networks are charting critical pathways, like the California Afterschool Network. They have begun seeking a standard occupational code (SOC) to gain an accurate count of youth workers in their state. Youth workers can be coded under many categories, including education or social workers. This still leaves out the many workers who do not work in mainstream national organizations that are regarded nationally or receive public funding, making tracking more difficult for youth workers in independent programs or street-based youth work. More dialogue and collaboration with other countries might also generate new directions to support youth workers. Scholars in the United Kingdom have created advocacy spaces for youth workers to make their needs more visible and to provide vital structural support.[30]

More research is one of our greatest tools for understanding the lived experiences of youth workers and providing specificity about their challenges based on their social positioning, ensuring these issues can be addressed. By uncovering the specific ways Black youth workers are made even more precarious by the youth work profession, I hope to unveil pathways for future researchers to explore how other racially minoritized and multiply oppressed youth workers navigate and experience the profession. Recent data reveal that in California, youth workers from immigrant backgrounds who identify as Latina earn less than their white counterparts.[31] Some youth work scholars have written about the plight of youth workers from immigrant and refugee backgrounds or mixed-status households.[32] In addition to understanding how youth workers interpret their experiences in the profession, further research that can systematically report accurate accounts of youth workers and their locations can make a significant contribution. The nature of work is stratified by race, class, citizenship, language, and gender; thus, it is essential to identify and understand how youth workers from diverse backgrounds engage in the profession. Youth workers most affected by structural oppression are present (and have always been present), educating, nurturing, guiding, supporting, and loving young people. They deserve a living wage to support themselves. They deserve to be seen and heard. They deserve our respect. They deserve our gratitude.

The Promise in Black Youth Work

I see profound promise in Black youth work. From my early experiences as a program participant, to youth worker, to my scholarship and engagement with organizations and state and city out-of-school networks around the country, I see innovation, creativity, and groups of dedicated people working tirelessly to support youth in their full humanity. I am immensely grateful for my personal and professional experiences working in community-based educational spaces and for the work of the scholars before me that have led me to write this book. I owe much to the scholarship that highlights the experiences of young people—particularly those marginalized by race, class, gender, sexuality, ability, or citizenship status—who have turned to youth work programs for refuge and peace. The advocacy and research of intermediary organizations and after-school networks that strive to tell the stories of youth workers and ensure they receive adequate wages and support have been truly inspiring. This work must continue.

The promise of Black youth work is rooted in a belief that Black folks have always held—that education is connected to liberation. Black youth workers should receive recognition and praise alongside Black schoolteachers, organizers, and activists; disruptors, agitators, and resisters; and hopeful and determined family and community members who have nurtured, affirmed, and validated the humanity of Black youth, guiding them through unwelcoming educational environments and fostering joyful, liberated spaces for learning. I hope this book ignites a conversation that includes everyone who is working for better educational futures for children and youth. I envision a society where all youth workers emerge from the shadows into the spotlight to receive the respect, gratitude, and appreciation they deserve.

Epilogue

Living, working, and learning with uncertainty is inevitable. As I write this epilogue, we are several months past the 2024 US presidential election. Now more than ever, it is crucial to fortify Black educational spaces in all their forms. The attacks on what and how students can learn—the banning of words like *race, equity, gender identity*, and more—will have tremendous consequences for all of us, especially for those who are most vulnerable and those committed to justice. How policy, institutions, and cultural spaces will shift remains to be seen; however, what is certain is that change, harm, and suffering will occur. Yet, as I have learned from the youth workers who spoke with me and my team, this inevitability does not have to be limiting. Just as harm and suffering exist, resistance and joy are ever-present. Black youth workers mentor and guide young people through perilous times. They teach, dream, and live through moments of uncertainty because uncertainty is always present. There is much to be learned from Black youth workers. What I hope you'll take from them is their deep commitment to dreaming of new futures despite the potential harm that may come. Freedom dreaming and freedom building go hand in hand. In the tradition of Black education for liberation, we must continue to fight, dream, and build.

Research amid "Uncertainty"
Black Precarity Across Time and Space

I struggle with the concept of uncertainty. In my first book, *Reclaiming Community: Race and the Uncertain Future of Youth Work*, I used the term *uncertain* to capture what felt like the unknown. I discussed the role of market-based education policy reforms that had been seeping into nonprofit community-based educational spaces for years. This term helped me name what threatened the sacredness of youth work—the imposing structures and logic that were making out-of-school spaces of respite and joy feel like the worst parts of "schooling." However, as I reflected, it became clear that *uncertainty* was probably an insufficient term. For those who lead precarious lives, those on the margins, and those who bear the weight of structural oppression, life is always uncertain. For Black folks, life is always uncertain.

"My safety is not always guaranteed," Olivia told me. She is correct. As a Black woman, her safety is never assured and is therefore uncertain. In recent years, we have faced a global health crisis, erosion of civil rights, a decline in bodily autonomy, an increase in mass shootings and hate crimes, an attempted coup, and relentless state violence, leading to some of the largest protests in the US and around the world. Scholars have sought to define these times as "unsettled moments,"[1] "ruptures," and "racial reckonings."[2] These terms have been used to make sense of these incidents that shifted our social fabric and fundamentally reoriented how we think about and interact with the world. For families, young people, and workers most affected by economic hardship, state surveillance, violence, and racist, xenophobic, and anti-Black discrimination, these moments were intensified.

As I conducted research for this book during these challenging social moments, I wondered what it might feel like to have the whole world speak about uncertainty as though it were a new occurrence, when opportunity, freedom, education, safety, and life itself have not always been guaranteed for Black people. Police violence, a global health pandemic, economic collapse, heightened disinformation leading to xenophobic and racist attacks, and social unrest have all contributed to instability in the fabric of our social lives. The relationship of Black people to precarity is rooted in chattel slavery and colonialism, being treated as objects and property, and seen as something other than human.[3] The reality of social and political shifts in the world undoubtedly shapes and reshapes institutions and how people exist in relation to one another. However, these shifts were exacerbated for Black people and other communities oppressed by the colossal weight of white supremacist cis-heteropatriarchal violence. I conducted research projects that spanned ten years. At every period of my research, there were unsettled moments or times of crisis in the cities where I met youth workers, as well as nationally. As a critical qualitative scholar, examining the social, historical, and political context of participants' worldviews is essential to my data collection and analysis. Holding together a view of the macro-level structures and systems that shape the lives of participants, the meso-level response of organizations and educational spaces that are influenced by the broader sociopolitical context, and the micro-level experiences, ways of being, and maneuvering through space with participants is vital to an analysis of critical bifocality.[4]

Black Youth Work Amid Racial Disparities: 2015–2020

In Pleasant Ridge, I began engaging with Black youth workers after a citywide report revealed data highlighting the racial disparities between Black and white residents. Additionally, there had been several incidents of police violence against Black children in the city, reflecting the escalating national unrest and the mobilization of the Black Lives Matter Movement following the murders of Trayvon Martin, Mike Brown, and Rekia Boyd, among others. Pleasant Ridge has just under 250,000 residents, of which roughly 75% are white, 8.7% Asian, 7% Latinx, 6.4% Black, 2.9% American Indian/Alaskan

Native, and 3.5% of more than two races. Other communities in Pleasant Ridge face racial and economic disparities. Yet, in recent years, media attention has focused on the racial disparities faced by the Black community. Although Pleasant Ridge is perceived to be a "nice" and "liberal" place, it is a city with a school district that continues to disregard the cries and organizing of Black youth who demand that cops be removed from schools. It is also a city where Black students continuously face verbal, emotional, and physical violence, as teachers are often outed for calling Black students racist slurs, and school officials have been identified for physically assaulting students. Pleasant Ridge, mirroring other "liberal" locations throughout the country, is also a place where Black youth have been denied entry into and violently removed by police from libraries, malls, and other public spaces. Given this context, the methodological lens for this study acknowledges the historical, cultural, and social context of Pleasant Ridge and how participants come to this study.[5]

INTERVIEWS AND OBSERVATIONS

With support from the National Academy of Education/Spencer Foundation, I began engaging in fieldwork in Pleasant Ridge by observing city events that discussed the racial disparities that came to light. My team and I attended panels, conferences, and meetings held by university researchers, school district personnel, community-based organizations, and concerned residents of Pleasant Ridge. We also collected print and digital media that featured headlines and stories about the racial disparities in the city, reported racist incidents, and neighborhood and city initiatives that attempted to address these disparities. We observed twenty-two events during the first two years of the study. Throughout the summer of 2015 and into the summer of 2016, I, or a member of my research team, attended various events in Pleasant Ridge. These events—ranging from twenty people to a few hundred in attendance— were sponsored by various community-based organizations, faith-based institutions, local universities, and activist organizations to discuss racism in Pleasant Ridge. I had formed relationships with several city organizations and many youth workers, and using community nominations,[6] a form of purposeful sampling,[7] I conducted sixteen interviews with youth workers from various youth work organizations. Fourteen identified as Black.[8] Of the Black youth workers interviewed, three worked for national youth organizations with local chapters in Pleasant Ridge, six worked in independent youth orga-

TABLE A.1 Participants Interviewed 2016–2020, Pleasant Ridge.

Name*	Age Range	Years in Field	Role in Field	Sector/Context
Beatrice	40–45	20+	Program coordinator	School district
Ben	25–30	8	Youth worker/intermediary	City and county
Brandon	25–30	8	Youth worker	National
Ellis	40–45	20+	Program coordinator/youth worker	National/school district/intermediary
Gerald	35–40	20	Youth worker/program founder	Independent
Gia	25–30	10+	Youth worker/ program coordinator/organizer	Independent
Hamilton	40–45	20+	Youth worker/coordinator	Independent
Lamar	40–45	20+	Scholar/youth worker/program founder/leader	Independent/higher education
Lawrence	50–55	30	Program leader/scholar	Independent/school district
Monica	40–45	15	Program coordinator/organizer	City and county/school district
Sam	30–35	15+	Youth coordinator/youth worker	Independent
Sarah	25–30	8	Youth worker	Independent
Sasha	30–35	5	Program development	National
Sky	25–30	10	Youth worker/program coordinator	Independent/school district
Tarik	25–30	10	Youth worker/program coordinator	National/school district
Wahid	35–40	20	Youth worker/program coordinator/scholar	City and county/independent

* All names are pseudonyms.

Source: Author.

nizations untethered to national programs, four worked with school districts, and three worked across school districts, city and county providers, and intermediary organizations. Because of the nature of youth work, participants straddled multiple settings and had various roles throughout their careers— from youth workers and program coordinators to program founders/leaders. Six identified as women, and ten identified as men. The participants in my study had a range of formal educational experiences ranging from some college to doctorate degrees. Some participants lived in Pleasant Ridge for as few as four years, while others were born and raised in the city.

Youth workers were selected because they engage Black youth in various forms of youth work. Semistructured interviews lasting between 60 and 120 minutes explored their understanding of anti-Black racism in Pleasant Ridge, how it might inform their educational and organizing work with Black youth, and how their organization engaged youth participants in dialogue about racial disparities and anti-Black racism. Analyzing citywide conversations about racism in Pleasant Ridge, triangulated with data from public media and interviews with youth workers, provided a comprehensive approach to studying how liberal discourses about racial disparities perpetuate anti-Black racism within community-based educational spaces. I frequently met with my research assistants to discuss interpretations of comments made during events and provide inter-coder reliability for the collected data.[9] All, except four interviews, were conducted in person.

EQUITY IN OUT-OF-SCHOOL TIME: 2020–2022

In 2020, I was invited by the Wallace Foundation to conduct a study concerning equity issues in out-of-school time. With coresearchers Ben Kirshner, Daniela DiGiacomo, Sam Mejias, and Deepa Vasudevan, I conducted a national interview project with youth workers, program leaders, policy influencers, and scholars of youth work.[10] These interviews with experts in the field took place at the height of the COVID-19 pandemic and the uprisings against state violence following the murders of George Floyd and Breonna Taylor. A team of graduate and youth researchers (high school and college students) conducted a youth participatory action research (YPAR) project alongside our interview study. We engaged fifty-eight experts in interviews and thirty-five focus group participants. Of those interviewed, the majority were women and white, with participants from Latine, Black, South Asian,

TABLE A.2 Participants Interviewed 2020–2022.

Name*	Age Range	Years in Field	Region	Role in Field	Organization Type
Alexis	40–45	20+	Southeast	Youth worker/scholar	City and county/independent/higher education
Bill	40–45	20+	Southwest	Program director	City and county
Braylen	40–45	25+	Midwest	Youth worker/scholar	Independent/national
Gloria	50–55	30+	West	Youth worker/Program Coordinator/leader	Independent /intermediary
Jerome	55–60	30+	Midwest	Program leader/scholar	Intermediary
Kaia	30–35	10	Southeast	Program founder/leader/scholar	Independent/faith-based
Leah	50–55	30+	Northeast	Program leader	College preparatory program/independent
Mason	30–35	15+	Southeast	Youth worker/ program founder/leader	Independent
Morris	45–50	30+	Midwest	Youth worker/program leader	City and county
Pat	55–60	30+	Southeast	Program director/scholar	Intermediary
Porsha	50–55	30+	Midwest	Program leader/scholar	Independent
Raisa	50–55	30+	Midwest	Youth worker/scholar	Street-based outreach/independent
Rihanna	35–40	15+	West	Youth worker/program leader	Independent
Sage	45–50	20+	West	Youth worker/leader/scholar	Independent
Sheryl	50–55	30+	Midwest	Program leader	City and county/intermediary
Tamir	40–45	25	Southeast	Program leader/organizer/scholar	Intermediary/Independent
Tina	35–40	20+	Northeast	Program director/youth worker	Independent/cultural institutions
Toussaint	30–35	10	West	Youth worker/organizer	Independent
Victoria	40–45	20+	Midwest	Intermediary leader/scholar	Independent
Walker	45–50	25+	Northeast	Program leader	Independent
Whitney	40–45	20+	Northeast	Intermediary leader	City and county/intermediary
Wynter	35–40	20+	West	Youth worker/program leader	Independent

* All names are pseudonyms.

Source: Author.

Southeast Asian, and Middle Eastern/North African backgrounds. Our focus group participants included youth workers engaging in organizations that support youth activism, youth from immigrant and refugee backgrounds, early childhood, LGBTQIA+ youth, and a group of out-of-school-time intermediary and policy influencers. These participants included men, women, nonbinary youth workers, and out-of-school time advocates from diverse racial and ethnic backgrounds.

Laboring in the Shadows features interviews with twenty-two youth workers and program leaders who identified as Black or of African descent, as well as several experts from academia and intermediary organizations, to provide important context about the arrangement of the field. Throughout their careers, these youth workers held front-facing positions, director positions, and were founders of youth work organizations of various types, including independent programs, national programs, street-based outreach programming, city and county providers, faith-based programs, and higher education. The average length of time in the field is twenty years. Fourteen identified as women, while eight were men. These youth workers represented every region of the US. All interviews were collected via Zoom, and participants were offered a flexible gift card for their participation.

ADDITIONAL INTERVIEWS WITH BLACK
YOUTH WORKERS: 2022–2023

The final stage of interviews occurred with Black youth workers around the country, who were picking up the pieces in their organizations, responding to all the forms of loss experienced during the pandemic, including relationships with peers and teachers, extracurricular activities, and human contact with loved ones outside of their households. Again, using purposeful sampling through community nominations, my team and I interviewed fifteen Black youth workers around the country. These youth workers engaged with youth in national organizations, independent programs, school districts, medical facilities, and city- and county-run programs. Ten identified as women, and five identified as men. This group's average length of time in the field was sixteen years.

All interviews except one were held via Zoom and lasted 60–120 minutes. Youth workers were compensated with a flexible gift card for their participation. During these interviews, youth workers reflected on issues of equity and

TABLE A.3 Participants Interviewed 2023–2024.

Name*	Age Range	Years in Field	Region	Role in Field	Organization Type
Bria	20–25	8	Midwest	Program coordinator	Independent/health and wellness
Chris	25–30	10	Midwest	Youth worker coordinator	National
Darren	35–40	10	Northeast	Youth worker/program coordinator	National/independent
Gabi	30–35	15	East Coast	Youth worker	Independent
Harriet	40+	30	Northeast	Early childhood youth worker	National
Hilario	35–40	15	Northeast	Program coordinator	National/independent/city and county
Hippolyta	35–40	15	Southeast	Program founder/leader	National/independent
Jamea	40–45	22	Midwest	Program founder/leader	Independent
Joy	40+	25	Midwest	Youth worker/program coordinator	National
Kim	35–40	20	West	Program founder/leader	Independent
Olivia	40–45	23	West	Program leader	School district/independent
Robeson	35–40	16	Northeast	Youth worker	Independent
Ruben	35–40	15	Northeast	Juvenile detention worker	School district /city and county
Waverly	20–25	9	Northeast	Youth worker/program coordinator	Independent
Zora	40+	20	Southeast	Youth worker/program coordinator	Independent

* All names are pseudonyms.

Source: Author.

anti-Black racism in nonprofit youth work. They shared their motivations for entering the field, their joys and challenges in the job, and what they envisioned for the youth they worked with and their own careers.

Bringing the Data Together: Analysis

Drawing inspiration from prior sociological studies bringing together research from over a ten-year period,[11] I analyzed and coded interviews from each research stage. I noticed recurring themes across each stage of research. Black youth workers shared similar motivations for entering the field and expressed everyday experiences with tokenization, racial microaggressions, and anti-Black racism. They had similar stories of trying to intervene on behalf of the Black students they worked with who encountered many instances of anti-Black racism and police violence in their schools or neighborhoods. Using Dedoose software, I created a data set of interviews with all Black youth workers from each period of research and the ethnographic observations from Pleasant Ridge. Using the constant comparative method,[12] interview transcripts and ethnographic fieldnotes were read and reread to generate relevant themes. Through an inductive process, open coding involved reviewing all transcripts for descriptive categories and developing and refining each category until no new information yielded any additional meaning. Following the systematic coding process, major themes were developed, collapsed, and modified to core themes and codes.

Precarity Across Time and Space: Research in Difficult Times

It did not occur to me initially to pull multiple stages of research together into a book project. However, reading through interviews of Black youth workers from every region of the country, I kept seeing recurring themes of precarity, power struggles, fear, retaliation, and utter grief from witnessing Black people being killed in local and national contexts over ten years, as well as critical hope, resistance, and joy. The ten years in which this data were collected parallels the rise of the Black Lives Matter Movement. These were unsettling moments to live through: appalling statistics reflecting deep racial and economic disparities disproportionately shaping Black children and youth in Pleasant Ridge, police violence against Black people, a global health pandemic, an attempted coup, and more police violence against Black people. Across time and space, during these unsettled moments, Black youth workers expressed the same concerns. The always of every day of anti-Black racism, compounded with a global health pandemic, shaped and reshaped Black youth work. As I reflect on my role in this research, I am reminded of the grace I needed as a researcher/youth worker/coparent and the grace and gratitude I needed to extend to Black youth workers interviewed.

EXTENDING GRACE AND GRATITUDE
IN THE RESEARCH PROCESS

Time is precious and fleeting. I worried that people would feel burdened by my request for interviews and exhausted from their long days of working online and having no separation from work and home—and, of course, carrying the grief of witnessing Black death on a loop. To my surprise, most people welcomed the opportunity to talk. Having to shift programming online (for those who were not forced to meet in person) led to innovation and partnerships that strengthened some aspects of their organizations—people wanted to share what they were doing and learning. I learned how youth workers pivoted to virtual programming, trying to preserve the uniqueness of their pedagogy and support for students experiencing loss and facing the reality that some youth workers had to be furloughed. In addition to moving programming online, youth workers immediately worked to ensure that their youth and their families had the economic support they needed to stay at home. In my interviews, I learned that many organizations provided mutual aid to youth and families, providing wi-fi access so that young people could attend school online. Because the pandemic hit during spring and early summer, prom and graduation season quickly approached. I talked with youth workers who creatively found ways to celebrate these significant life events in the lives of teenagers. They did graduation and prom caravans, driving by young people's homes, cheering and celebrating young people for their accomplishments. These creative celebrations honored their hard work and provided joy during a difficult time.

As programs were providing mutual aid, planning virtual proms and graduations, and trying to continue the normal functioning of their organization's programs, the world became witness to the execution of George Floyd. As more information emerged about the murders of Breonna Taylor,

Ahmaud Arbery, Ezekiel Ford, Tony McDade, Rayshard Brooks, and others, more people across the globe were compelled to act, to resist, and to make their voices heard against blatant injustice and police violence. The suffering and harm seemed relentless Processing the anti-Black state violence and subsequently engaging in social action to resist state violence were also added to the long list of things youth workers were doing to support young people at this time. It is within this context that this research was conducted, which profoundly impacted how youth workers could show up for interviews. It shifted how I showed up to interviews too. For example, during the interviews with Pleasant Ridge youth workers, before they started, there was typically a conversation about what it felt like to exist in Pleasant Ridge as a Black person. During interviews between 2020 and 2021, there were tears, disbelief, and outrage. The interview space became a container to hold anger and grief. In the last stage of research, Black youth workers extended grace to me as I was battling illnesses, and we were all witnessing more violence on vulnerable communities, especially children as victims of gun violence.

Nurturing young people's hopes, desires, and dreams is critical to the identities of the youth workers who shared their stories with me. In most of my interviews, there was a release of pent-up emotions and a strong desire to discuss their experiences, share their ideas, air grievances, and articulate their visions and dreams for Black youth. In turn, listening to them became a release for me as well. I welcomed youth workers into our conversations in whatever way they *needed* to show up. They often felt fatigued and overwhelmed, coming straight from a meeting or preparing for one after our conversation. The interview process allowed them to reflect not only on their days but also on their journeys into youth work and what they envisioned for their future. At each moment of data collection, there were crises that youth workers had to manage to protect themselves and the youth they worked with. Still, they were dedicated to youth and enthusiastic about participating in conversations with my team because they love what they do and want respect and support for the field. Youth workers provide grace to the young people they serve every day. And this research process across so many moments of crises serves as a reminder to extend not only gratitude and grace to youth workers but also to all those who work in professions that care for the most vulnerable among us.

Notes

Preface

1. Bianca J. Baldridge, "On Educational Advocacy and Cultural Work: Situating Community-Based Youth Work [ers] in Broader Educational Discourse," *Teachers College Record* 120, no. 2 (February 2018): 1–28.

2. The after-school workforce is comprised of youth workers who may be volunteers or paid staff members in nonprofit youth-serving organizations, credentialed teachers, social workers, and other professionals.

3. Karen Pittman, "Moving Beyond Where and When to the People and Practices That Impact Youth," *Journal of Youth Development* 13, no. 4 (2018): 1–4.

4. Arne L. Kalleberg, Barbara F Reskin, and Ken Hudson, "Bad Jobs in America: Standard and Nonstandard Employment Relations and Job Quality in the United States," *American Sociological Review* 65, no. 2 (2000): 256–278.

5. Christina Sharpe, *In the Wake: On Blackness and Being* (Duke University Press, 2016); Michael J. Dumas, "Against the Dark: Antiblackness in Education Policy and Discourse," *Theory into Practice* 55, no. 1 (2016): 11–19.; Moon-Kie Jung and João H. Costa Vargas, eds. *Antiblackness* (Duke University Press, 2021); kihana miraya ross and Jarvis R. Givens, "The Clearing: On Black Education Studies and the Problem of 'Antiblackness,'" *Harvard Educational Review* 93, no. 2 (2023): 149–172.

6. Association for Child & Youth Care Practice, Inc., accessed July 30, 2024, https://acycp.org/; National Center for Educational Statistics, accessed July 30, 2024, https://nces.ed.gov/.

7. Nick Juravich. *Para Power: How Paraprofessional Labor Changed Education* (University of Illinois Press, 2024). Ruth Milkman, "Stratification Among In-Home Care Workers in the United States," *Critical Sociology* 49, no. 1 (2023): 11–22.

8. Sarah Jaffe, *Work Won't Love You Back: How Devotion to Our Jobs Keeps Us Exploited, Exhausted, and Alone* (Bold Type Books, 2021).

9. Bianca J. Baldridge, "On Educational Advocacy and Cultural Work."

10. Jaffe, *Work Won't Love You Back*.

11. Damien M. Sojoyner, *Joy and Pain: A Story of Black Life and Liberation in Five Albums* (University of California Press, 2022).

Introduction

1. All names of youth workers interviewed are pseudonyms.

2. Shirley Brice Heath and Milbrey W. McLaughlin, "The Best of Both Worlds: Connecting Schools and Community Youth Organizations for All-Day, All-Year Learning," *Educational Administration Quarterly* 30, no. 3 (1994): 278–300; Barton J. Hirsch, Nancy L. Deutsch, and David L. DuBois, *After-School Centers and Youth Development: Case Studies of Success and Failure* (Cambridge University Press, 2011); Deborah Lowe Vandell, "Afterschool Program Quality and Student Outcomes: Reflections on Positive Key Findings on Learning and Development from Recent Research," in *Expanding Minds and Opportunities: Leveraging the Power of Afterschool and Summer Learning for Student Success*, ed. Terry K. Peterson, 10–16 (Collaborative Communications Group, 2013); Karen J. Pittman, Merita Irby, Nicole Yohalem, and Alicia Wilson-Ahlstrom, "Blurring the Lines for Learning: The Role of Out-of-School Programs as Complements to Formal Learning," *New Directions for Youth Development* 2004, no. 101 (2004): 19–41.

3. Barbara Rogoff, Maureen Callanan, Kris D. Gutiérrez, and Frederick Erickson, "The Organization of Informal Learning," *Review of Research in Education* 40, no. 1 (2016): 356–401.

4. Bianca J. Baldridge, "On Educational Advocacy and Cultural Work: Situating Community-Based Youth Work[ers] in a Broader Educational Discourse," *Teachers College Record* 120, no. 2 (2018): 1–28.

5. Robert Halpern, "A Different Kind of Child Development Institution: The History of After-School Programs for Low-Income Children," *Teachers College Record* 104, no. 3 (March 2002): 178–211; Soo Ah Kwon, *Uncivil Youth: Race, Activism, and Affirmative Governmentality* (Duke University Press, 2013).

6. For comparison, according to the Pew Research Center, there are roughly three million federal workers (excluding ex-military and U.S postal service workers), which is the fifteenth largest workforce in the country.

7. Association of Child & Youth Care Practice, Inc., https://acycp.org/; Afterschool Alliance, "America After 3pm 2020 National Report: Demand Grows, Opportunity Shrinks," *America after 3pm*, 2020, https://afterschoolalliance.org/documents/AA3PM-2020/AA3PM-National-Report.pdf.

8. Baldridge, Bianca J. "The Youthwork Paradox: A Case for Studying the Complexity of Community-Based Youth Work in Education Research." *Educational Researcher* 49, no. 8 (2020): 618–625.

9. Jennifer R. Wolch, "The Shadow State: Transformations in the Voluntary Sector," in *The Power of Geography*, ed. Jennifer R. Wolch and Michael Dear (Routledge, 2014), 197–221.

10. Ruth Wilson Gilmore, "In the Shadow of the Shadow State," *S&F Online* 13, no. 2 (Spring 2016); Dylan Rodriguez, "The Political Logic of the Non-Profit Industrial Complex," in *The Revolution Will Not Be Funded: Beyond the Non-Profit Industrial Complex*, ed. INCITE! Women of Color Against Violence, 21–40 (Duke University Press, 2007).

11. Nick Juravich, *Para Power: How Paraprofessional Labor Changed Education* (University of Illinois Press, 2024).

12. Daphne Berry and Myrtle P. Bell, "Worker Cooperatives: Alternative Governance for Caring and Precarious Work," *Equality, Diversity and Inclusion: An International Journal* 37, no. 4 (2018): 376–391; LaTonya J. Trotter, *More Than Medicine: Nurse Practitioners and the Problems They Solve for Patients, Health Care Organizations, and the State* (Cornell University Press, 2020).

13. Gilmore, "In the Shadow of the Shadow State."

14. Rachel Meyer, "Precarious Workers and Collective Efficacy," *Critical Sociology* 43, no. 7/8 (2017): 1125–1141; Michael Heathfield and Dana Fusco, "Honoring and Supporting Youth Work Intellectuals," in *The Changing Landscape of Youth Work: Theory and Practice for an Evolving Field*, ed. Kristen M. Pozzoboni and Ben Kirshner, 127–146 (Information Age Publishing, 2016); Rebecka Bloomer, Lesley M. Harris, Aishia A. Brown, and Shantel Crosby, "Exploring the Promotion of Youth Voice in Community-Based Youth Development Programmes," *Child & Family Social Work* 28, no. 2 (2023): 291–301.

15. Dana Fusco, ed., *Advancing Youth Work: Current Trends, Critical Questions* (Routledge, 2012).

16. Fusco, *Advancing Youth Work*.

17. Richard Lofton, "'I Was Called Everything but a Student': Blackness and the Social Death of Student Status," *Social Problems* (2023): spad033; Michael J. Dumas, "'Losing an Arm': Schooling as a Site of Black Suffering." *Race Ethnicity and Education* 17, no. 1 (2014): 1–29.

18. Economic Policy Institute, "EPI's Family Budget Calculator," accessed March 14, 2025, https://www.epi.org/publication/epis-family-budget-calculator/.

19. Massachusetts Institute of Technology, "MIT Living Wage Calculator," accessed March 14, 2025, https://livingwage.mit.edu/.

20. Karen Pittman, "Moving Beyond Where and When to the People and Practices That Impact Youth," *Journal of Youth Development* 13, no. 4 (2018): 1–4.

21. Vajra Watson, *Learning to Liberate: Community-Based Solutions to the Crisis in Urban Education* (Routledge, 2012).

22. Reed W. Larson, Kathrin C. Walker, Natalie Rusk, and Lisa B. Diaz, "Understanding Youth Development from the Practitioner's Point of View: A Call for Research on Effective Practice," *Applied Developmental Science* 19, no. 2 (2015): 74–86.

23. Nicole P. Marwell, *Bargaining for Brooklyn: Community Organizations in the Entrepreneurial City* (University of Chicago Press, 2009).

24. Walter Powell, "What Is the Non-Profit Sector?" in *The Nonprofit Sector: A Research Handbook*, ed. Walter W. Powell and Patricia Bromley, 3–23 (Stanford University Press, 2020).

25. Powell, "What Is the Non-Profit Sector?"

26. Jose Eos Trinidad, *Subtle Webs: How Local Organizations Shape US Education* (Oxford University Press, 2024).

27. Helmut K. Anheier, *Nonprofit Organizations: Theory, Management, Policy* (Routledge, 2014), 9.

28. Powell, "What Is the Non-Profit Sector?"

29. Powell, "What Is the Non-Profit Sector?"

30. Trinidad, *Subtle Webs.*

31. Sarah Jaffe, *Work Won't Love You Back: How Devotion to Our Jobs Keeps Us Exploited, Exhausted, and Alone* (Bold Type Books, 2021).

32. Eunice Han and Emma Garcia, "The Effect of Teachers' Unions on Teacher Stress: Evidence from District-Teacher Matched Data," *Labor Studies Journal* 48, no. 1 (2023): 35–69.

33. Quentin Brummet, Emily K. Penner, Nikolas Pharris-Ciurej, and Sonya R. Porter, "After School: An Examination of the Career Paths and Earnings of Former Teachers," *Educational Evaluation and Policy Analysis* (2024), https://doi.org/10.3102/01623737241227906; Terrenda White, "Teachers of Color and Urban Charter Schools: Race, School Culture, and Teacher Turnover in the Charter Sector," *Journal of Transformative Leadership & Policy Studies* 7, no. 1 (2018): 27–42.

34. Elizabeth Todd-Breland, *A Political Education: Black Politics and Education Reform in Chicago Since the 1960s* (University of North Carolina Press, 2018.)

35. Jaffe, *Work Won't Love You Back.*

36. Michalinos Zembylas, "The Ethics and Politics of Precarity: Risks and Productive Possibilities of a Critical Pedagogy for Precarity," *Studies in Philosophy and Education* 38, no. 2 (2019): 95–111; Guy Standing. The *Precariat: The New Dangerous Class* (Bloomsbury Academic, 2011).

37. Enobong Hannah Branch and Caroline Hanley, "A Racial-Gender Lens on Precarious Nonstandard Employment," in *Precarious Work*, vol. 31, 183–213 (Emerald Publishing, 2017), https://doi.org/10.1108/S0277–283320170000031006.

38. Rodriguez, "The Political Logic of the Non-Profit Industrial Complex"; Gilmore, "In the Shadow of the Shadow State"; Rodriguez, "The Political Logic of the Non-Profit Industrial Complex.

39. Rodriguez, "The Political Logic of the Non-Profit Industrial Complex," 21.

40. Baldridge, "On Educational Advocacy and Cultural Work." Jal Mehta and Sarah Fine, *In Search of Deeper Learning: The Quest to Remake the American High School* (Harvard University Press, 2019).

41. Georgia Hall, Jan Gallagher Hall, and Elizabeth Starr, eds., *The Heartbeat of the Youth Development Field: Professional Journeys of Growth, Connection, and Transformation* (IAP, 2022).

42. Afterschool Alliance, "America after 3pm 2020 National Report."

43. Baldridge, "On Educational Advocacy and Cultural Work."

44. Deepa Sriya Vasudevan, "'Because We Care': Youth Worker Identity and Persistence in Precarious Work," PhD diss. (Harvard University, 2019); Em K. Ma-

loney, "The Influence of Occupational Identity on Emotional Experience," *American Behavioral Scientist* 67, no. 1 (2023): 100–124; Lisa Hoogstra, Barbara Schneider, and Fengbin Chang, "Young Adult Occupational Identity and Well-Being: Influences of Postsecondary Education and Work," *Sociological Focus* 34, no. 4 (2001): 337–356.

45. Vasudevan, "'Because We Care.'"

46. Vasudevan, "'Because We Care.'"

47. Jaffe, *Work Won't Love You Back.*

48. Jaffe, *Work Won't Love You Back.*

49. Baldridge, "The Youthwork Paradox."

50. Bianca J. Baldridge, "Relocating the Deficit: Reimagining Black Youth in Neoliberal Times," *American Educational Research Journal* 51, no. 3 (2014): 440–472.

51. Baldridge, "The Youthwork Paradox"; Victor Ray, "A Theory of Racialized Organizations," *American Sociological Review* 84, no. 1 (2019): 26–53.

52. Bianca J. Baldridge, Marc Lamont Hill, and James Earl Davis, "New Possibilities: (Re)engaging Black Male Youth Within Community-Based Educational Spaces," in *The Education of Black Males in a "Post-Racial" World*, ed. Anthony L. Brown (London: Routledge, 2013), 201. Susan T. Gooden, Lindsey L. Evans, Michael L. Perkins, Caper Gooden, and Yali Pang. "Examining Youth Outcomes of African American–Led Nonprofits," *Nonprofit and Voluntary Sector Quarterly* 47, no. 4 suppl (2018): 34S–54S.

53. Baldridge, "The Youthwork Paradox."

54. Baldridge, "The Youthwork Paradox."

55. Baldridge, "The Youthwork Paradox"; Katie Johnston-Goodstar, "Decolonizing Youth Development: Re-imagining Youthwork for Indigenous Youth Futures," *AlterNative: An International Journal of Indigenous Peoples* 16, no. 4 (November 2020): 378–386.

56. Bronwyn Bevan, Deborah Maroney, and Megan Brown, "The Power of Us: How Better Understanding the Youth Fields Workforce Can Help Communities Thrive," *Afterschool Matters*, no. 37 (2023).

57. Laura M. Kennedy, Lindsay McHolme, and Carrie Symons, "Refugee-Background Youth Workers as Agents of Social Change: Building Bridging Relationships One Story at a Time," *Journal of Higher Education Outreach and Engagement* 28, no. 1 (2024).

58. Joseph L. Mahoney, Maria E. Parente, and Edward F. Zigler, "Afterschool Programs in America: Origins, Growth, Popularity, and Politics," *Journal of Youth Development* 4, no. 3 (2009): 23–42.

59. Halpern, "A Different Kind of Child Development Institution"; Rachel Klepper, "Staying Late: Afterschool Programs for Children in New York City, 1930–1965," PhD diss. (Columbia University, 2024).

60. Klepper, "Staying Late"; Michael Hines, "'They Do Not Know How to Play': Reformers' Expectations and Children's Realities on the First Progressive Playgrounds of Chicago," *Journal of the History of Childhood and Youth* 10, no. 2 (2017): 206–227.

61. Halpern, "A Different Kind of Child Development Institution"; Klepper, "Staying Late."

62. Klepper, "Staying Late."

63. Shawn Ginwright, *Black Youth Rising: Activism and Radical Healing in Urban America* (Teachers College Press, 2010).

64. Soo Ah Kwon, *Uncivil Youth: Race, Activism, and Affirmative Governmentality* (Duke University Press, 2013).

65. Carnegie Foundation Report, "A Matter of Time: Risk and Opportunity in the Non-School Hours," Carnegie Corporation of New York, December 1992, https://www.carnegie.org/publications/a-matter-of-time-risk-and-opportunity-in-the-non school-hours/.

66. Kwon, *Uncivil Youth.*

67. Michelle Alexander, "The New Jim Crow," *Ohio State Journal of Criminal Law* 9, no. 1 (2011); Mark Warren, *Willful Defiance: The Movement to Dismantle the School-to-Prison Pipeline* (Oxford University Press, 2022).

68. Shawn Ginwright and Julio Cammarota, "Youth Activism in the Urban Community: Learning Critical Civic Praxis Within Community Organizations," *International Journal of Qualitative Studies in Education* 20, no. 6 (October 2007): 693–710; Ranita Ray, *The Making of a Teenage Service Class: Poverty and Mobility in an American City* (University of California Press, 2017); Damien Sojoyner, *Joy and Pain: A Story of Black Liberation in Five Albums* (University of California Press, 2022).

69. Victor Rios, "The Racial Politics of Youth Crime," in *Behind Bars: Latino/as and Prison in the United States*, ed. Suzanne Oboler (New York: Palgrave Macmillan, 2009), 97–111.

70. Aisha Harris, "The Central Park Five: We Were Just Baby Boys," *New York Times*, May 30, 2019, https://www.nytimes.com/2019/05/30/arts/television/when-they -see-us.html.

71. Kwon, *Uncivil Youth*, 9.

72. Ray, *The Making of a Teenage Service Class.*

73. Bianca J. Baldridge, "Relocating the Deficit: Reimagining Black Youth in Neoliberal Times," *American Educational Research Journal* 51, no. 3 (June 2014): 440–472.

74. *The Principal*, directed by Christopher Cain (ML Delphi Premier Productions, 1987); *Dangerous Minds*, directed by John N. Smith (Hollywood Pictures, Don Simpson/Jerry Bruckheimer Films, 1995); *Freedom Writers*, directed by Richard LaGravenese (MTV Films, Jersey Films, 2S Films, 2007).

75. Bianca J. Baldridge, " 'It's Like This Myth of the Supernegro': Resisting Narratives of Damage and Struggle in the Neoliberal Educational Policy Context," *Race Ethnicity and Education* 20, no. 6 (2017): 784; *Coach Carter*, directed by Thomas Carter (MTV Films, Tollin/Robbins Productions, 2005); *Lean on Me*, directed by John G. Avildsen (Norman Twain Productions, 1989).

76. Michael Singh, *Good Boys, Bad Hombres: The Racial Politics of Mentoring Latino Boys in Schools* (University of Minnesota Press, 2024)

77. Baldridge, "Relocating the Deficit;" Singh, *Good Boys, Bad Hombres.*

78. Vandell, "Afterschool Program Quality and Student Outcomes."

79. Halpern, "A Different Kind of Child Development Institution." Klepper, "Staying Late."

80. Aishia Brown, Corliss Outley, and Harrison Pinckney, "Examining the Use of Leisure for the Sociopolitical Development of Black Youth in Out-of-School Time Programs," *Leisure Sciences* 40, no. 7 (January 2018): 686–696.

81. Gloria Ladson-Billings, "Toward a Theory of Culturally Relevant Pedagogy," *American Educational Research Journal* 32, no. 3 (1995): 465–491.

82. Michael Dumas, "Against the Dark: Antiblackness in Education Policy and Discourse," *Theory into Practice* 55, no. 1 (2016): 11–19; Jarvis Givens, *Fugitive Pedagogy: Carter G. Woodson and the Art of Black Teaching* (Harvard University Press, 2021).

83. Jarvis R. Givens, *School Clothes: A Collective Memoir of Black Student Witness* (Beacon Press, 2023); Gholnecsar E. Muhammad, "The Literacy Development and Practices Within African American Literary Societies," *Black History Bulletin* 75, no. 1 (2012): 6–13.

84. Maisha T. Winn, *Futuring Black Lives: Independent Black Institutions and the Literary Imaginary* (Vanderbilt University Press, 2025).

85. Givens, *Fugitive Pedagogy*; Jarvis R. Givens, "Literate Slave, Fugitive Slave: A Note on the Ethical Dilemma of Black Education," in *The Future Is Black*, ed. Carl A. Grant, Ashley N. Woodson, and Michael J. Dumas, 22–30 (Routledge, 2020); James Anderson, *The Education of Blacks in the South* (University of North Carolina Press, 1988).

86. Fikile Nxumalo and kihana miraya ross, "Envisioning Black Space in Environmental Education for Young Children," *Race Ethnicity and Education* 22, no. 4 (2019): 502–524.

87. Gloria Ladson-Billings, "From the Achievement Gap to the Education Debt: Understanding Achievement in US Schools," *Educational Researcher* 35, no. 7 (2006): 3–12; Bettina L. Love, *We Want to Do More Than Survive: Abolitionist Teaching and the Pursuit of Educational Freedom* (Beacon Press, 2019); Dumas, "Against the Dark"; Michael Dumas and kihana ross, " 'Be Real Black for Me': Imagining BlackCrit in Education," *Urban Education* 51, no. 4 (2016): 415–442.

88. James D. Anderson, *The Education of Blacks in the South, 1860–1935* (University of North Carolina Press, 1988); Gloria Ladson-Billings, "Landing on the Wrong Note: The Price We Paid for Brown," *Educational Researcher* 33, no. 7 (2004): 3–13; Michael Fultz, "The Displacement of Black Educators Post-Brown: An Overview and Analysis," *History of Education Quarterly* 44, no. 1 (2004): 11–45; Vanessa Siddle Walker, *Their Highest Potential: An African American School Community in the Segregated South* (University of North Carolina Press, 2000).

89. Givens, *Fugitive Pedagogy*; Evelyn Brooks Higginbotham, *Righteous Discontent: The Women's Movement in the Black Baptist Church, 1880–1920* (Harvard University Press, 1994). Maisha Winn, "Futures Matter: Creating Just Futures in This Age of Hyper-Incarceration," *Peabody Journal of Education* 96, no. 5 (2021): 527–529.

90. Givens, *Fugitive Pedagogy*, 89.

91. Noliwe M. Rooks, *A Passionate Mind in Relentless Pursuit: The Vision of Mary McLeod Bethune* (Penguin Press, 2024).

92. Rooks, *A Passionate Mind in Relentless Pursuit*.

93. Anderson, *The Education of Blacks in the South*; Givens, *Fugitive Pedagogy*; Baldridge, *Reclaiming Community*; Charles Payne, *I've Got the Light of Freedom: The Organizing Tradition and the Mississippi Freedom Struggle* (University of California Press, 2007).

94. Ginwright, *Black Youth Rising*.

95. Daniel Perlstein, "Freedom, Liberation, Accommodation: Politics and Pedagogy in SNCC and the Black Panther Party," in *Teach Freedom: Education for Liberation in the African-American Tradition*, ed. Charles M. Payne and Carol Sills Strickland (Teachers College Press, 2008), 77.

96. Perlstein, "Freedom, Liberation, Accommodation."

97. Joy Ann Williams. "Community Control with a Black Nationalist Twist: The Black Panther Party's Educational Programs," *Counterpoints* 237 (2005): 137–157.

98. Payne, *I've Got the Light of Freedom*; Russell Rickford, *We Are an African People: Independent Education, Black Power, and the Radical Imagination* (Oxford University Press, 2016).

99. Karida L. Brown, *The Battle for the Black Mind* (Legacy Lit, 2025).

100. Judith Butler, *Precarious Life: The Powers of Mourning and Violence* (Verso Books, 2004).

101. Butler, *Precarious Life*.

102. Arne L. Kalleberg, "Precarious Work, Insecure Workers: Employment Relations In Transition," *American Sociological Review* 74, no. 1 (2009): 1–22; Zembylas, "The Ethics and Politics of Precarity."

103. Baldridge, "'It's Like This Myth of the Supernegro.'"

104. Sojoyner, *Joy and Pain*.

105. Sojoyner, *Joy and Pain*; Bill Fletcher Jr., "Whither the Black Worker?" *Labor Studies Journal* 47, no. 4 (2022): 488–492.

106. Sojoyner, *Joy and Pain*; Sean Hill II, "Precarity in the Era of #BlackLivesMatter," *WSQ: Women's Studies Quarterly* 45, no. 3 (2017): 94–109.

107. Givens, *Fugitive Pedagogy*; Sojoyner, *Joy and Pain*.

108. Django Paris, "Culturally Sustaining Pedagogy: A Needed Change in Stance, Terminology, and Practice," *Educational Researcher* 41, no. 3 (April 2012): 93–97.

109. Pleasant Ridge is a pseudonym as are all sites mentioned.

110. Kevin Quashie, *Black Aliveness, or of a Poetics of Being* (Duke University Press, 2021); Elizabeth Alexander, *The Black Interior: Essays* (Graywolf Press, 2004).

111. All names are pseudonyms to protect the identities of participants. Descriptions of participants, their specific roles and places of work and elements of their backgrounds have been disguised.

112. Robin D. G. Kelley, *Freedom Dreams: The Black Radical Imagination* (Beacon Press, 2022).

113. Gloria Ladson-Billings, "Toward a Theory of Culturally Relevant Pedagogy 2.0."

114. Givens, *Fugitive Pedagogy*; Harney Stefano and Fred Moten, *The Undercommons: Fugitive Planning and Black Study* (Minor Compositions, 2013).

115. Quashie, *Black Aliveness*; Christina Sharpe, "Black Studies: In the Wake," *The Black Scholar* 44, no. 2 (October 2014): 59–69; Sylvia Wynter, "A Black Studies Manifest," *Forum N.H.I.: Knowledge for the 21st Century* 1, no. 1 (1994): 3–11; Saidiya V. Hartman and Frank B. Wilderson, "The Position of the Unthought," *Qui Parle* 13, no. 2 (Spring/Summer 2003): 183–201.

116. Sojoyner, *Joy and Pain*.

117. bell hooks, *Teaching to Transgress: Education as the Practice of Freedom* (Routledge, 1994).

118. hooks, *Teaching to Transgress*.

Chapter 1

1. Bronwyn Bevan, Deborah Moroney, and Megan Brown, "The Power of Us: How Better Understanding the Youth Fields Workforce Can Help Communities Thrive," *Afterschool Matters* 37 (Fall 2023): 1–2.

2. Bianca J. Baldridge, "On Educational Advocacy and Cultural Work: Situating Community-Based Youth Work[ers] in Broader Educational Discourse," *Teachers College Record* 120, no. 2 (2018): 1–28.

3. Deepa Sriya Vasudevan, " 'Because We Care': Youth Worker Identity and Persistence in Precarious Work," PhD diss. (Harvard University, 2019).

4. Carnegie Foundation Report, "A Matter of Time: Risk and Opportunity in the Non-School Hours," Carnegie Corporation of New York, December 1992, https://www.carnegie.org/publications/a-matter-of-time-risk-and-opportunity-in-the-non school-hours/.

5. Soo Ah Kwon, *Uncivil Youth: Race, Activism, and Affirmative Governmentality* (Duke University Press, 2013).

6. Kwon, *Uncivil Youth*.

7. Jennifer R. Wolch, *The Shadow State: Government and Voluntary Sector in Transition* (The Free Press, 1990).

8. Baldridge, "On Educational Advocacy"; Milbrey W. McLaughlin, *You Can't Be What You Can't See: The Power of Opportunity to Change Young Lives* (Harvard Education Press, 2018); Barbara J. Hirsch, Nancy L. Deutsch, and David L. DuBois, *After-School Centers and Youth Development: Case Studies of Success and Failure* (Cambridge University Press, 2011).

9. Ruth W. Gilmore, "In the Shadow of the Shadow State," in INCITE! Women of Color Against Violence, ed. *The Revolution Will Not Be Funded*.

10. Gilmore, "In the Shadow of the Shadow State"; Amy Brown, *A Good Investment?: Philanthropy and the Marketing of Race in an Urban Public School* (University of Minnesota Press, 2015); Bianca J. Baldridge, "Relocating the Deficit: Reimagining Black Youth in Neoliberal Times," *American Educational Research Journal* 51, no. 3 (2014): 440–472.

11. Bianca J. Baldridge, "The Youthwork Paradox: A Case for Studying the Com-

plexity of Community-Based Youth Work in Education Research," *Educational Researcher* 49, no. 8 (2020): 618–625.

12. Arlene E. Edwards, "Community Mothering: The Relationship Between Mothering and the Community Work of Black Women," *Journal of the Motherhood Initiative for Research and Community Involvement* 2, no. 2 (2000), https://jarm.journals.yorku.ca/index.php/jarm/article/view/2141; Patricia Hill Collins, *Black Feminist Thought : Knowledge, Consciousness, and the Politics of Empowerment* (Unwin Hyman, 1990); Zakiya Luna, " 'Other Mother' of a Generation: On bell hooks and Living Black Feminism," *Ms. Magazine*, December 23, 2021, https://msmagazine.com/2021/12/23/other-mother-of-a-generation-on-bell-hooks-and-living-black-feminism/.

13. Shantá R. Robinson, "Homeless Youth of Color and the Shaping of Aspirations: The (Re)productive Role of Institutions," *Urban Education* 57, no. 8 (2022): 1299–1328.

14. Kathleen M. Millar, "Toward a Critical Politics of Precarity," *Sociology Compass* 11, no. 6 (2017).

15. Judith Butler, *Precarious Life: The Powers of Mourning and Violence* (Verso Books, 2004).

16. Pierre Bourdieu, *Acts of Resistance: Against the Tyranny of the Market* (The New Press, 1998); Guy Standing, *The Precariat: The New Dangerous Class* (Bloomsbury Academic, 2011).

17. Tayyab Mahmud, "Precarious Existence and Capitalism: A Permanent State of Exception," *Southwestern Law Review* 44, no. 2 (2015): 699–726.

18. Arne L. Kalleberg, "Precarious Work, Insecure Workers: Employment Relations in Transition," *American Sociological Review* 74, no. 1 (2009): 1–22.; Enobong Hannah Branch and Caroline Hanley, "A Racial-Gender Lens on Precarious Nonstandard Employment," in *Precarious Work*, vol. 31, 183–213 (Emerald Publishing, 2017); Vasudevan, " 'Because We Care.' "

19. Catriona Mackenzie, Wendy Rogers, and Susan Dodds. "Introduction: What Is Vulnerability and Why Does It Matter for Moral Theory?," in *Vulnerability: New Essays in Ethics and Feminist Philosophy*, ed. Catriona Mackenzie, Wendy Rogers, and Susan Dodds, 1–29 (Oxford University Press, 2014); Michalinos Zembylas, "The Ethics and Politics of Precarity: Risks and Productive Possibilities of a Critical Pedagogy for Precarity," *Studies in Philosophy and Education* 38, no. 2 (2019): 95–111.

20. Bianca J. Baldridge et al., "Out-of-School Time Programs in the United States in an Era of Racial Reckoning: Insights on Equity from Practitioners, Scholars, Policy Influencers, and Young People," *Educational Researcher* 53, no. 4 (2024): 201–212; Dana Fusco, ed., *Advancing Youth Work: Current Trends, Critical Questions* (Jossey-Bass, 2012).

21. Vasudevan, " 'Because We Care,' " 1–2; Nicole Yohalem, Karen Pittman, and Sharon Lovick Edwards, *Strengthening the Youth Development/After-School Workforce: Lessons Learned and Implications for Funders* (The Forum for Youth Investment, 2010).

22. Adam S. Minsky, "40 Million Student Loan Borrowers Hit by Trio of Trump Orders—Here's Where Things Stand," *Forbes*, March 25, 2025, https://www.forbes.

com/sites/adamminsky/2025/03/25/40-million-student-loan-borrowers-hit-by-trio-of
-trump-orders---heres-where-things-stand/.

23. Vasudevan, "'Because We Care.'"

24. AmeriCorps, accessed March 27, 2025, https://americorps.gov/.

25. Vasudevan, "'Because We Care'"; Dana Fusco, "On Becoming an Academic Profession," in *Advancing Youth Work: Current Trends, Critical Questions*, ed. Dana Fusco (Routledge, 2012); Rebecka Bloomer, Aishia A. Brown, Andrew M. Winters and Anna Domiray, "'Trying to Be Everything Else': Examining the Challenges Experienced by Youth Development Workers," *Children and Youth Services Review* 129 (2021).

26. Erica Rosenfeld Halverson, Kailea Saplan, Sam Mejias, and Caitlin Martin, "What We Learn About Learning from Out-of-School Time Arts Education," *Review of Research in Education* 47, no. 1 (2023): 360–404.

27. Quentin Brummet, Emily K. Penner, Nikolas Pharris-Ciurej, and Sonya R. Porter, "After School: An Examination of the Career Paths and Earnings of Former Teachers," *Educational Evaluation and Policy Analysis* (2024), https://doi.org/10.3102/01623737241227906; Nick Juravich, *Para Power: How Paraprofessional Labor Changed Education* (University of Illinois Press, 2024); Johanna S. Quinn and Myra Marx Ferree, "Schools as Workplaces: Intersectional Regimes of Inequality," *Gender, Work & Organization* 26, no. 12 (2019): 1806–1815.

Chapter 2

1. All names of organizations are pseudonyms.

2. Enobong Hannah Branch and Caroline Hanley, "A Racial-Gender Lens on Precarious Nonstandard Employment," in *Precarious Work*, vol. 31, 183–213 (Emerald Publishing, 2017); Bill Fletcher Jr. "Whither the Black Worker?" *Labor Studies Journal* 47, no. 4 (2022): 488–492.

3. Adam McCann, "State Economies with the Most Racial Equality in 2024," WalletHub, June 11, 2024, https://wallethub.com/edu/state-economies-with-most-racial-equality/75810.

4. 2020 Census Data, [State Data] https://data.census.gov/profile/.

5. Charles Tilly, *Durable Inequality* (University of California Press, 1999); Amanda E. Lewis and John B. Diamond, *Despite the Best Intentions: How Racial Inequality Thrives in Good Schools* (Oxford University Press, 2015).

6. Derrick Bell, "Racial Realism," *Connecticut Law Review* 24 (1991): 363; Derrick Bell, *Faces at the Bottom of the Well: The Permanence of Racism* (New York: Basic Books, 1992).

7. Fletcher, "Whither the Black Worker?"

8. Fletcher, "Whither the Black Worker?"; Branch and Hanley, "A Racial-Gender Lens on Precarious Nonstandard Employment."

9. Eduardo Bonilla-Silva, *Racism Without Racists: Color-Blind Racism and the Persistence of Racial Inequality in America* (Rowman & Littlefield, 2021); Crystal M. Fleming, *How to Be Less Stupid About Race: On Racism, White Supremacy, and the Racial*

Divide (Beacon Press, 2018.); Toni Morrison, *Playing in the Dark: Whiteness and the Literary Imagination* (Vintage Books, 2004); See Toni Morrison, interview by Charlie Rose, January 19, 1998,

10. Fleming, *How to Be Less Stupid About Race.*

11. Ashley L. Smith-Purviance, "Masked Violence Against Black Women and Girls," *Feminist Studies* 47, no. 1 (2021): 175–200; Connie Wun, "Against Captivity: Black Girls and School Discipline Policies in the Afterlife of Slavery," *Educational Policy* 30, no. 1 (2016): 171–196; Michael J. Dumas, "'Losing an Arm': Schooling as a Site of Black Suffering," *Race, Ethnicity and Education* 17, no. 1 (2014): 1–29, https://doi.org/10.1080/13613324.2013.850412.

12. Eduardo Bonilla-Silva, "More Than Prejudice: Restatement, Reflections, and New Directions in Critical Race Theory," *Sociology of Race and Ethnicity* 1, no. 1 (2015): 73–87.

13. Dumas, "'Losing an Arm,'" 1–29.

14. Michael J. Dumas and kihana miraya ross, "'Be Real Black for Me': Imagining BlackCrit in Education," *Urban Education* 51, no. 4 (April 2016): 415–42, https://doi.org/10.1177/0042085916628611; Connie Wun, "Unaccounted Foundations: Black Girls, Anti-Black Racism, and Punishment in Schools," *Critical Sociology* 42, no. 4–5 (2016): 737–750; Smith-Purviance, "Masked Violence Against Black Women and Girls."

15. Baldridge, Bianca J., Nathan Beck, Juan Carlos Medina, and Marlo A. Reeves. "Toward a New Understanding of Community-Based Education: The Role of Community-Based Educational Spaces in Disrupting Inequality for Minoritized Youth," *Review of Research in Education* 41, no. 1 (2017): 381–402, https://doi.org/10.3102/0091732X16688622.

16. Justin A. Coles, "A BlackCrit Re/Imagining of Urban Schooling Social Education Through Black Youth Enactments of Black Storywork," *Urban Education* 58, no. 6 (2023): 1180–1209.; Shawn Ginwright, *Black Youth Rising: Activism and Radical Healing in Urban America* (Teachers College Press, 2009).

17. Baldridge et al., "Toward a New Understanding," 2017.

18. Antwi A. Akom, "Reexamining Resistance as Oppositional Behavior: The Nation of Islam and the Creation of a Black Achievement Ideology," *Sociology of Education* (2003): 305–325; Jarvis Givens, *Fugitive Pedagogy: Carter G. Woodson and the Art of Black Teaching* (Harvard University Press, 2021); Gloria Ladson-Billings, "Toward a Theory of Culturally Relevant Pedagogy," *American Educational Research Journal* 32, no. 3 (1995): 465–491; Maisha T. Winn and Nim Tottenham, "Looking Back to Look Forward: Leveraging Historical Models for Future-Oriented Caregiving," *Dædalus* 154, no. 1 (2025): 70–81.

19. Bianca J. Baldridge, "Relocating the Deficit: Reimagining Black Youth in Neoliberal Times," *American Educational Research Journal* 51, no. 3 (2014): 440–472; Soo Ah Kwon, *Uncivil Youth: Race, Activism, and Affirmative Governmentality* (Duke University Press, 2013).

20. Abbie Cohen, "Stuck Between a Rock and a Hard Place: An Investigation

into a Youth-Serving Community-Based Organization, Philanthropy, and Urban Public Schools," *Children & Schools* 46, no. 3 (2024): 183–193; Michael V. Singh, *Good Boys, Bad Hombres: The Racial Politics of Mentoring Latino Boys in Schools* (University of Minnesota Press, 2024).

21. Baldridge, "Relocating the Deficit"; Gregory Wilson, "An Invisible Impediment to Progress: Perceptions of Racialization in the Nonprofit Sector," *Nonprofit and Voluntary Sector Quarterly* (2024), http://dx.doi.org/10.1177/08997640241252650.

22. Patricia Hill Collins, *Black Feminist Thought: Knowledge, Consciousness, and the Politics of Empowerment* (Routledge, 2022); Tanya Golash-Boza, "A Critical and Comprehensive Sociological Theory of Race and Racism," *Sociology of Race and Ethnicity* 2, no. 2 (2016): 129–141; Mary Pattillo, *Black on the Block: The Politics of Race and Class in the City* (University of Chicago Press, 2010).

23. John C. Turner and S. Alexander Haslam, "Social Identity, Organizations, and Leadership," in *Groups at Work: Social Identity, Organizations, and Leadership*, ed. Marlene E. Turner (Psychology Press, 2014).

24. Bianca J. Baldridge, "The Youthwork Paradox: A Case for Studying the Complexity of Community-Based Youth Work in Education Research," *Educational Researcher* 49, no. 8 (2020): 618–625.

25. Erica O. Turner and Abigail J. Beneke, "'Softening School Resource Officers': The Extension of Police Presence in Schools in an Era of Black Lives Matter, School Shootings, and Rising Inequality," *Race Ethnicity and Education* 23, no. 2 (2020): 221–240; Wun, "Unaccounted Foundations"; Savannah Shange, "Progressive Dystopia: Multiracial Coalition and the Carceral State," PhD diss. (University of Pennsylvania, 2017).

26. Victor Ray, "A Theory of Racialized Organizations," *American Sociological Review* 84, no. 1 (2019): 26–53.

27. Susan T. Gooden, Lindsey L. Evans, Michael L. Perkins, Caper Gooden, and Yali Pang, "Examining Youth Outcomes of African American–Led Nonprofits," *Nonprofit and Voluntary Sector Quarterly* 47, no. suppl. va4 (2018): 34S–54S.

28. Karen Pittman, "Moving Beyond Where and When to the People and Practices That Impact Youth," *Journal of Youth Development* 13, no. 4 (2018): 1–4.

29. Dale Curry, Andrew J. Schneider-Muñoz, Frank Eckles, and Carol Stuart, "Assessing Youth Worker Competence: National Child and Youth Worker Certification," in *Advancing Youth Work: Current Trends, Critical Questions*, ed. Dana Fusco (Routledge, 2012); Nicole Yohalem and Karen Pittman, "Putting Youth Work on the Map," in *Forum for Youth Investment* (Forum for Youth Investment, 2006).

30. Fusco, *Advancing Youth Work*.

31. Lynne M. Borden, Michael Conn, Casey D. Mull, and Michele Wilkens, "The Youth Development Workforce: The People, the Profession, and the Possibilities," *Journal of Youth Development* 15, no. 1 (2020): 1–8.

32. Bianca J. Baldridge, "'It's Like This Myth of the Supernegro': Resisting Narratives of Damage and Struggle in the Neoliberal Educational Policy Context," *Race*

Ethnicity and Education 20, no. 6 (2017): 781–795; Kevin L. Clay, "'Despite the Odds': Unpacking the Politics of Black Resilience Neoliberalism," *American Educational Research Journal* 56, no. 1 (2019): 75–110.

33. Amanda E. Lewis and John B. Diamond, *Despite the Best Intentions: How Racial Inequality Thrives in Good Schools* (Oxford University Press, 2025); Savannah Shange, *Progressive Dystopia: Abolition, Antiblackness, and Schooling in San Francisco* (Duke University Press, 2020).

34. Ray, "A Theory of Racialized Organizations."

35. Nicole P. Marwell, "Privatizing the Welfare State: Nonprofit Community-Based Organizations as Political Actors," *American Sociological Review* 69, no. 2 (2004): 265–91.; Gregory D. Wilson, "An Invisible Impediment to Progress: Perceptions of Racialization in the Nonprofit Sector," *Nonprofit and Voluntary Sector Quarterly* 54, no. 9 (2024), https://doi.org/10.1177/08997640241252650; Ray, "A Theory of Racialized Organizations."

Chapter 3

1. Robin D. G. Kelley, *Freedom Dreams: The Black Radical Imagination*, 2nd ed. (Beacon Press, 2021).

2. Larry Buchanan, Quoctrung Bui, and Jugal K. Patel, "Black Lives Matter May Be the Largest Movement in US History," *New York Times*, July 3, 3030, https://www.nytimes.com/interactive/2020/07/03/us/george-floyd-protests-crowd-size.html.

3. Tracy Jan, Jena McGregor, and Meghan Hoyer, "Corporate America's $50 Billion Promise," *Washington Post*, August 23, 2021, https://www.washingtonpost.com/business/interactive/2021/george-floyd-corporate-america-racial-justice/.

4. Fikile Nxumalo and kihana miraya ross, "Envisioning Black Space in Environmental Education for Young Children," *Race Ethnicity and Education* 22, no. 4 (2019): 502–524.

5. Maisha T. Winn, *Futuring Black Lives: Independent Black Institutions and the Literary Imagination* (Vanderbilt University Press, 2025).

6. Bianca J. Baldridge, "On Educational Advocacy and Cultural Work: Situating Community-Based Youth Work[ers] in Broader Educational Discourse," *Teachers College Record* 120, no. 2 (2018): 1–28.

7. Kelley, *Freedom Dreams*.

8. Veronica Terriquez, "How Youth Organizing Groups Educate Toward a Multiracial Democracy in California," University of California, Los Angeles, March 2023, https://idea.gseis.ucla.edu/publications/educating-toward-a-multiracial-democracy; Ben Kirshner, *Youth Activism in an Era of Education Inequality* (New York University Press, 2015); Shawn Ginwright, *Black Youth Rising: Activism and Radical Healing in Urban America* (Teachers College Press, 2010).

9. Kelley, *Freedom Dreams*, 60.

10. Bianca J. Baldridge, "The Youthwork Paradox: A Case for Studying the Complexity of Community-Based Youth Work in Education Research," *Educational Researcher* 49, no. 8 (2020): 618–625.

11. Christina Sharpe, *In the Wake: On Blackness and Being* (Duke University Press, 2016).

12. Brian D. McKenzie, "Religious Social Networks, Indirect Mobilization, and African-American Political Participation," *Political Research Quarterly* 57, no. 4 (2004): 621–632; Mary Pattillo, "Church Culture as a Strategy of Action in the Black Community," *American Sociological Review* 63, no. 6 (1998): 767–784.

13. Patricia Hill Collins, "Black Women and Motherhood [1991]," in *Justice and Care: Essential Readings in Feminist Ethics*, ed. Virginia Held, 117–136 (Routledge, 1995).

14. Buchanan, Bui, and Patel, "Black Lives Matter"; Tage S. Rai, Jun Zi, and Peter DeScioli, "Coalitional Psychology on the Playground: Competition and Dominance Influence Children's Conflict Tactics," *Proceedings of the National Academy of Sciences* 118, no. 50 (2021): e2109860118, https://doi.org/10.1073/pnas.2109860118.

15. Khalil Gibran Muhammad, *The Condemnation of Blackness: Race, Crime, and the Making of Modern Urban America* (Harvard University Press, 2019).

16. Derron Wallace, "Safe Routes to School? Black Caribbean Youth Negotiating Police Surveillance in London and New York City," *Harvard Educational Review* 88, no. 3 (2018): 261–286.

17. Amnesty International, *USA: The World Is Watching: Mass Violations by U.S. Police of Black Lives Matter Protestors' Rights* (Amnesty International Ltd., August 4, 2020), https://www.amnesty.org/en/documents/amr51/2807/2020/en/.

18. Vargas, João Costa, and Joy James. "Refusing Blackness-as-Victimization: Trayvon Martin and the Black Cyborgs," in *Pursuing Trayvon Martin: Historical Contexts and Contemporary Manifestations of Racial Dynamics*, ed. George Yancy and Janine Jones (Lexington Press, 2012), 193–204, 193.

19. kihana miraya ross, "Anti-Blackness in Education and the Possibilities of Redress: Toward Educational Reparations," *Amerikastudien/American Studies* 66, no. 1 (2021): 229–233.; Christina Sharpe, *In the Wake: On Blackness and Being* (Duke University Press, 2016).

20. Chezare A. Warren, "From Morning to Mourning: A Meditation on Possibility in Black Education," *Equity & Excellence in Education* 54, no. 1 (2021): 92–102.

21. Deion S. Hawkins, "'After Philando, I Had to Take a Sick Day to Recover': Psychological Distress, Trauma, and Police Brutality in the Black Community," in *Emergent Health Communication Scholarship from and about African American, Latino/a/x, and American Indian/Alaskan Native Peoples*, ed. Angela Cooke-Jackson (Routledge, 2024), 10, https://doi.org/10.4324/9731032661285.

22. Uriel Serrano, David C. Turner III, Gabriel Regalado, and Alejandro Banuelos. "Towards Community-Rooted Research and Praxis: Reflections on the BSS Safety and Youth Justice Project," *Social Sciences* 11, no. 5 (2022): 195.

23. Bridget J. Goosby and Chelsea Heidbrink, "The Transgenerational Consequences of Discrimination on African-American Health Outcomes," *Sociology Compass* 7, no. 8 (2013): 630–643.

24. David R. Williams, "Stress and the Mental Health of Populations of Color:

Advancing Our Understanding of Race-Related Stressors," *Journal of Health and Social Behavior* 59, no. 4 (2018): 466–485.

25. Ben Kirshner and Shawn Ginwright, "Youth Organizing as a Developmental Context for African American and Latino Adolescents," *Child Development Perspectives* 6, no. 3 (2012): 288–294; Roderick J. Watts, Nat Chioke Williams, and Robert J. Jagers, "Sociopolitical Development," *American Journal of Community Psychology* 31, no. 1/2 (2003): 185–194; Roderick J. Watts and Carlos P. Hipolito-Delgado. "Thinking Ourselves to Liberation?: Advancing Sociopolitical Action in Critical Consciousness," *The Urban Review* 47 (2015): 847–867.

26. Craig Martin Peck, *"Educate to Liberate:" The Black Panther Party and Political Education* (Stanford University Press, 2001).

27. Shawn Ginwright and Julio Cammarota, "New Terrain in Youth Development: The Promise of a Social Justice Approach," *Social Justice* 29, no. 4 (90 (2002): 82–95.

28. Daniel Perlstein, "Freedom, Liberation, Accommodation: Politics and Pedagogy in SNCC and the Black Panther Party," in *Teach Freedom: Education for Liberation in the African-American Tradition*, ed. Charles M. Payne and Carol Sills Strickland, 75–94 (New York: Teachers College Press, 2008).

29. Aldon D. Morris, *The Origins of the Civil Rights Movement* (Simon and Schuster, 1984); Perlstein, "Freedom, Liberation, Accommodation."

30. Gloria Ladson-Billings, "Culturally Relevant Pedagogy 2.0: a.k.a. The Remix," *Harvard Educational Review* 84, no. 1 (April 2014): 74–84, https://doi.org/10.17763/haer.84.1.p2rj131485484751.

31. David Gillborn, *White Lies: Racism, Education and Critical Race Theory* (Taylor & Francis, 2024); Rashawn Ray and Alexandra Gibbons. "Why Are States Banning Critical Race Theory?," Brookings Institute, November 2021, https://www.brookings.edu/articles/why-are-states-banning-critical-race-theory/.

32. Watts and Hipolito-Delgado, "Thinking Ourselves to Liberation?"

33. Kevin L. Clay, "'Despite the Odds': Unpacking the Politics of Black Resilience Neoliberalism," *American Educational Research Journal* 56, no. 1 (2019): 75–110.

34. Kirshner, *Youth Activism in an Era of Education Inequality*; Juan C. Medina, Bianca J. Baldridge, and Tanya Wiggins, "Critical Reflections on Tensions in Authentic Youth–Adult Partnerships," in *At Our Best: Building Youth-Adult Partnerships in Out-of-School Time Settings*, ed. Gretchen Brion-Meisels, Jessica Tseming Fei, and Deepa Sriya Vasudevan, 61–82 (Information Age Publishing, 2021); Nancy Lesko, "Denaturalizing Adolescence: The Politics of Contemporary Representations," *Youth & Society* 28, no. 2 (1996): 139–161, https://doi.org/10.1177/0044118X96028002001.

35. Kirshner, *Youth Activism in an Era of Education Inequality*, 12.

36. Ginwright and Cammarota, "New Terrain in Youth Development; Merle McGee, "Critical Youth Development," in *Changemakers! Practitioners Advance Equity and Access in Out-of-School Time Programs*, ed. Sara Hill and Femi Vance (Information Age Publishing, 2019), 93–108.

37. Jeffrey M. Duncan-Andrade and Ernest Morrell, "Youth Participatory Action

Research as Critical Pedagogy," *Counterpoints* 285 (2008): 105–131; Ginwright and Cammarota, "New Terrain in Youth Development"; McGee, "Critical Youth Development."

38. Bic Ngo and Stacey J. Lee, "Navigating Social Justice in the Current Historical Moment." *International Journal of Qualitative Studies in Education* 33, no. 2 (2020): 135–139.

39. Gloria Ladson-Billings. "I'm Here for the Hard Re-Set: Post Pandemic Pedagogy to Preserve Our Culture," *Equity & Excellence in Education* 5, no. 1 (2021): 68–78; Fernando M. Reimers, "Learning from a Pandemic: The Impact of COVID-19 on Education Around the World," in *Primary and Secondary Education During Covid-19: Disruptions to Educational Opportunity During a Pandemic,* ed. Fernando M. Reimers, 1–37 (Springer, 2022).

40. Bianca J. Baldridge and Alexandros Orphanides, "Are the Kids Alright? Youth Perspectives on Schooling, Learning, and Community, *Stanford University Public Scholarship Collaborative,* May 21, 2023, https://publicscholarshiptestonly.sites. stanford.edu/news/are-kids-alright-youth-perspectives-schooling-learning-and -community.

41. Juliana Kim, "The Missing Hours: 7 Students on Losing a Year of After-School Activities," *New York Times,* March 14, 2021, https://www.nytimes.com/2021/ 03/14/us/nyc-after-school-activities-reopening.html.

42. World Health Organization Data, "WHO COVID-19 Dashboard," accessed March 2025, https://data.who.int/dashboards/covid19/deaths.

43. David Steingart, "The Importance of Prioritizing Emotional Wellness over Academic Achievement," National Alliance on Mental Illness, December 12, 2022, https://www.nami.org/bipolar-and-related-disorders/the-importance-of-prioritizing -emotional-wellness-over-academic-achievement/; Laura Hamilton and Betheny Gross, "How Has the Pandemic Affected Students' Social-Emotional Well-Being? A Review of the Evidence to Date," Center on Reinventing Public Education, August 2021, https://eric.ed.gov/?id=ED614131.

44. Kirshner, *Youth Activism in an Era of Education Inequality*; Shawn Ginwright and Julio Cammarota, "Youth Activism in the Urban Community: Learning Critical Civic Praxis Within Community Organizations," *International Journal of Qualitative Studies in Education* 20, no. 6 (October 2007): 693–710; David C. Turner, "The (Good) Trouble with Black Boys: Organizing with Black Boys and Young Men in George Floyd's America," *Theory into Practice* 60, no. 4 (2021): 422–433.

45. Kirshner, *Youth Activism in an Era of Education Inequality*; Terriquez, "Training Young Activists."

46. Roderick L. Carey, Thomas Akiva, Haya Abdellatif, and Kendell A. Daughtry, "'And School Won't Teach Me That!' Urban Youth Activism Programs as Transformative Sites for Critical Adolescent Learning," *Journal of Youth Studies* 24, no. 7 (2021): 941–960; Kirshner and Ginwright, "Youth Organizing," 290.

47. Leah M. Watson, "The Anti- 'Critical Race Theory' Campaign: Classroom Censorship and Racial Backlash by Another Name," *Harvard Civil Rights-Civil Liberties*

Law Review 58 (2023): 487–549; Sean Cahill and Matthew Pettus, *Trump-Pence Administration Policies Undermine LGBTQ Health Equity* (The Fenway Institute, 2020), https:// fenwayhealth.org/wp-content/uploads/TFIP-37_Policy-Brief-Cover-Trump-Biden -LGTQIA-equality-HIV-health-and-racial-justice-Full-Brief.pdf; Gillborn, *White Lies*.

48. John B. Diamond, "Race and White Supremacy in the Sociology of Education: Shifting the Intellectual Gaze," in *Education in a New Society: Renewing the Sociology of Education*, ed. Jal Mehta and Scott Davies, 345–362 (University of Chicago Press, 2018).

49. Watts, Williams, and Jagers, "Sociopolitical Development"; Watts and Hipolito-Delgado, "Thinking Ourselves to Liberation?"

50. Charles M. Payne, *I've Got the Light of Freedom: The Organizing Tradition and the Mississippi Freedom Struggle* (University of California Press, 2007).

51. Ladson-Billings, "Culturally Relevant Pedagogy 2.0"; Ginwright, *Black Youth Rising*.

52. Gregory Wilson, "Towards a Racialized Nonprofit Industrial Complex," *Academy of Management Proceedings* 2024, no. 1 (2024): article 17065, https://doi.org/10 .5465/AMPROC.2024.17065; Ruth Wilson Gilmore, "In the Shadow of the Shadow State," in *The Revolution Will Not Be Funded: Beyond the Non-Profit Industrial Complex*, ed. INCITE! Women of Color Against Violence, 41–52 (Duke University Press, 2017), https://doi.org/10.1515/9780822373001-005; Dylan Rodríguez, "The Political Logic of the Non-Profit Industrial Complex," In *The Revolution Will Not Be Funded*, 21–40, https://doi.org/10.1515/9780822373001-004; Kirshner, *Youth Activism*; Soo Ah Kwon, *Uncivil Youth: Race, Activism, and Affirmative Governmentality* (Duke University Press, 2013), https://doi.org/10.1215/9780822399094.

53. Kwon, *Uncivil Youth*.

54. Bianca J. Baldridge, *Reclaiming Community: Race and the Uncertain Future of Youth Work* (Stanford University Press, 2020); Kwon, *Uncivil Youth*.

55. Abbie Cohen, "Stuck Between a Rock and a Hard Place: An Investigation into a Youth-Serving Community-Based Organization, Philanthropy, and Urban Public Schools," *Children & Schools*, 46, no. 3 (2024): 183–193; Robin D. G. Kelley, "Racial Capitalism: An Unfinished History," in *The South African Tradition of Racial Capitalism*, ed. Marcel Paret and Zachary Levenson, 160–166 (Routledge, 2024); Jodi Melamed, "Racial Capitalism," *Critical Ethnic Studies* 1, no. 1 (2015): 76–85.

56. Robert L. Allen, *Black Awakening in Capitalist America: An Analytic History* (Anchor Books, 1969).

57. Rodriguez, "The Political Logic"; Gilmore, "In the Shadow."

58. Bianca J. Baldridge, "Relocating the Deficit: Reimagining Black Youth in Neoliberal Times," *American Educational Research Journal* 51, no. 3 (2014): 440–472.

59. Pew Research Center, "Support for the Black Lives Matter Movement Has Dropped Considerably from Its Peak in 2020," Pew Research Center's Social & Demographic Trends, June 14, 2023, https://www.pewresearch.org/social-trends/2023/ 06/14/support-for-the-black-lives-matter-movement-has-dropped-considerably-from -its-peak-in-2020/.

60. Enobong Hannah Branch and Caroline Hanley, "A Racial-Gender Lens on Precarious Nonstandard Employment," in *Precarious Work*, vol. 31, 183–213 (Emerald Publishing, 2017).

61. Bianca J. Baldridge, "'It's Like This Myth of the Supernegro': Resisting Narratives of Damage and Struggle in the Neoliberal Educational Policy Context," *Race Ethnicity and Education* 20, no. 6 (2017): 781–795.

62. Kelley, *Freedom Dreams*.

63. Caitlynn Peetz, "Schools Take a $3 Billion Hit from the Culture Wars. Here's How It Breaks Down," *Education Week*, October 30, 2024. https://www.edweek.org/leadership/schools-take-a-3-billion-hit-from-the-culture-wars-heres-how-it-breaks-down/2024/10.

64. Gillborn, *White Lies*.

65. Uriel Serrano, David C. Turner III, Gabriel Regalado, and Alejandro Banuelos, "Towards Community Rooted Research and Praxis: Reflections on the BSS Safety and Youth Justice Project," *Social Sciences* 11, no. 5 (2022): 195; Terriquez, "Training Young Activists"; Miguel N. Abad, "'Stop the Monster, Build the Marvel': Movement Vulnerability, Youth Organizing and Abolitionist Praxis in Late Liberal San Francisco," *Journal of Youth Studies* 27, no. 5 (2024): 741–757.

66. Baldridge, *Reclaiming Community*; Ginwright, *Black Youth Rising*; Nancy L. Deutsch and Barton J. Hirsch, "A Place to Call Home: Youth Organizations in the Lives of Inner-City Adolescents," in *Understanding Early Adolescent Self and Identity: Applications and Interventions*, ed. Thomas M. Brinthaupt and Richard P. Lipka, 293–320 (State University of New York Press, 2012), https://doi.org/10.1515/9780791488751-011.

67. Shawn Ginwright, *Hope and Healing in Urban Education: How Urban Activists and Teachers Are Reclaiming Matters of the Heart* (Routledge, 2015).

68. Manuel Luis Espinoz and Shirin Vossoughi, "Perceiving Learning Anew: Social Interaction, Dignity, and Educational Rights," *Harvard Educational Review* 84, no. 3 (2014): 285–313; Kelley, *Freedom Dreams*.

69. Tyrone C. Howard, "Culturally Relevant Teaching: A Pivot for Pedagogical Transformation and Racial Reckoning," *The Educational Forum* 85, no. 4, (2021): 406–415.

70. Vargas and James, "Refusing Blackness-as-Victimization," 193.

71. Michael J., Dumas and kihana miraya ross, "'Be Real Black for Me': Imagining BlackCrit in Education," *Urban Education* 51, no. 4 (2016): 415–442, https://doi.org/10.1177/0042085916628611; Vargas and James, "Refusing Blackness-as-Victimization," 193; Moon-Kie Jung and João H. Costa Vargas, "Antiblackness of the Social and the Human," in *Antiblackness*, ed. Moon-Kie Jung and João H. Costa Vargas, 1–14 (Duke University Press, 2021).

72. Kelley, *Freedom Dreams*; Sharpe, *In the Wake*.

73. Saidiya Hartman, *Lose Your Mother: A Journey Along the Atlantic Slave Route* (Farrar, Straus and Giroux, 2008).

Chapter 4

1. Pedro A. Noguera, *The Trouble with Black Boys: . . . and Other Reflections on Race, Equity, and the Future of Public Education* (Wiley, 2009); Victor M. Rios, *Punished: Policing the Lives of Black and Latino Boys* (New York University Press, 2011); Forrest Stuart, *Ballad of the Bullet: Gangs, Drill Music, and the Power of Online Infamy* (Princeton University Press, 2020).

2. Prudence L. Carter, *Keepin' It Real: School Success Beyond Black and White* (Oxford University Press, 2005); Stuart, *Ballad of the Bullet.*

3. Eve Tuck and K. Wayne Yang, "R-Words: Refusing Research," in *Humanizing Research: Decolonizing Qualitative Inquiry with Youth and Communities*, ed. Django Paris and Maisha T. Winn, 223–247 (Sage, 2014).

4. Kevin Lawrence Henry Jr., "Feasting on Blackness: Educational Parasitism, Necropolicy, and Black Thought," *International Journal of Qualitative Studies in Education* (2023): 1–17.

5. Jarvis Givens, *Fugitive Pedagogy: Carter G. Woodson and the Art of Black Teaching* (Harvard University Press, 2021); Charles M. Payne, *I've Got the Light of Freedom: The Organizing Tradition and the Mississippi Freedom Struggle* (University of California Press, 2007); Karida L. Brown, *The Battle for the Black Mind* (Legacy Lit, 2025).

6. Rebecka Bloomer, Aishia A. Brown, Andrew M. Winters, and Anna Domiray, "'Trying to Be Everything Else': Examining the Challenges Experienced by Youth Development Workers," *Children and Youth Services Review* 129 (2021).

7. Gregory Wilson, "Towards a Racialized Nonprofit Industrial Complex," *Academy of Management Proceedings* 2024, no. 1 (2024): article 17065, https://doi.org/10.5465/AMPROC.2024.17065.

8. Christina Sharpe, *In the Wake: On Blackness and Being* (Duke University Press, 2016).

9. Kevin Quashie, *Black Aliveness, or of a Poetics of Being* (Duke University Press, 2021).

10. Merle McGee, "Critical Youth Development: Living and Learning at the Intersections of Life," in *Changemakers! Practitioners Advance Equity and Access in Out-of-School Time Programs*, ed. Sara Hill and Femi Vance (Information Age Publishing, Inc., 2019), 93.

11. Shawn Ginwright and Julio Cammarota, "New Terrain in Youth Development: The Promise of a Social Justice Approach," *Social Justice* 29, no. 4 (2002): 82–95.

12. Joi A. Spencer and Kerri Ullucci, *Anti-Blackness at School: Creating Affirming Educational Spaces for African American Students* (Teachers College Press, 2022); A. A. Akom, "Reexamining Resistance as Oppositional Behavior: The Nation of Islam and the Creation of a Black Achievement Ideology," *Sociology of Education* 76, no. 4 (October 2003): 305–325.

13. Shawn Ginwright, "Black Youth Activism and the Role of Critical Social Capital in Black Community Organizations," *American Behavioral Scientist* 51, no. 3 (2007): 403–418, https://doi.org/10.1177/0002764207306068.

14. Bianca J. Baldridge, "Negotiating Anti-Black Racism in 'Liberal' Contexts: The Experiences of Black Youth Workers in Community-Based Educational Spaces," *Race Ethnicity and Education* 23, no. 6 (2020): 747–766. Ginwright and Cammarota, "New Terrain in Youth Development."

15. Daniel Perlstein, "Freedom, Liberation, Accommodation: Politics and Pedagogy in SNCC and the Black Panther Party," in *Teach Freedom: Education for Liberation in the African-American Tradition*, ed. Charles M. Payne and Carol Sills Strickland, 75–94. (Teachers College Press, 2008).

16. Bianca J. Baldridge, *Reclaiming Community: Race and the Uncertain Future of Youth Work* (Stanford University Press, 2019); Barton J. Hirsch, Nancy L. Deutsch, and David L. DuBois, *After-School Centers and Youth Development: Case Studies of Success and Failure* (Cambridge University Press, 2011); Shawn Ginwright, *Black Youth Rising: Activism and Radical Healing in Urban America* (Teachers College Press, 2010).

17. Baldridge, *Reclaiming Community*.

18. Perlstein, "Freedom, Liberation, Accommodation."

19. Roderick J. Watts and Carlos P. Hipolito-Delgado, "Thinking Ourselves to Liberation?: Advancing Sociopolitical Action in Critical Consciousness," *The Urban Review* 47 (2015): 847–867.

20. Maisha T. Winn, *Futuring Black Lives: Independent Black Institutions and the Literary Imagination* (Vanderbilt University Press, 2025).

21. Gretchen Brion-Meisels, Jessica Tseming Fei, and Deepa Sriya Vasudevan, "Introduction," in *At Our Best: Building Youth-Adult Partnerships in Out-of-School Time Settings*, ed. Gretchen Brion-Meisels, Jessica Tseming Fei, and Deepa Sriya Vasudevan, 1–22 (Information Age Publishing, 2020); Ginwright, *Black Youth Rising*; Bianca J. Baldridge, Baldridge, N. Beck, J. C. Medina, and M. A. Reeves, "Toward a New Understanding of Community-Based Education: The Role of Community-Based Educational Spaces in Disrupting Inequality for Minoritized Youth," *Review of Research in Education* 41, no. 1 (2017): 381–402, https://doi.org/10.3102/0091732X166886 22.

22. Bianca J. Baldridge, "The Youthwork Paradox: A Case for Studying the Complexity of Community-Based Youth Work in Education Research," *Educational Researcher* 49, no. 8 (2020): 618–625.

23. Robert L. Allen, *Black Awakening in Capitalist America: An Analytic History* (Anchor Books, 1969); Claire Dunning, "No Strings Attached: Philanthropy, Race, and Donor Control from Black Power to Black Lives Matter," *Nonprofit and Voluntary Sector Quarterly* 52, no. 1 (2023): 29–49.

24. Bianca J. Baldridge, "Relocating the Deficit: Reimagining Black Youth in Neoliberal Times," *American Educational Research Journal* 51, no. 3 (2014): 440–472.

25. Eve Tuck, "Suspending Damage: A Letter to Communities," *Harvard Educational Review* 79, no. 3 (2009): 409–428.

26. Bianca J. Baldridge, "'It's Like This Myth of the Supernegro': Resisting Narratives of Damage and Struggle in the Neoliberal Educational Policy Context," *Race Ethnicity and Education* 20, no. 6 (2017): 781–795.

27. Gregory Wilson, "An Invisible Impediment to Progress: Perceptions of Racialization in the Nonprofit Sector," *Nonprofit and Voluntary Sector Quarterly* 54, no. 9 (2024), http://dx.doi.org/10.1177/08997640241252650.

28. Baldridge, "'It's Like This Myth of the Supernegro,'" 781–795.

29. Baldridge, "The Youthwork Paradox"; Baldridge, "Relocating the Deficit."

30. Bianca J. Baldridge, "On Educational Advocacy and Cultural Work: Situating Community-Based Youth Work[ers] in Broader Educational Discourse," *Teachers College Record* 120, no. 2 (2018): 1–28, https://doi.org/10.1177/016146811812000206.

31. Ruth Wilson Gilmore, "In the Shadow of the Shadow State," in *The Revolution Will Not Be Funded: Beyond the Non-Profit Industrial Complex*, ed. INCITE! Women of Color Against Violence, 41–52 (Duke University Press, 2017); Dylan Rodriguez, "The Political Logic of the Non-Profit Industrial Complex," in *The Revolution Will Not Be Funded: Beyond the Non-Profit Industrial Complex.*

32. Wilson, "An Invisible Impediment to Progress."

33. Rodriguez, "The Political Logic of the Non-Profit Industrial Complex"; Erica Kohl-Arenas, *The Self-Help Myth: How Philanthropy Fails to Alleviate Poverty* (University of California Press, 2016), http://www.jstor.org/stable/10.1525/j.ctt19632k8.

34. Allen, *Black Awakening*; Baldridge, "Relocating the Deficit."

35. Baldridge, *Reclaiming Community.*

36. Baldridge, "Relocating the Deficit"; Wilson, "Towards a Racialized Nonprofit Industrial Complex."

37. Baldridge, *Reclaiming Community.*

38. Baldridge, "Relocating the Deficit," 440–472.

39. Richard Valencia, *The Evolution of Deficit Thinking: Educational Thought and Practice* (Routledge, 2012); Baldridge, "Relocating the Deficit."

40. Baldridge, "Relocating the Deficit."

41. Baldridge, "Relocating the Deficit"; Wilson, "Towards a Racialized Nonprofit Industrial Complex."

42. Baldridge, "Relocating the Deficit."

43. Maxine McKinney de Royston, Tia C. Madkins, Jarvis R. Givens, and Na'ilah Suad Nasir, "'I'm a Teacher, I'm Gonna Always Protect You': Understanding Black Educators' Protection of Black Children," *American Educational Research Journal* 58, no. 1 (2021): 68–106.

44. Bronwyn Bevan, Deborah Maroney, and Megan Brown, "The Power of Us: How Better Understanding the Youth Fields Workforce Can Help Communities Thrive," *Afterschool Matters* 37 (2023): 1–4.

45. Enobong Hannah Branch and Caroline Hanley, "A Racial-Gender Lens on Precarious Nonstandard Employment," in *Precarious Work*, vol. 31, 183–213 (Emerald Publishing, 2017).

46. Kathleen Newman-Bremang, "Reclaiming Audre Lorde's Radical Self Care," *Unbothered*, Refinery 29, May 28, 2021, https://www.refinery29.com/en-us/2021/05/10493153/reclaiming-self-care-audre-lorde-black-women-community-care.

47. Angela Rose Black and Suz Switzer, "Mindfulness for the People: Radically

Re-Imagining the Mindfulness Movement," in *Beyond White Mindfulness: Critical Perspectives on Racism, Well-Being, and Liberation*, ed. Crystal M. Fleming, Veronica Y. Womack, and Jeffrey Proulx, 140–152 (Routledge, 2022).

48. Tricia Hersey, *Rest Is Resistance: A Manifesto* (Hachette, 2022).

49. Ashley R. Hall and Tiffany J. Bell, "The Pedagogy of Renewal: Black Women, Reclaiming Joy, and Self-Care as Praxis," *Journal of Communication Pedagogy* 6, no. 1 (2022): 3.

50. Moya Bailey, *Misogynoir Transformed: Black Women's Digital Resistance* (New York University Press, 2021).

51. Sarah Jaffe, *Work Won't Love You Back: How Devotion to Our Jobs Keeps Us Exploited, Exhausted, and Alone* (Bold Type Books, 2021).

52. Michael Heathfield and Dana Fusco, "Honoring and Supporting Youth Work Intellectuals," in *The Changing Landscape of Youth Work: Theory and Practice for an Evolving Field*, ed. Kristen M. Pozzoboni and Ben Kirshner, 127–146 (Information Age Publishing, 2016).

53. Rebecka Bloomer, Aishia A. Brown, Andrew M. Winters, and Anna Domiray. ""Trying to Be Everything Else': Examining the Challenges Experienced by Youth Development Workers," *Children and Youth Services Review* 129 (2021): 106–213.

54. Sean W. Barford and William J. Whelton, "Understanding Burnout in Child and Youth Care Workers," *Child & Youth Care Forum* 39 (2010): 271–287.

55. Ed Brockenbrough, " 'The Discipline Stop': Black Male Teachers and the Politics of Urban School Discipline," *Education and Urban Society* 47, no. 5 (2015): 499–522.

56. Deepa Sriya Vasudevan, " 'Because We Care': Youth Worker Identity and Persistence in Precarious Work," PhD diss. (Harvard University, 2019); Heathfield and Fusco, "Honoring and Supporting Youth Work Intellectuals."

57. Rosabeth Moss Kanter, *Work and Family in the United States: A Critical Review and Agenda for Research and Policy* (Russell Sage Foundation, 1977).

58. Heathfield and Fusco, "Honoring and Supporting Youth Work Intellectuals."

59. Bianca J. Baldridge, David K. DiGiacomo, Ben Kirshner, Silvia Mejias, and Deepa S. Vasudevan. "Out-of-School Time Programs in the United States in an Era of Racial Reckoning: Insights on Equity from Practitioners, Scholars, Policy Influencers, and Young People," *Educational Researcher* 53 no. 4 (2024): 201–212.

60. Vasudevan, " 'Because We Care' "; Baldridge, *Reclaiming Community*; Dana Fusco, "On Becoming an Academic Profession," in *Advancing Youth Work: Current Trends, Critical Questions*, ed. Dana Fusco (Routledge, 2012).

61. Baldridge, "On Educational Advocacy and Cultural Work."

62. Baldridge, "On Educational Advocacy and Cultural Work."

63. John B. Diamond and Louis M. Gomez, "Disrupting White Supremacy and Anti-Black Racism in Educational Organizations," *Educational Researcher* (2023), https://doi.org/10.3102/0013189X231161054.

64. Javon Johnson, "Black Joy in the Time of Ferguson," *QED: A Journal in GLBTQ Worldmaking* 2, no. 2 (2015): 177–183.

65. Erin Cech, *The Trouble with Passion: How Searching for Fulfillment at Work Fosters Inequality* (University of California Press, 2021).

66. Jaffe, *Work Won't Love You Back.*

67. Brion-Meisels, Fei, and Vasudevan, eds., *At Our Best*; Juan C. Medina, Tanya Wiggins, and Bianca J. Baldridge, "Critical Reflections on Tensions in Authentic Youth-Adult Partnerships," in *At Our Best*, 61.

68. Uriel Serrano, David C. Turner III, Gabriel Regalado, and Alejandro Banuelos, "Towards Community Rooted Research and Praxis: Reflections on the BSS Safety and Youth Justice Project," *Social Sciences* 11, no. 5 (2022): 195. Medina, Baldridge, and Wiggins, "Critical Reflections on Tensions in Authentic Youth-Adult Partnerships."

69. Ricardo B. Stanton-Salazar, "A Social Capital Framework for the Study of Institutional Agents and Their Role in the Empowerment of Low-Status Students and Youth," *Youth & Society* 43, no. 3 (2011): 1066–1109.

Chapter 5

1. Bianca J. Baldridge, "Relocating the Deficit: Reimagining Black Youth in Neoliberal Times," *American Educational Research Journal* 51, no. 3 (2014): 440–472.

2. Bianca J. Baldridge, "Lifting Up Youth Work," Spencer Foundation, July 27, 2020, https://www.spencer.org/news/lifting-up-youth-work.

3. Bianca J. Baldridge, N. Beck, J. C. Medina, and M. A. Reeves, "Toward a New Understanding of Community-Based Education: The Role of Community-Based Educational Spaces in Disrupting Inequality for Minoritized Youth." *Review of Research in Education* 41, no. 1 (2017): 381–402, https://doi.org/10.3102/0091732X16688 622.

4. Bianca J. Baldridge, *Reclaiming Community: Race and the Uncertain Future of Youth Work* (Stanford University Press, 2019); Milbrey McLaughlin, "Community Counts: How Youth Organizations Matter for Youth Development," The Public Education Network, 2000, http://www.publiceducation.org; Barton J. Hirsch et al., "After-School Programs for High School Students: An Evaluation of After School Matters," Technical Report, Wallace Foundation, 2011, https://wallacefoundation.org/report/after-school-programs-high-school-students-evaluation-after-school-matters-evaluation-after; Dana Fusco, ed., *Advancing Youth Work: Current Trends, Critical Questions* (Jossey-Bass, 2012); Martellis D. Avent and K. S. U. Jayaratne, "Factors Limiting Youth Participation in 4-H and Other Youth Development Programs in Underserved Communities," *The Journal of Extension* 55, no. 4 (2017): 14.

5. Baldridge, *Reclaiming Community.*

6. Victor Ray, "A Theory of Racialized Organizations," *American Sociological Review* 84, no. 1 (2019): 26–53.

7. Gregory Wilson, "An Invisible Impediment to Progress: Perceptions of Racialization in the Nonprofit Sector," *Nonprofit and Voluntary Sector Quarterly* 54, no. 9 (2024), http://dx.doi.org/10.1177/08997640241252650.

8. Sarah Jaffe, *Work Won't Love You Back: How Devotion to Our Jobs Keeps Us Exploited, Exhausted, and Alone* (Bold Type Books, 2021).

9. Damien Sojoyner, *Joy and Pain: A Story of Black Liberation in Five Albums* (University of California Press, 2022); Jarvis Givens, *Fugitive Pedagogy: Carter G. Woodson and the Art of Black Teaching* (Harvard University Press, 2021); Michael Fultz, "The Displacement of Black Educators Post-Brown: An Overview and Analysis," *History of Education Quarterly* 44, no. 1 (2004): 11–45; Gloria Ladson-Billings, "Landing on the Wrong Note: The Price We Paid for Brown," *Educational Researcher* 33, no.7 (2004): 3–13.

10. McLaughlin, "Community Counts"; Malcolm Woodland, "After-School Programs: A Resource for Young Black Males and Other Urban Youth," *Urban Education* 51, no. 7 (2016): 770–796.

11. Shawn Ginwright and Taj James, "From Assets to Agents of Change: Social Justice, Organizing, and Youth Development," in *Youth Participation: Improving Institutions and Communities*, ed. B. Kirshner, J. L. O'Donoghue, and M. McLaughlin, 27–46 (Jossey-Bass, 2002).

12. Carl A. Grant, Keffrelyn D. Brown, and Anthony L. Brown. *Black Intellectual Thought in Education: The Missing Traditions of Anna Julia Cooper, Carter G. Woodson, and Alain Leroy Locke* (Routledge, 2015).

13. Saidiya Hartman, *Lose Your Mother: A Journey Along the Atlantic Slave Route* (Macmillan, 2008).

14. Krystal L. Williams, Alethia Russell, and Kiara Summerville, "Centering Blackness: An Examination of Culturally-Affirming Pedagogy and Practices Enacted by HBCU Administrators and Faculty Members," *Innovative Higher Education* 46, no. 6 (2021): 733–757.

15. Maisha T. Winn, "Paradigm Shifting for Black Girls: Toward a Futures Matter Stance," in *Investing in the Educational Success of Black Women and Girls*, ed. Lori D. Patton, Venus Evans-Winters, Charlotte Jacob, 227–240 (Routledge, 2022).

16. Robin D. G. Kelley, *Freedom Dreams: The Black Radical Imagination*, 2nd ed. (Beacon Press, 2021).

17. Fabio Rojas, *From Black Power to Black Studies: How a Radical Social Movement Became an Academic Discipline* (JHU Press, 2010).

18. Womack, *Afrofuturism*.

19. Womack, *Afrofuturism*; Elizabeth Alexander. *The Black Interior: Essays* (Graywolf Press, 2004).

20. Maisha T. Winn, *Futuring Black Lives: Independent Black Institutions and the Literary Imaginary* (Vanderbilt University Press, 2025).

21. Maisha T. Winn, "Futures Matter: Creating Just Futures in This Age of Hyper-Incarceration," *Peabody Journal of Education* 96, no. 5 (2021): 527–539, 533.

22. Winn, "Futures Matter," 533.

23. kihana miraya ross, "Antiblackness in Education and the Possibility of Redress: Toward Educational Reparations," *American Studies* 66, no. 1 (2021): 229–233.

24. Baldridge, "Relocating the Deficit."

25. Awad Ibrahim and Shirley Steinberg, *Critical Youth Studies Reader* (Peter Lang, 2014).

26. Shawn Ginwright, *Hope and Healing in Urban Education: How Urban Activists and Teachers Are Reclaiming Matters of the Heart* (Routledge, 2015).

27. Michael Heathfield and Dana Fusco, "Honoring and Supporting Youth Work Individuals," in *The Changing Landscape of Youth Work: Theory and Practice for an Evolving Field*, ed. Kristen M. Pozzoboni and Ben Kirschner, 127–146 (Information Age Publishing, 2016); Baldridge, "Reclaiming Community."

28. Derrick Brooms, "Black Otherfathering in the Educational Experiences of Black Males in a Single-Sex Urban High School," *Teachers College Record* 119, no. 11 (2017): 1–46.

Conclusion

1. Enobong Hannah Branch and Caroline Hanley, *Work in Black and White: Striving for the American Dream* (Russell Sage Foundation, 2022); Arne L. Kalleberg, "Precarious Work, Insecure Workers: Employment Relations in Transition." *American Sociological Review* 74, no. 1 (2009): 1–22.

2. Bianca J. Baldridge, *Reclaiming Community: Race and the Uncertain Future of Youth Work* (Stanford University Press, 2019).

3. Jarvis Givens, *Fugitive Pedagogy: Carter G. Woodson and the Art of Black Teaching* (Harvard University Press, 2021).

4. Jarvis R. Givens, *School Clothes: A Collective Memoir of Black Student Witness* (Beacon Press, 2023); Khalil Gibran Muhammad, *The Condemnation of Blackness: Race, Crime, and the Making of Modern Urban America* (Harvard University Press, 2019); Karida L. Brown, *The Battle for the Black Mind* (Legacy Lit, 2025).

5. Deepa Sriya Vasudevan, " 'Because We Care': Youth Worker Identity and Persistence in Precarious Work," PhD diss. (Harvard University, 2019).

6. Baldridge, *Reclaiming Community.*

7. Damien Sojoyner, *Joy and Pain: A Story of Black Liberation in Five Albums* (University of California Press, 2022).

8. Sonja Teupen, "Material Poverty and Symbolic Precarity," in *Cultural Psychology: An Introduction*, 297–305 (Springer Fachmedien Wiesbaden, 2024).

9. At the federal level, there is funding for organizations designated as 21st Century Community Learning Centers (CCLCs), which began as part of the Clinton administration in the 1990s to support urban and rural youth academically and to prepare them for higher education and the workforce. Programs like GEAR Up and Upward Bound are part of these federal efforts. These monies are provided by the federal government and distributed to states. States then decide how schools and organizations will apply for or receive the funding. This is a small amount of money, but it does help many programs. Other federal programs that support supplementary education and after-school opportunities provide small amounts of money that programs use to provide snacks and meals to students during their programming time before or after school and during weekend or summer programs.

10. Tayyab Mahmud. "Precarious Existence and Capitalism: A Permanent State of Exception," *Southwestern University Law Review* 44 (2014): 699; Guy Standing, *The*

Precariat: The New Dangerous Class (Bloomsbury Academic, 2011); Lucas Van Milders, "Precarity/Coloniality," *Theory & Event* 24, no. 4 (2021): 1068–1089; Moon-Kie Jung. "The Enslaved, the Worker, and Du Bois's Black Reconstruction: Toward an Under-discipline of Antisociology," *Sociology of Race and Ethnicity* 5, no. 2 (2019): 157–168; Bill Fletcher Jr. "Whither the Black Worker?" *Labor Studies Journal* 47, no. 4 (2022): 488–492.

11. Saidiya Hartman, *Lose Your Mother: A Journey Along the Atlantic Slave Route* (Macmillan, 2008).

12. Jung, "The Enslaved, the Worker, and DuBois's Black Reconstruction."

13. Jung, "The Enslaved, the Worker, and DuBois's Black Reconstruction"; Hartman, *Lose Your Mother.*

14. Kalleberg, "Precarious Work, Insecure Workers"; Catriona MacKenzie, Wendy Rogers, and Susan Dodds. "Introduction: What Is Vulnerability and Why Does It Matter for Moral Theory?" in *Vulnerability: New Essays in Ethics and Feminist Philosophy*, ed. Catriona Mackenzie, Wendy Rogers, and Susan Dodds, 1–29 (Oxford University Press, 2014). Standing, *The Precariat*; Michalinos Zembylas, "The Ethics and Politics of Precarity: Risks and Productive Possibilities of a Critical Pedagogy for Precarity," *Studies in Philosophy and Education* 38, no. 2 (2019): 95–111.

15. Bianca J. Baldridge, "'It's Like This Myth of the Supernegro': Resisting Narratives of Damage and Struggle in the Neoliberal Educational Policy Context," *Race Ethnicity and Education* 20, no. 6 (2017): 781–795.

16. Michael J. Dumas, "'Losing an Arm': Schooling as a Site of Black Suffering," *Race, Ethnicity and Education* 17, no 1 (2014): 1–29, https://doi.org/10.1080/13613324 .2013.850412.

17. Fletcher, "Whither the Black Worker?"

18. Shawn Ginwright and Julio Cammarota, "New Terrain in Youth Development: The Promise of a Social Justice Approach," *Social Justice* 29, no. 4 (2002): 82–95.; Merle McGee, "Critical Youth Development: Living and Learning at the Intersections of Life," in *Changemakers! Practitioners Advance Equity and Access in Out-of-School Time Programs*, ed. Sara Hill and Femi Vance (Information Age Publishing, 2019).

19. Veronica Terriquez. "Training Young Activists: Grassroots Organizing and Youths' Civic and Political Trajectories," *Sociological Perspectives* 58, no. 2 (2015): 223–242; Uriel Serrano, May Lin, Jamileh Ebrahimi, Jose Orellana, Rosanai Paniagua, and Veronica Terriquez, "In Millennial Footsteps: California Social Movement Organizations for Generation Z," *Sociological Perspectives* (2021), https://doi.org/10.1177/07311214211010565; Mark R. Warren, Meredith Mira, and Thomas Nikundiwe, "Youth Organizing: From Youth Development to School Reform," *New Directions for Youth Development*, no. 117 (2008): 27–42.

20. Michael J. Dumas and kihana miraya ross, "'Be Real Black for Me': Imagining BlackCrit in Education," *Urban Education* 51, no. 4 (2016): 415–442. https://doi.org/10.1177/0042085916628611; Christina Sharpe, *In the Wake: On Blackness and Being* (Duke University Press, 2016).

21. João Costa Vargas and Joy James, "Refusing Blackness-As-Victimization: Trayvon Martin and the Black Cyborgs, in *Pursuing Trayvon Martin: Historical Contexts and Contemporary Manifestations of Racial Dynamics*, ed. Georgy Yancy and Janine Jones (Lexington Books, 2013), 193–204.

22. kihana miraya ross, "Call It What It Is: Anti-Blackness," *New York Times*, June 4, 2020.

23. Michael Dumas, "Against the Dark: Antiblackness in Education Policy and Discourse," *Theory into Practice* 55, no. 1 (2016): 11–19; Frantz Fanon, *The Wretched of the Earth*, trans. Richard Philcox (Grove Press, 2004). Originally published in 1961.

24. Givens, *Fugitive Pedagogy*.

25. ross, "Antiblackness in Education."

26. Jane Quinn, "Transforming Afterschool Programs into 'Engines of Development': A Policy Analysis of the Federal 21st Century Community Learning Centers," PhD diss. (City University of New York, 2022).

27. Afterschool Alliance, "America After 3pm 2020 National Report: Demand Grows, Opportunity Shrinks," *America after 3pm*, 2020, https://afterschoolalliance.org/documents/AA3PM-2020/AA3PM-National-Report.pdf.

28. Every Hour Counts, *Lighting the Path Forward: How Afterschool Intermediaries Have Supported Youth and Communities During the Pandemic*, 2023, https://drive.google.com/file/d/18oAVPNRqqYeWLnLG4MhG5x0PLOOlvZvQ/view.

29. Bronwyn Bevan, Deborah Moroney, and Megan Brown. "The Power of Us: How Better Understanding the Youth Fields Workforce Can Help Communities Thrive," *Afterschool Matters* 37 (2023): 1–3.

30. Tania de St Croix, *Grassroots Youth Work* (Policy Press, 2016).

31. Bevan, Maroney, and Brown, "The Power of Us Survey."

32. Jen Couch, "Together We Walk: The Importance of Relationship in Youth Work with Refugee Young People," in *The Sage Handbook of Youth Work Practice*, ed. Dana Fusco, Fin Cullen, Kathy Edwards, Pam Alldred, 213–225 (Sage, 2018); Vasudevan, *Because We Care*.

Appendix

1. John B. Diamond and Louis M. Gomez, "Disrupting White Supremacy and Anti-Black Racism in Educational Organizations," *Educational Researcher* (2023), https://doi.org/10.3102/0013189X231161054.

2. Tyrone C. Howard, "Culturally Relevant Teaching: A Pivot for Pedagogical Transformation and Racial Reckoning," *The Educational Forum* 85, no. 4, (2021): 406–415.

3. Michael J. Dumas and kihana miraya ross, " 'Be Real Black for Me': Imagining BlackCrit in Education," *Urban Education* 51, no. 4 (2016): 415–442, https://doi.org/10.1177/0042085916628611; Moon-Kie Jung, "The Enslaved, the Worker, and Du Bois's Black Reconstruction: Toward an Underdiscipline of Antisociology," *Sociology of Race and Ethnicity* 5, no. 2 (2019): 157–168; Damien Sojoyner, *Joy and Pain: A Story of Black Liberation in Five Albums* (University of California Press, 2022).

4. Lois Weis and Michelle Fine, "Critical Bifocality and Circuits of Privilege: Expanding Critical Ethnographic Theory and Design," *Harvard Educational Review* 82, no. 2 (2012): 173–201.

5. Soyini D. Madison, *Critical Ethnography: Method, Ethics, and Performance* (Sage, 2011).

6. Gloria Ladson Billings, *The Dreamkeepers: Successful Teachers of African American Children* (Wiley, 2022).

7. Michael Quinn Patton, "Sampling, Qualitative (Purposeful)," in *The Blackwell Encyclopedia of Sociology*, ed. George Ritzer (Blackwell, 2007).

8. The decision to include these two participants was based on their positions in the city and within the Pleasant Ridge School District, and as advocates for Black youth.

9. John L. Campbell, Charles Quincy, Jordan Osserman, and Ove K. Pedersen, "Coding In-Depth Semistructured Interviews: Problems of Unitization and Intercoder Reliability and Agreement," *Sociological Methods & Research* 42, no. 3 (2013): 294–320.

10. Bianca J. Baldridge, Daniele DiGiacomo, Ben Kirshner, Sam Mejias, and Deepa Vasudevan, "Out-of-School Time Programs in the United States in an Era of Racial Reckoning: Insights on Equity from Practitioners, Scholars, Policy Influencers, and Young People," *Educational Researcher* 53, no. 4 (2024): 201–212.

11. Annette Lareau, "Invisible Inequality: Social Class and Childrearing in Black Families and White Families," *American Sociological Review* 67, no. 5 (2002): 747–776.

12. Barney G. Glaser, "The Constant Comparative Method of Qualitative Analysis," *Social Problems* 12, no. 4 (1965): 436–445.

Bibliography

Abad, Miguel N. "'Stop the Monster, Build the Marvel': Movement Vulnerability, Youth Organizing and Abolitionist Praxis in Late Liberal San Francisco." *Journal of Youth Studies* 27, no. 5 (2024): 741–757.

Abdallah, Chahrazad, Sadhvi Dar, Joshua Kalemba, and Ali Mir. "Anti-Blackness in Management and Organization Studies: Challenging Racial Capitalism in Organizing and Knowledge Production." *Organization* 32, no. 2 (2025): 167–179.

Afterschool Alliance. "America After 3pm 2020 National Report: Demand Grows, Opportunity Shrinks." *America After 3pm*, 2020. https://afterschoolalliance.org/documents/AA3PM-2020/AA3PM-National-Report.pdf.

Akom, Antwi A. "Reexamining Resistance as Oppositional Behavior: The Nation of Islam and the Creation of a Black Achievement Ideology." *Sociology of Education* (2003): 305–325.

Alexander, Elizabeth. *The Black Interior: Essays.* Graywolf Press, 2004.

Alexander, Michelle. "The New Jim Crow." *Ohio State Journal of Criminal Law* 9, no. 1 (2011): 7.

Allen, Robert L. *Black Awakening in Capitalist America: An Analytic History.* Anchor Books, 1969.

Alter, Alexandra, and Elizabeth A. Harris. "Publishing Pledged to Diversify: Change Has Been Slow." *New York Times*, February 28, 2024. https://www.nytimes.com/2024/02/28/books/publishing-books-poc-dei.html.

Amnesty International. *USA: The World Is Watching: Mass Violations by U.S. Police of Black Lives Matter Protestors' Rights.* London: Amnesty International Ltd., August 4, 2020. https://www.amnesty.org/en/documents/amr51/2807/2020/en/.

Anderson, James D. *The Education of Blacks in the South, 1860–1935.* University of North Carolina Press, 1988.

Anheier, Helmut K. *Nonprofit Organizations: Theory, Management, Policy*. Routledge, 2014.

Association for Child & Youth Care Practice, Inc. "Association for Child & Youth Care Practice." Accessed on July 30, 2024, https://acycp.org/.

Avent, Martellis D., and K. S. U. Jayaratne. "Factors Limiting Youth Participation in 4-H and Other Youth Development Programs in Underserved Communities." *Journal of Extension* 55, no. 4 (2017): 14.

Avildsen, John G. (director). *Lean on Me*. Norman Twain Productions, 1989. 1 hr., 48 min.

Ibrahim, Awad, and Shirley Steinberg. *Critical Youth Studies Reader*. Peter Lang, 2014.

Bell, Derrick. *Faces at the Bottom of the Well: The Permanence of Racism*. New York: BasicBooks, 1992.

Bell, Derrick. "Racial Realism." *Connecticut Law Review* 24 (1991): 363.

Bailey, Moya. "Misogynoir Transformed: Black Women's Digital Resistance." In *Misogynoir Transformed*. New York University Press, 2021.

Baldridge, Bianca J. "'It's Like This Myth of the Supernegro': Resisting Narratives of Damage and Struggle in the Neoliberal Educational Policy Context." *Race Ethnicity and Education* 20, no. 6 (2017): 781–795.

Bianca J. Baldridge, "Lifting Up Youth Work," *Spencer Foundation*, July 27, 2020, https://www.spencer.org/news/lifting-up-youth-work.

Baldridge, Bianca J. "Negotiating Anti-Black Racism in 'Liberal' Contexts: The Experiences of Black Youth Workers in Community-Based Educational Spaces." *Race Ethnicity and Education* 23, no. 6 (2020): 747–766.

Baldridge, Bianca J. "On Educational Advocacy and Cultural Work: Situating Community-Based Youth Work[ers] in Broader Educational Discourse." *Teachers College Record* 120, no. 2 (2018): 1–28.

Baldridge, Bianca J. *Reclaiming Community: Race and the Uncertain Future of Youth Work*. Stanford University Press, 2020.

Baldridge, Bianca J. "Relocating the Deficit: Reimagining Black Youth in Neoliberal Times." *American Educational Research Journal* 51, no. 3 (2014): 440–472.

Baldridge, Bianca J. "The Youthwork Paradox: A Case for Studying the Complexity of Community-Based Youth Work in Education Research." *Educational Researcher* 49, no. 8 (2020): 618–625.

Baldridge, Bianca J., Nathan Beck, Juan Carlos Medina, and Marlo A. Reeves. "Toward a New Understanding of Community-Based Education: The Role of Community-Based Educational Spaces in Disrupting Inequality for Minoritized Youth." *Review of Research in Education* 41, no. 1 (2017): 381–402. https://doi.org/10.3102/0091732X16688622.

Baldridge, Bianca J., Daniela K. DiGiacomo, Ben Kirshner, Sam Mejias, and Deepa S. Vasudevan. "Out-of-School Time Programs in the United States in an Era of Racial Reckoning: Insights on Equity from Practitioners, Scholars,

Policy Influencers, and Young People." *Educational Researcher* 53, no. 4 (2024): 201–212.

Baldridge, Bianca J., Marc Lamont Hill, and James Earl Davis. "New Possibilities: (Re) Engaging Black Male Youth Within Community-Based Educational Spaces." In *The Education of Black Males in a "Post-Racial" World*, edited by Anthony L. Brown and Jamel K. Donner, 121–136. Routledge, 2013.

Baldridge, Bianca J., and Alexandros Orphanides. "Are the Kids Alright? Youth Perspectives on Schooling, Learning, and Community." *Stanford University Public Scholarship Collaborative*, May 21, 2023. https://publicscholarshiptestonly.sites.stanford.edu/news/are-kids-alright-youth-perspectives-schooling-learning-and-community.

Barford, Sean W., and William J. Whelton. "Understanding Burnout in Child and Youth Care Workers." *Child & Youth Care Forum* 39 (2010): 271–287.

Berry, Daphne, and Myrtle P. Bell. "Worker Cooperatives: Alternative Governance for Caring and Precarious Work." *Equality, Diversity and Inclusion: An International Journal* 37, no. 4 (2013): 376–391.

Bevan, Bronwyn, Deborah Moroney, and Megan Brown. "The Power of Us: How Better Understanding the Youth Fields Workforce Can Help Communities Thrive." *Afterschool Matters* 37 (2023): 1–3.

Black, Angela Rose, and Suz Switzer. "Mindfulness for the People: Radically Re-Imagining the Mindfulness Movement." In *Beyond White Mindfulness: Critical Perspectives on Racism, Well-Being, and Liberation*, edited by Crystal M. Fleming, Veronica Y. Womack, and Jeffrey Proulx, 140–152. Routledge, 2022.

Bloomer, Rebecka, Aishia A. Brown, Andrew M. Winters, and Anna Domiray. "'Trying to Be Everything Else': Examining the Challenges Experienced by Youth Development Workers." *Children and Youth Services Review* 129 (2021).

Bloomer, Rebecka, Lesley M. Harris, Aishia A. Brown, and Shantel Crosby. "Exploring the Promotion of Youth Voice in Community-Based Youth Development Programmes." *Child & Family Social Work* 28, no. 2 (2023): 291–301.

Bonilla-Silva, Eduardo. "More Than Prejudice: Restatement, Reflections, and New Directions in Critical Race Theory." *Sociology of Race and Ethnicity* 1, no. 1 (2015): 73–87.

Bonilla-Silva, Eduardo. *Racism Without Racists: Color-Blind Racism and the Persistence of Racial Inequality in America*. Rowman & Littlefield, 2021.

Borden, Lynne M., Michael Conn, Casey D. Mull, and Michele Wilkens. "The Youth Development Workforce: The People, the Profession, and the Possibilities." *Journal of Youth Development* 15, no. 1 (2020): 1–8.

Bourdieu, Pierre. *Acts of Resistance: Against the Tyranny of the Market*. The New Press, 1988.

Branch, Enobong Hannah, and Caroline Hanley. "A Racial-Gender Lens on Precarious Nonstandard Employment." In *Precarious Work*, vol. 31, 183–213. Emerald Publishing, 2017. https://doi.org/10.1108/S0277-283320170000031006.

Branch, Enobong Hannah, and Caroline Hanley. *Work in Black and White: Striving for the American Dream*. Russell Sage Foundation, 2022.

Brion-Meisels, Gretchen, Jessica Tseming Fei, and Deepa Sriya Vasudevan, eds. *At Our Best: Building Youth-Adult Partnerships in Out-of-School Time Settings*. IAP, 2020.

Brockenbrough, Ed. "'The Discipline Stop': Black Male Teachers and the Politics of Urban School Discipline." *Education and Urban Society* 47, no. 5 (2015): 499–522.

Brooms, Derrick R. "Black Otherfathering in the Educational Experiences of Black Males in a Single-Sex Urban High School." *Teachers College Record* 119, no. 11 (2017): 1–46.

Brown, Aishia A., Corliss W. Outley, and Harrison P. Pinckney. "Examining the Use of Leisure for the Sociopolitical Development of Black Youth in Out-of-School Time Programs." *Leisure Sciences* 40, no. 7 (2018): 686–696.

Brown, Amy. *A Good Investment?: Philanthropy and the Marketing of Race in an Urban Public School*. University of Minnesota Press, 2015.

Brown, Karida, L. *The Battle for the Black Mind*. Legacy Lit, 2025.

Brummet, Quentin, Emily K. Penner, Nikolas Pharris-Ciurej, and Sonya R. Porter. "After School: An Examination of the Career Paths and Earnings of Former Teachers." *Educational Evaluation and Policy Analysis* 47, no. 2 (2024). https://doi.org/10.3102/01623737241227906.

Buchanan, Larry, Quoctrung Bui, and Jugal K. Patel. "Black Lives Matter May Be the Largest Movement in U.S. History." *New York Times*, July 3, 2020. https://www.nytimes.com/interactive/2020/07/03/us/george-floyd-protests-crowd-size.html.

Butler, Judith. *Precarious Life: The Powers of Mourning and Violence*. Verso Books, 2004.

Butler, Judith. "Precarious Life, Vulnerability, and the Ethics of Cohabitation." *Journal of Speculative Philosophy* 26, no. 2 (2012): 134–151.

Cahill, Sean, and Matthew Pettus. "Trump-Pence Administration Policies Undermine LGBTQ Health Equity." The Fenway Institute, 2020. https://fenwayhealth.org/wp-content/uploads/TFIP-37_Policy-Brief-Cover-Trump-Biden-LGTQIA-equality-HIV-health-and-racial-justice-Full-Brief.pdf.

Cain, Christopher (director). *The Principal*. ML Delphi Premier Productions, 1987. 1 hr., 49 min.

Campbell, John L., Charles Quincy, Jordan Osserman, and Ove K. Pedersen. "Coding In-Depth Semistructured Interviews: Problems of Unitization and Intercoder Reliability and Agreement." *Sociological Methods & Research* 42, no. 3 (2013): 294–320.

Carey, Roderick L., Thomas Akiva, Haya Abdellatif, and Kendell A. Daughtry. "'And School Won't Teach Me That!' Urban Youth Activism Programs as Transformative Sites for Critical Adolescent Learning." *Journal of Youth Studies* 24, no. 7 (2021): 941–960.

Carnegie Foundation Report. "A Matter of Time: Risk and Opportunity in the Non-School Hours." *The Carnegie Corporation of New York*, December 1992. https://www.carnegie org/publications/a-matter-of-time-risk-and-opportunity -in-the-nonschool-hours/.

Carter, Prudence L. *Keepin' It Real: School Success Beyond Black and White*. Oxford University Press, 2005.

Carter, Thomas (director). *Coach Carter*. MTV Films, Tollin/Robbins Productions, 2005. 2 hr., 16 min.

Cech, Erin. *The Trouble with Passion: How Searching for Fulfillment at Work Fosters Inequality*. University of California Press, 2021.

Clay, Kevin L. "'Despite the Odds': Unpacking the Politics of Black Resilience Neoliberalism." *American Educational Research Journal* 56, no. 1 (2019): 75–110.

Cohen, Abbie. "Stuck Between a Rock and a Hard Place: An Investigation into a Youth-Serving Community-Based Organization, Philanthropy, and Urban Public Schools." *Children and Schools* 46, no. 3 (2024): 183–193.

Coles, Justin A. "A BlackCrit Re/Imagining of Urban Schooling Social Education Through Black Youth Enactments of Black Storywork." *Urban Education* 58, no. 6 (2023): 1180–1209.

Coles, Justin A., and Turette Powell. "A BlackCrit Analysis on Black Urban Youth and Suspension Disproportionality as Anti-Black Symbolic Violence." *Race Ethnicity and Education* 23, no. 1 (2020): 113–133.

Collins, Patricia Hill. *Black Feminist Thought: Knowledge, Consciousness, and the Politics of Empowerment*. Unwin Hyman, 1990.

Collins, Patricia Hill. "Black Women and Motherhood [1991]." In *Justice and Care: Essential Readings in Feminist Ethics*, edited by Virginia Held, 117–136. Routledge, 1995.

Couch, Jen. "Together We Walk: The Importance of Relationship in Youth Work with Refugee Young People." In *The Sage Handbook of Youth Work Practice*, edited by Dana Fusco, Fin Cullen, Kathy Edwards, Pam Alldred, 213–225. Sage Publications Ltd., 2018.

Curry, Dale, Andrew J. Schneider-Muñoz, Frank Eckles, and Carol Stuart. "Assessing Youth Worker Competence: National Child and Youth Worker Certification." In *Advancing Youth Work: Current Trends, Critical Questions*, edited by Dana Fusco. Routledge, 2012.

de St Croix, Tania. *Grassroots Youth Work*. Policy Press, 2016.

de St Croix, Tania. "Youth Work, Performativity and the New Youth Impact Agenda: Getting Paid for Numbers?" *Journal of Education Policy* 33, no. 3 (2018): 414–438.

Deutsch, Nancy L., and Hirsch, Barton J. "A Place to Call Home: Youth Organizations in the Lives of Inner-City Adolescents," In *Understanding Early Adolescent Self and Identity: Applications and Interventions*, edited by Thomas M. Brinthaupt and Richard P. Lipka, 293–320. State University of New York Press, 2012. https://doi.org/10.1515/9780791488751-011.

Diamond, John B., and Louis M. Gomez. "Disrupting White Supremacy and Anti-Black Racism in Educational Organizations." *Educational Researcher* (2023). https://doi.org/10.3102/0013189X231161054.

Diamond, John B. "Race and White Supremacy in the Sociology of Education: Shifting the Intellectual Gaze." In *Education in a New Society: Renewing the Sociology of Education*, edited by Jal Mehta and Scott Davies, 345–362. University of Chicago Press, 2018.

Dumas, Michael J. "Against the Dark: Antiblackness in Education Policy and Discourse." *Theory into Practice* 55, no. 1 (2016): 11–19.

Dumas, Michael J. "'Losing an Arm': Schooling as a Site of Black Suffering." *Race Ethnicity and Education* 17, no. 1 (2014): 1–29. https://doi.org/10.1080/13613324.2013.850412.

Dumas, Michael J., and kihana miraya ross. "'Be Real Black for Me': Imagining BlackCrit in Education." *Urban Education* 51, no. 4 (2016): 415–442.

Duncan-Andrade, Jeffrey M., and Ernest Morrell. "Youth Participatory Action Research as Critical Pedagogy." *Counterpoints* 285 (2008): 105–131.

Dunning, Claire. "No Strings Attached: Philanthropy, Race, and Donor Control from Black Power to Black Lives Matter." *Nonprofit and Voluntary Sector Quarterly* 52, no. 1 (2023): 29–49.

Economic Policy Institute. "EPI's Family Budget Calculator." Accessed March 14, 2025. https://www.epi.org/publication/epis-family-budget-calculator/.

Edwards, Arlene E. "Community Mothering: The Relationship Between Mothering and the Community Work of Black Women." *Journal of the Motherhood Initiative for Research and Community Involvement* 2, no. 2 (2000). https://jarm.journals.yorku.ca/index.php/jarm/article/view/2141.

Espinoza, Manuel Luis, and Shirin Vossoughi. "Perceiving Learning Anew: Social Interaction, Dignity, and Educational Rights." *Harvard Educational Review* 84, no. 3 (2014): 285–313.

Every Hour Counts. *Lighting the Path Forward: How Afterschool Intermediaries Have Supported Youth and Communities During the Pandemic*, 2023. https://drive.google.com/file/d/18oAVPNRqqYeWLnLG4MhG5x0PLOOlvZvQ/view.

Fanon, Frantz. *The Wretched of the Earth*. Translated by Richard Philcox. Grove Press, 2004. Originally published in 1961.

Fleming, Crystal M. *How to Be Less Stupid About Race: On Racism, White Supremacy, and the Racial Divide*. Beacon Press, 2018.

Fletcher, Bill, Jr. "Whither the Black Worker?" *Labor Studies Journal* 47, no. 4 (2022): 488–492.

Fultz, Michael. "The Displacement of Black Educators Post-Brown: An Overview and Analysis." *History of Education Quarterly* 44, no. 1 (2004): 11–45.

Fusco, Dana, ed. *Advancing Youth Work: Current Trends, Critical Questions*. Routledge, 2012.

Gillborn, David. *White Lies: Racism, Education and Critical Race Theory*. Taylor & Francis, 2024.

Gilmore, Ruth Wilson. "In the Shadow of the Shadow State." *S&F Online* 13, no. 2 (Spring 2016).

Ginwright, Shawn. *Black Youth Rising: Activism and Radical Healing in Urban America*. Teachers College Press, 2010.

Ginwright, Shawn. *Hope and Healing in Urban Education: How Urban Activists and Teachers Are Reclaiming Matters of the Heart*. Routledge, 2015.

Ginwright, Shawn, and Julio Cammarota. "New Terrain in Youth Development: The Promise of a Social Justice Approach." *Social Justice* 29, no. 4 (2002): 82–95.

Ginwright, Shawn, and Julio Cammarota. "Youth Activism in the Urban Community: Learning Critical Civic Praxis Within Community Organizations." *International Journal of Qualitative Studies in Education* 20, no. 6 (October 2007): 693–710.

Ginwright, Shawn, and Taj James. "From Assets to Agents of Change: Social Justice, Organizing, and Youth Development." In *Youth Participation: Improving Institutions and Communities*, edited by B. Kirshner, J. L. O'Donoghue, and M. McLaughlin. Jossey-Bass, 2022

Givens, Jarvis R. *Fugitive Pedagogy: Carter G. Woodson and the Art of Black Teaching*. Harvard University Press, 2021.

Givens, Jarvis R. "Literate Slave, Fugitive Slave: A Note on the Ethical Dilemma of Black Education." In *The Future Is Black*, edited by Carl A. Grant, Ashley N. Woodson, and Michael J. Dumas, 22–30. Routledge, 2020.

Givens, Jarvis R. *School Clothes: A Collective Memoir of Black Student Witness*. Beacon Press, 2023.

Glaser, Barney G. "The Constant Comparative Method of Qualitative Analysis." *Social Problems* 12, no. 4 (1965): 436–445.

Golash-Boza, Tanya. "A Critical and Comprehensive Sociological Theory of Race and Racism." *Sociology of Race and Ethnicity* 2, no. 2 (2016): 129–141.

Gooden, Susan T., Lindsey L. Evans, Michael L. Perkins, Caper Gooden, and Yali Pang. "Examining Youth Outcomes of African American–Led Nonprofits." *Nonprofit and Voluntary Sector Quarterly* 47, no. 4 suppl (2018): 34S–54S.

Goosby, Bridget J., and Chelsea Heidbrink. "The Transgenerational Consequences of Discrimination on African-American Health Outcomes." *Sociology Compass* 7, no. 8 (2013): 630–643.

Grant, Carl A., Keffrelyn D. Brown, and Anthony L. Brown. *Black Intellectual Thought in Education: The Missing Traditions of Anna Julia Cooper, Carter G. Woodson, and Alain Leroy Locke*. Routledge, 2015.

Gutiérrez, Kris D., and Barbara Rogoff. "Cultural Ways of Learning: Individual Traits or Repertoires of Practice." *Educational Researcher* 32, no. 5 (2003): 19–25.

Hall, Ashley R., and Tiffany J. Bell. "The Pedagogy of Renewal: Black Women, Reclaiming Joy, and Self-Care as Praxis." *Journal of Communication Pedagogy* 6, no. 1 (2022): 3.

Hall, Georgia, Jan Gallagher Hall, and Elizabeth Starr, eds. *The Heartbeat of the Youth Development Field: Professional Journeys of Growth, Connection, and Transformation*. IAP, 2022.

Halpern, Robert. "A Different Kind of Child Development Institution: The History of After-School Programs for Low-Income Children." *Teachers College Record* 104, no. 2 (2002): 178–211.

Halverson, Erica Rosenfeld, Kailea Saplan, Sam Mejias, and Caitlin Martin. "What We Learn About Learning from Out-of-School Time Arts Education." *Review of Research in Education* 47, no. 1 (2023): 360–404.

Hamilton, Laura, and Betheny Gross. "How Has the Pandemic Affected Students' Social-Emotional Well-Being? A Review of the Evidence to Date." Center on Reinventing Public Education, August 2021. https://eric.ed.gov/?id=ED614131.

Han, Eunice S., and Emma García. "The Effect of Teachers' Unions on Teacher Stress: Evidence from District-Teacher Matched Data." *Labor Studies Journal* 48, no. 1 (2023): 35–69.

Harney, Stefano, and Fred Moten. *The Undercommons: Fugitive Planning and Black Study*. Minor Compositions, 2013.

Harris, Aisha. "The Central Park Five: We Were Just Baby Boys." *New York Times*, May 30, 2019. https://www.nytimes.com/2019/05/30/arts/television/when-they-see-us.html.

Harris, Elizabeth A. "People Are Marching Against Racism. They're Also Reading About It." *New York Times*, June 5, 2020. https://www.nytimes.com/2020/06/05/books/antiracism-books-race-racism.html.

Hartman, Saidiya. *Lose Your Mother: A Journey Along the Atlantic Slave Route*. Farrar, Straus and Giroux, 2008.

Hartman, Saidiya V., and Frank B. Wilderson. "The Position of the Unthought." *Qui Parle* 13, no. 2 (Spring/Summer 2003): 183–201.

Hawkins, Deion S. "'After Philando, I Had to Take a Sick Day to Recover': Psychological Distress, Trauma, and Police Brutality in the Black Community." In *Emergent Health Communication Scholarship from and about African American, Latino/a/x, and American Indian/Alaskan Native Peoples*, edited by Angela Cooke-Jackson. Routledge, 2024. https://doi.org/10.4324/9781032661285.

Heath, Shirley Brice, and Milbrey W. McLaughlin. "The Best of Both Worlds: Connecting Schools and Community Youth Organizations for All-Day, All-Year Learning." *Educational Administration Quarterly* 30, no. 3 (1994): 278–300.

Heathfield, Michael, and Dana Fusco. "Honoring and Supporting Youth Work Intellectuals." In *The Changing Landscape of Youth Work: Theory and Practice for an Evolving Field*, edited by Kristen M. Pozzoboni and Ben Kirshner, 127–146. Information Age Publishing, Inc., 2016.

Henry, Kevin Lawrence, Jr. "Feasting on Blackness: Educational Parasitism, Necropolicy, and Black Thought." *International Journal of Qualitative Studies in Education* (2023): 1–17.

Hersey, Tricia. *Rest Is Resistance: A Manifesto*. Hachette UK, 2022.

Higginbotham, Evelyn Brooks. *Righteous Discontent: The Women's Movement in the Black Baptist Church, 1880–1920*, Harvard University Press, 2019.

Hill, Sean, II. "Precarity in the Era of #BlackLivesMatter." *WSQ: Women's Studies Quarterly* 45, no. 3 (2017): 94–109.

Hines, Michael. "'They Do Not Know How to Play': Reformers' Expectations and Children's Realities on the First Progressive Playgrounds of Chicago." *Journal of the History of Childhood and Youth* 10, no. 2 (2017): 206–227.

Hirsch, Barton J., Nancy L. Deutsch, and David L. DuBois. *After-School Centers and Youth Development: Case Studies of Success and Failure.* Cambridge University Press, 2011.

Hirsch, Barton J., Larry V. Hedges, JulieAnn Stawicki, and Megan A. Mekinda. "After-School Programs for High School Students: An Evaluation of After School Matters." Wallace Foundation, June 2011, https://wallacefoundation.org/report/after-school-programs-high-school-students-evaluation-after-school-matters-evaluation-after.

Hoogstra, Lisa, Barbara Schneider, and Fengbin Chang. "Young Adult Occupational Identity and Well-Being: Influences of Postsecondary Education and Work." *Sociological Focus* 34, no. 4 (2001): 337–356.

hooks, bell. *Teaching to Transgress: Education as the Practice of Freedom.* Routledge, 1994.

Howard, Tyrone C. "Culturally Relevant Teaching: A Pivot for Pedagogical Transformation and Racial Reckoning," *The Educational Forum* 85, no. 4 (2021): 406–415.

Insecure, created by Issa Rae and Larry Wilmore, aired on HBO, 2016.

Jaffe, Sarah. *Work Won't Love You Back: How Devotion to Our Jobs Keeps Us Exploited, Exhausted, and Alone.* Bold Type Books, 2021.

Jan, Tracy, Jena McGregor, and Meghan Hoyer. "Corporate America's $50 Billion Promise." *Washington Post*, August 23, 2021. https://www.washingtonpost.com/business/interactive/2021/george-floyd-corporate-america-racial-justice/.

Johnson, Javon. "Black Joy in the Time of Ferguson." *QED: A Journal in GLBTQ Worldmaking* 2, no. 2 (2015): 177–183.

Johnston-Goodstar, Katie. "Decolonizing Youth Development: Re-Imagining Youthwork for Indigenous Youth Futures." *AlterNative: An International Journal of Indigenous Peoples* 16, no. 4 (2020): 378–386.

Jones, Marshall B. "The Multiple Sources of Mission Drift." *Nonprofit and Voluntary Sector Quarterly* 36, no. 2 (2007): 299–307.

Jung, Moon-Kie. "The Enslaved, the Worker, and Du Bois's Black Reconstruction: Toward an Underdiscipline of Antisociology." *Sociology of Race and Ethnicity* 5, no. 2 (2019): 157–168.

Jung, Moon-Kie, and João H. Costa Vargas, eds. *Antiblackness.* Duke University Press, 2021.

Juravich, Nick. *Para Power: How Paraprofessional Labor Changed Education.* University of Illinois Press, 2024.

Kalleberg, Arne L. "Precarious Work, Insecure Workers: Employment Relations in Transition." *American Sociological Review* 74, no. 1 (2009): 1–22.

Kalleberg, Arne L., Barbara F. Reskin, and Ken Hudson, "Bad Jobs in America: Standard and Nonstandard Employment Relations and Job Quality in the United States." *American Sociological Review* 65, no. 2 (2000): 256–278.

Kanter, Rosabeth Moss. "Work and Family in the United States: A Critical Review and Agenda for Research and Policy." *Family Business Review* 2, no. 1 (1989): 77–114.

Kelley, Robin D. G. *Freedom Dreams: The Black Radical Imagination.* Beacon Press, 2022.

Kelley, Robin D. G. "Racial Capitalism: An Unfinished History." In *The South African Tradition of Racial Capitalism,* edited by Marcel Paret and Zachary Levenson, 160–166. Routledge, 2024.

Kennedy, Laura M., Lindsay McHolme, and Carrie Symons. "Refugee-Background Youth Workers as Agents of Social Change: Building Bridging Relationships One Story at a Time." *Journal of Higher Education Outreach and Engagement* 28, no. 1 (2024).

Kim, Juliana. "The Missing Hours: 7 Students on Losing a Year of After-School Activities." *New York Times,* March 14, 2021. https://www.nytimes.com/2021/03/14/us/nyc-after-school-activities-reopening.html.

Kirshner, Ben. *Youth Activism in an Era of Education Inequality.* Vol. 2. New York University Press, 2015.

Kirshner, Ben, and Shawn Ginwright. "Youth Organizing as a Developmental Context for African American and Latino Adolescents." *Child Development Perspectives* 6, no. 3 (2012): 288–294.

Klepper, Rachel. "Staying Late: Afterschool Programs for Children in New York City, 1930–1965." PhD diss., Columbia University, 2024.

Kohl-Arenas, Erica. *The Self-Help Myth: How Philanthropy Fails to Alleviate Poverty.* University of California Press, 2016. http://www.jstor.org/stable/10.1525/j.ctt19632k8.

Kwon, Soo Ah. *Uncivil Youth: Race, Activism, and Affirmative Governmentality.* Duke University Press, 2013.

Ladson-Billings, Gloria. *The Dreamkeepers: Successful Teachers of African American Children.* Wiley, 2022.

Ladson-Billings, Gloria. "From the Achievement Gap to the Education Debt: Understanding Achievement in US Schools." *Educational Researcher* 35, no. 7 (2006): 3–12.

Ladson-Billings, Gloria. "I'm Here for the Hard Re-Set: Post Pandemic Pedagogy to Preserve Our Culture." *Equity & Excellence in Education* 54, no. 1 (2021): 68–78.

Ladson-Billings, Gloria. "It's Your World, I'm Just Trying to Explain It: Understanding Our Epistemological and Methodological Challenges." *Qualitative Inquiry* 9, no. 1 (2003): 5–12.

Ladson-Billings, Gloria. "Landing on the Wrong Note: The Price We Paid for Brown." *Educational Researcher* 33, no. 7 (2004): 3–13.

Ladson-Billings, Gloria. "Toward a Theory of Culturally Relevant Pedagogy." *American Educational Research Journal* 32, no. 3 (1995): 465–491.

LaGravenese, Richard (director). *Freedom Writers*. MTV Films, Jersey Films, 2S Films, 2007. 2 hr., 3 min.

Lareau, Annette. "Invisible Inequality: Social Class and Childrearing in Black Families and White Families." *American Sociological Review* 67, no. 5 (2002): 747–776.

Larson, Reed W., Kathrin C. Walker, Natalie Rusk, and Lisa B. Diaz. "Understanding Youth Development from the Practitioner's Point of View: A Call for Research on Effective Practice." *Applied Developmental Science* 19, no. 2 (2015): 74–86.

Lee, Stacey J., Choua P. Xiong, Linda M. Pheng, and Mai Neng Vang. "'Asians for Black Lives, not Asians for Asians': Building Southeast Asian American and Black Solidarity." *Anthropology & Education Quarterly* 51, no. 4 (2020): 405–421.

Lesko, Nancy. "Denaturalizing Adolescence: The Politics of Contemporary Representations." *Youth & Society* 28, no. 2 (1996): 139–161. https://doi.org/10.1177/0044118X96028002001.

Lewis, Amanda E., and John B. Diamond. *Despite the Best Intentions: How Racial Inequality Thrives in Good Schools*. Oxford University Press, 2015.

Lofton, Richard. "'I Was Called Everything but a Student': Blackness and the Social Death of Student Status." *Social Problems* (2023): spad033.

Lorde, Audre. "A Burst of Light: Living with Cancer." In *A Burst of Light and Other Essays*. Women's Press, 1992.

Love, Bettina L. *We Want to Do More Than Survive: Abolitionist Teaching and the Pursuit of Educational Freedom*. Boston: Beacon Press, 2019.

Luna, Zakiya. "'Other Mother' of a Generation: On bell hooks and Living Black Feminism." *Ms. Magazine*, December 23, 2021. https://msmagazine.com/2021/12/23/other-mother-of-a-generation-on-bell-hooks-and-living-black-feminism/.

Mackenzie, Catriona, Wendy Rogers, and Susan Dodds. "Introduction: What Is Vulnerability and Why Does It Matter for Moral Theory?" *Vulnerability: New Essays in Ethics and Feminist Philosophy*, edited by Catriona Mackenzie, Wendy Rogers, and Susan Dodds, 1–29. Oxford University Press, 2014.

Madison, Soyini D. *Critical Ethnography: Method, Ethics, And Performance*. Sage, 2011.

Mahmud, Tayyab. "Precarious Existence and Capitalism: A Permanent State of Exception." *Southwestern University Law Review* 44, no. 4 (2014): 699–726.

Mahoney, Joseph L., Maria E. Parente, and Edward F. Zigler. "Afterschool Programs in America: Origins, Growth, Popularity, and Politics." *Journal of Youth Development* 4, no. 3 (2009): 23–42.

Maloney, Em K. "The Influence of Occupational Identity on Emotional Experience." *American Behavioral Scientist* 67, no. 1 (2023): 100–124.

Marwell, Nicole P. *Bargaining for Brooklyn: Community Organizations in the Entrepreneurial City*. University of Chicago Press, 2009.

Marwell, Nicole P. "Privatizing the Welfare State: Nonprofit Community-Based Organizations as Political Actors." *American Sociological Review* 69, no. 2 (2004): 265–291.

Massachusetts Institute of Technology. "MIT Living Wage Calculator." Accessed March 14, 2025. https://livingwage.mit.edu/.

McCann, Adam. "State Economies with the Most Racial Equality in 2024." WalletHub, June 11, 2024. https://wallethub.com/edu/state-economies-with-most-racial-equality/75810.

McGee, Merle. "Critical Youth Development: Living and Learning at the Intersections of Life." In *Changemakers! Practitioners Advance Equity and Access in Out-of-School Time Programs*, edited by Sara Hill and Femi Vance. Information Age Publishing, 2019.

McKenzie, Brian D. "Religious Social Networks, Indirect Mobilization, and African-American Political Participation." *Political Research Quarterly* 57, no. 4 (2004): 621–632.

McKinney de Royston, Maxine, Tia C. Madkins, Jarvis R. Givens, and Na'ilah Suad Nasir. "'I'm a Teacher, I'm Gonna Always Protect You': Understanding Black Educators' Protection of Black Children." *American Educational Research Journal* 58, no. 1 (2021): 68–106.

McLaughlin, Milbrey W. "Community Counts: How Youth Organizations Matter for Youth Development." The Public Education Network, 2000. http://www.publiceducation.org.

McLaughlin, Milbrey W. *You Can't Be What You Can't See: The Power of Opportunity to Change Young Lives*. Harvard Education Press, 2018.

Medina, Juan. C., Tanya Wiggins, and Bianca J. Baldridge, "Critical Reflections on Tensions in Authentic Youth-Adult Partnerships." In *At Our Best: Building Youth-Adult Partnerships in Out-of-School Time Settings*, edited by Gretchen Brion-Meisels, Jessica Tseming Fei and Deepa Sriya Vasudevan. Information Age Publishing, 2020.

Mehta, Jal, and Sarah Fine. *In Search of Deeper Learning: The Quest to Remake the American High School*. Harvard University Press, 2019.

Melamed, Jodi. "Racial Capitalism." *Critical Ethnic Studies* 1, no. 1 (2015): 76–85.

Meyer, Rachel. "Precarious Workers and Collective Efficacy." *Critical Sociology* 43, no. 7/8 (2017): 1125–1141.

Milkman, Ruth. "Stratification Among In-Home Care Workers in the United States." *Critical Sociology* 49, no. 1 (2023): 11–22.

Millar, Kathleen M. "Toward a Critical Politics of Precarity." *Sociology Compass* 11, no. 6 (2017): e12483.

Minsky, Adam S. "40 Million Student Loan Borrowers Hit by Trio of Trump Orders—Here's Where Things Stand." *Forbes*, March 25, 2025. https://www.forbes.com/sites/adamminsky/2025/03/25/40-million-student-loan-borrowers-hit-by-trio-of-trump-orders---heres-where-things-stand/.

Morris, Aldon D. *The Origins of the Civil Rights Movement*. Simon and Schuster, 1984.

Morrison, Toni. Interview by Charlie Rose. *Charlie Rose*, PBS, January 19, 1998. Audio, 29:35. https://charlierose.com/videos/17664.

Morrison, Toni. *Playing in the Dark: Whiteness and the Literary Imagination*. Vintage Books, 2004.

Muhammad, Gholnecsar E. "The Literacy Development and Practices Within African American Literary Societies." *Black History Bulletin* 75, no. 1 (2012): 6–13.

Muhammad, Khalil Gibran. *The Condemnation of Blackness: Race, Crime, and the Making of Modern Urban America*. Harvard University Press, 2019.

National Center for Education Statistics (home page), Institute of Education Sciences (IES), US Department of Education. Accessed July 30, 2024. https://nces.ed.gov/.

Newman-Bremang, Kathleen. "Reclaiming Audre Lorde's Radical Self-Care." *Unbothered*, Refinery 29, May 28, 2021, https://www.refinery29.com/en-us/2021/05/10493153/reclaiming-self-care-audre-lorde-black-women-community-care.

Ngo, Bic, and Stacey J. Lee. "Navigating Social Justice in the Current Historical Moment." *International Journal of Qualitative Studies in Education* 33, no. 2 (2020): 135–139.

Noguera, Pedro A. *The Trouble with Black Boys . . . And Other Reflections on Race, Equity, and the Future of Public Education*. Wiley, 2009.

Nxumalo, Fikile, and kihana miraya ross. "Envisioning Black Space in Environmental Education for Young Children." *Race Ethnicity and Education* 22, no. 4 (2019): 502–524.

Paris, Django. "Culturally Sustaining Pedagogy: A Needed Change in Stance, Terminology, and Practice." *Educational Researcher* 41, no. 3 (April 2012): 93–97.

Pattillo, Mary. *Black on the Block: The Politics of Race and Class in the City*. University of Chicago Press, 2010.

Pattillo, Mary. "Church Culture as a Strategy of Action in the Black Community." *American Sociological Review* 63, no. 6 (1998): 767–784.

Patton, Michael Quinn. "Sampling, Qualitative (Purposeful)." *The Blackwell Encyclopedia of Sociology*, edited by George Ritzer. Blackwell, 2007.

Payne, Charles M. *I've Got the Light of Freedom: The Organizing Tradition and the Mississippi Freedom Struggle*. University of California Press, 2007.

Peetz, Caitlynn. "Schools Take a $3 Billion Hit from the Culture Wars. Here's How It Breaks Down." *Education Week*, October 30, 2024. https://www.edweek.org/leadership/schools-take-a-3-billion-hit-from-the-culture-wars-heres-how-it-breaks-down/2024/10.

Perlstein, Daniel. "Freedom, Liberation, Accommodation: Politics and Pedagogy in SNCC and the Black Panther Party." In *Teach Freedom: Education for Liberation in the African-American Tradition*, edited by Charles M. Payne and Carol Sills Strickland, 75–94. Teachers College Press, 2008.

Pew Research Center, "Support for the Black Lives Matter Movement Has Dropped Considerably from Its Peak in 2020." Pew Research Center's Social & Demographic Trends, June 14, 2023, https://www.pewresearch.org/social-trends/2023/06/14/support-for-the-black-lives-matter-movement-has-dropped-considerably-from-its-peak-in-2020/.

Pittman, Karen. "Moving Beyond Where and When to the People and Practices That Impact Youth." *Journal of Youth Development* 13, no. 4 (2018): 1–4.

Pittman, Karen J., Merita Irby, Nicole Yohalem, and Alicia Wilson-Ahlstrom. "Blurring the Lines for Learning: The Role of Out-of-School Programs as Complements to Formal Learning." *New Directions for Youth Development*, no. 101 (2004): 19–41.

Powell, Walter W., and Patricia Bromley, eds. *The Nonprofit Sector: A Research Handbook*. Stanford University Press, 2020.

Powell, Walter. "What Is the Nonprofit Sector?" In *The Nonprofit Sector: A Research Handbook*, 3rd. ed., edited by Walter W. Powell and Patricia Bromley, 3–23. Stanford University Press, 2020.

Quashie, Kevin. *Black Aliveness, or a Poetics of Being*. Duke University Press, 2021.

Quinn, Jane. "Transforming Afterschool Programs into 'Engines of Development': A Policy Analysis of the Federal 21st Century Community Learning Centers." PhD diss., City University of New York, 2022.

Quinn, Johanna S., and Myra Marx Ferree, "Schools as Workplaces: Intersectional Regimes of Inequality." *Gender, Work & Organization* 26, no. 12 (2019): 1806–1815.

Rai, Tage S., Jun Zi, and Peter DeScioli, "Coalitional Psychology on the Playground: Competition and Dominance Influence Children's Conflict Tactics," *Proceedings of the National Academy of Sciences* 118, no. 50 (2021): e2109860118. https://doi.org/10.1073/pnas.2109860118.

Ray, Ranita. *The Making of a Teenage Service Class: Poverty and Mobility in an American City*. University of California Press, 2017.

Ray, Rashawn, and Alexandra Gibbons. "Why Are States Banning Critical Race Theory?" Brookings Institute, November 2021. https://www.brookings.edu/articles/why-are-states-banning-critical-race-theory/.

Ray, Victor. "A Theory of Racialized Organizations." *American Sociological Review* 84, no. 1 (2019): 26–53.

Reimers, Fernando M. "Learning from a Pandemic: The Impact of COVID-19 on Education Around the World." In *Primary and Secondary Education During Covid-19: Disruptions to Educational Opportunity During a Pandemic*, edited by Fernando M. Reimers, 1–37. Springer, 2022.

Rickford, Russell. *We Are an African People: Independent Education, Black Power, and the Radical Imagination*. Oxford University Press, 2016.

Rios, Victor M. *Punished: Policing the Lives of Black and Latino Boys*. New York University Press, 2011.

Rios, Victor M. "The Racial Politics of Youth Crime." In *Behind Bars: Latino/as and Prison in the United States*, edited by Suzanne Oboler, 97–111. Palgrave Macmillan, 2009.

Robinson, Shantá R. "Homeless Youth of Color and the Shaping of Aspirations: The (Re)productive role of Institutions." *Urban Education* 57, no. 8 (2022): 1299–1328.

Rodriguez, Dylan. "The Political Logic of the Non-Profit Industrial Complex." In *The*

Revolution Will Not Be Funded: Beyond the Non-Profit Industrial Complex, edited by INCITE! Women of Color Against Violence, 21–40. Duke University Press, 2007.

Rogoff, Barbara, Maureen Callanan, Kris D. Gutiérrez, and Frederick Erickson. "The Organization of Informal Learning." *Review of Research in Education* 40, no. 1 (2016): 356–401.

Rojas, Fabio. *From Black Power to Black Studies: How a Radical Social Movement Became an Academic Discipline*. Johns Hopkins University Press, 2010.

Rooks, Noliwe M. *A Passionate Mind in Relentless Pursuit: The Vision of Mary McLeod Bethune*. Penguin Press, 2024.

ross, kihana miraya. "Antiblackness in Education and the Possibility of Redress: Toward Educational Reparations." *American Studies* 66, no. 1 (2021): 229–233.

ross, kihana miraya. "Call It What It Is: Anti-Blackness." *New York Times,* June 4, 2020.

ross, kihana miraya, and Jarvis R. Givens. "The Clearing: On Black Education Studies and the Problem of 'Antiblackness.'" *Harvard Educational Review* 93, no. 2 (2023): 149–172.

Serrano, Uriel, May Lin, Jamileh Ebrahimi, Jose Orellana, Rosanai Paniagua, and Veronica Terriquez. "In Millennial Footsteps: California Social Movement Organizations for Generation Z." *Sociological Perspectives* (2021). https://doi.org/10.1177/07311214211010565.

Serrano, Uriel, David C. Turner III, Gabriel Regalado, and Alejandro Banuelos. "Towards Community-Rooted Research and Praxis: Reflections on the BSS Safety and Youth Justice Project." *Social Sciences* 11, no. 5 (2022): 195.

Shange, Savannah. "Progressive Dystopia: Multiracial Coalition and the Carceral State." PhD diss., University of Pennsylvania, 2017.

Sharpe, Christina. "Black Studies: In the Wake." *The Black Scholar* 44, no. 2 (2014): 59–69.

Sharpe, Christina. *In the Wake: On Blackness and Being*. Duke University Press, 2016.

Singh, Michael V. *Good Boys, Bad Hombres: The Racial Politics of Mentoring Latino Boys in Schools*. University of Minnesota Press, 2024.

Smith, John N. *Dangerous Minds*. Hollywood Pictures, Don Simpson/Jerry Bruckheimer Films, 1995. 1 hr., 39 min.

Smith-Purviance, Ashley L. "Massed Violence Against Black Women and Girls." *Feminist Studies* 47, no. 1 (2021): 175–200.

Sojoyner, Damien M. *Joy and Pain: A Story of Black Life and Liberation in Five Albums*. University of California Press, 2022.

Spencer, Joi A., and Kerri D. Ullucci. *Anti-Blackness at School: Creating Affirming Educational Spaces for African American Students*. Teachers College Press, 2022.

Standing, Guy. *The Precariat: The New Dangerous Class*. Bloomsbury Academic, 2011.

Stanton-Salazar, Ricardo D. "A Social Capital Framework for the Study of Institutional Agents and Their Role in the Empowerment of Low-Status Students and Youth." *Youth & Society* 43, no. 3 (2011): 1066–1109.

Steingart, David. "The Importance of Prioritizing Emotional Wellness over Academic Achievement." National Alliance on Mental Illness, December 12, 2022. https://www.nami.org/bipolar-and-related-disorders/the-importance-of-prioritizing-emotional-wellness-over-academic-achievement/.

Stuart, Forrest. *Ballad of the Bullet: Gangs, Drill Music, and the Power of Online Infamy.* Princeton University Press, 2020.

Terriquez, Veronica. "How Youth Organizing Groups Educate Toward a Multiracial Democracy in California." University of California, Los Angeles, March 2023, https://idea.gseis.ucla.edu/publications/educating-toward-a-multiracial-democracy.

Terriquez, Veronica. "Training Young Activists: Grassroots Organizing and Youths' Civic and Political Trajectories." *Sociological Perspectives* 58, no. 2 (2015): 223–242.

Teupen, Sonja. "Material Poverty and Symbolic Precarity." In *Cultural Psychology: An Introduction*, edited by Uwe Wolfradt, Lars Allolio-Näcke, and Paul Sebastian Ruppel, 297–305. Springer Fachmedien Wiesbaden, 2024.

Tilly, Charles. *Durable Inequality.* University of California Press, 1999.

Todd-Breland, Elizabeth. *A Political Education: Black Politics and Education Reform in Chicago Since the 1960s.* University of North Carolina Press, 2018.

Trinidad, Jose Eos. *Subtle Webs: How Local Organizations Shape US Education.* Oxford University Press, 2024.

Trotter, LaTonya J. *More Than Medicine: Nurse Practitioners and the Problems They Solve for Patients, Health Care Organizations, and the State.* Cornell University Press, 2020.

Tuck, Eve. "Suspending Damage: A Letter to Communities." *Harvard Educational Review* 79, no. 3 (2009): 409–428.

Tuck, Eve, and K. Wayne Yang. "R-Words: Refusing Research." In *Humanizing Research: Decolonizing Qualitative Inquiry with Youth and Communities*, edited by Django Paris and Maisha T. Winn, 223–247. Sage, 2014.

Turner, David C. "The (Good) Trouble with Black Boys: Organizing with Black Boys and Young Men in George Floyd's America." *Theory into Practice* 60, no. 4 (2021): 422–433.

Turner, Erica O., and Abigail J. Beneke. "'Softening' School Resource Officers: The Extension of Police Presence in Schools in an Era of Black Lives Matter, School Shootings, and Rising Inequality." *Race Ethnicity and Education* 23, no. 2 (2020): 221–240.

Turner, John C., and S. Alexander Haslam. "Social Identity, Organizations, and Leadership." In *Groups at Work*: *Social Identity, Organizations, and Leadership*, edited by Marlene E. Turner, 25–65. Psychology Press, 2014.

Valencia, Richard R. *The Evolution of Deficit Thinking: Educational Thought and Practice.* Routledge, 2012.

Vandell, Deborah Lowe. "Afterschool Program Quality and Student Outcomes: Reflections on Positive Key Findings on Learning and Development from Recent Research." In *Expanding Minds and Opportunities*: *Leveraging the Power of*

Afterschool and Summer Learning for Student Success, edited by Terry K. Peterson, 10–16. Collaborative Communications Group, 2013.

Vargas, João Costa, and Joy A. James. "Refusing Blackness-as-Victimization: Trayvon Martin and the Black Cyborgs." In *Pursuing Trayvon Martin: Historical Contexts and Contemporary Manifestations of Racial Dynamics*, edited by George Yancy and Janine Jones. Lexington Press, 2012.

Vasudevan, Deepa Sriya. "'Because We Care': Youth Worker Identity and Persistence in Precarious Work." PhD diss., Harvard University, 2019.

Walker, Vanessa Siddle. *Their Highest Potential: An African American School Community in the Segregated South*. University of North Carolina Press, 2000.

Wallace, Derron. "Safe Routes to School? Black Caribbean Youth Negotiating Police Surveillance in London and New York City." *Harvard Educational Review* 88, no. 3 (2018): 261–286.

Warren, Chezare A. "From Morning to Mourning: A Meditation on Possibility in Black Education." *Equity & Excellence in Education* 54, no. 1 (2021): 92–102.

Warren, Mark R. *Willful Defiance: The Movement to Dismantle the School-to-Prison Pipeline*. Oxford University Press, 2022.

Warren, Mark R., Meredith Mira, and Thomas Nikundiwe. "Youth Organizing: From Youth Development to School Reform." *New Directions for Youth Development*, no. 117 (2008): 27–42.

Watson, Leah M. "The Anti- 'Critical Race Theory' Campaign: Classroom Censorship and Racial Backlash by Another Name." *Harvard Civil Rights-Civil Liberties Law Review* 58 (2023): 487–549.

Watson, Vajra. *Learning to Liberate. Community-Based Solutions to the Crisis in Urban Education*. Routledge, 2012.

Watts, Roderick J., and Carlos P. Hipolito-Delgado. "Thinking Ourselves to Liberation?: Advancing Sociopolitical Action in Critical Consciousness." *The Urban Review* 47 (2015): 847–867.

Watts, Roderick J., Nat Chioke Williams, and Robert J. Jagers. "Sociopolitical Development." *American Journal of Community Psychology* 31, no. 1–2 (2003): 185–194.

Weis, Lois, and Michelle Fine. "Critical Bifocality and Circuits of Privilege: Expanding Critical Ethnographic Theory and Design." *Harvard Educational Review* 82, no. 2 (2012): 173–201.

White, Terrenda. "Teachers of Color and Urban Charter Schools: Race, School Culture, and Teacher Turnover in the Charter Sector." *Journal of Transformative Leadership & Policy Studies* 7, no 1 (2018): 27–42.

Williams, David R. "Stress and the Mental Health of Populations of Color: Advancing Our Understanding of Race-Related Stressors." *Journal of Health and Social Behavior* 59, no. 4 (2018): 466–485.

Williams, Krystal L., Alethia Russell, and Kiara Summerville. "Centering Blackness: An Examination of Culturally Affirming Pedagogy and Practices Enacted by HBCU Administrators and Faculty Members." *Innovative Higher Education* 46, no. 6 (2021): 733–757.

Williamson, Joy Ann. "Community Control with a Black Nationalist Twist: The Black Panther Party's Educational Programs." *Counterpoints* 237 (2005): 137–157.

Wilson, Gregory D. "An Invisible Impediment to Progress: Perceptions of Racialization in the Nonprofit Sector." *Nonprofit and Voluntary Sector Quarterly* 54, no. 9 (2024), http://dx.doi.org/10.1177/08997640241252650.

Wilson, Gregory. "Towards a Racialized Nonprofit Industrial Complex." In *Academy of Management Proceedings* 2024, no. 1 (2024): 17065.

Winn, Maisha T. *Futuring Black Lives: Independent Black Institutions and the Literary Imaginary*. Vanderbilt University Press, 2025.

Winn, Maisha T. "Futures Matter: Creating Just Futures in This Age of Hyper-Incarceration." *Peabody Journal of Education* 96, no. 5 (2021): 527–539.

Winn, Maisha T. "Paradigm Shifting for Black Girls: Toward a Futures Matter Stance." In *Investing in the Educational Success of Black Women and Girls*, edited by Lori D. Patton, Venus Evans-Winters, Charlotte Jacob, pp. 227–240. Routledge, 2022.

Winn, Maisha T., and Nim Tottenham. "Looking Back to Look Forward: Leveraging Historical Models for Future-Oriented Caregiving." *Dædalus* 154, no. 1 (2025): 70–81.

Wolch, Jennifer R. *The Shadow State: Government and Voluntary Sector in Transition*. Foundation Center, 1990.

Wolch, Jennifer R., "The Shadow State: Transformations in the Voluntary Sector." In *The Power of Geography*, edited by Jennifer R. Wolch and Michael Dear, 197–221. Routledge, 2014.

Woodland, Malcolm H. "After-School Programs: A Resource for Young Black Males and Other Urban Youth." *Urban Education* 51, no. 7 (2016): 770–796.

Womack, Ytasha L. *Afrofuturism: The World of Black Sci-Fi and Fantasy Culture*. Chicago Review Press, 2013.

Wun, Connie. "Against Captivity: Black Girls and School Discipline Policies in the Afterlife of Slavery." *Educational Policy* 30, no. 1 (2016): 171–196.

Wun, Connie. "Unaccounted Foundations: Black Girls, Anti-Black Racism, and Punishment in Schools." *Critical Sociology* 42, no. 4/5 (2016): 737–750.

Wynter, Silvia. "A Black Studies Manifesto." *Forum N.H.I. Forum: Knowledge for the 21st Century* 1, no. 1 (1994): 3–11.

Yohalem, Nicole, and Karen Pittman. "Putting Youth Work on the Map." In *Forum for Youth Investment*. Forum for Youth Investment, 2006.

Yohalem, Nicole, Karen Pittman, and Sharon Lovick Edwards. *Strengthening the Youth Development/After-School Workforce: Lessons Learned and Implications for Funders*. Forum for Youth Investment, 2010.

Zembylas, Michalinos. "The Ethics and Politics of Precarity: Risks and Productive Possibilities of a Critical Pedagogy for Precarity." *Studies in Philosophy and Education* 38, no. 2 (2019): 95–111.

Index

The authorized representative in the EU for product safety and compliance is:
Mare Nostrum Group
B.V Doelen 72
4831 GR Breda
The Netherlands

www.ingramcontent.com/pod-product-compliance
Lightning Source LLC
Chambersburg PA
CBHW020857270326
41928CB00006B/742